THE CONCEPTUAL REPRESENTATION AND THE MEASUREMENT OF PSYCHOLOGICAL FORCES

BY KURT LEWIN

Professor of Child Psychology, Iowa Child Welfare Research Station,
State·University of Iowa, Iowa City, Iowa

Martino Publishing
Mansfield Centre, CT
2013

Martino Publishing
P.O. Box 373,
Mansfield Centre, CT 06250 USA

ISBN   978-1-61427-519-0

© *2013 Martino Publishing*

Cover design by T. Matarazzo

Printed in the United States of America On 100% Acid-Free Paper

THE CONCEPTUAL REPRESENTATION
AND THE MEASUREMENT OF
PSYCHOLOGICAL FORCES

BY KURT LEWIN

*Professor of Child Psychology, Iowa Child Welfare Research Station,
State University of Iowa, Iowa City, Iowa*

DUKE UNIVERSITY PRESS
Durham, N. C.
1938

PRINTED IN THE UNITED STATES OF AMERICA, BY
THE SEEMAN PRINTERY, INC., DURHAM, N. C.

PREFACE

The following considerations are intended to be the first part of a "Vector Psychology" which should be viewed together with *Topological Psychology* as an outline of a conceptual framework of psychology.

I do not wish here to repeat the motivation of such an undertaking, which I have outlined in extenso in the book mentioned. However, I might make a few remarks about points on which some misunderstanding seems to exist.

1. Neither the *Topological Psychology* nor the following monograph is intended to be a textbook; that is, to sum up the findings of experimental research. They rather are intended to define and characterize certain sets of concepts. To judge the practical usefulness of these concepts, the reader will have to turn to the numerous experiments making use of these concepts. However, in this monograph I have been able to refer widely to experiments as examples and I have tried to cover at least some of the experimental fields in question more systematically.

2. To my surprise, quite often I am meeting people who assume that topological psychology means representing psychological problems in physical terms. Since I cannot imagine how one can stress the necessity and the right of psychological concepts (as against any other kind of concepts) in psychology more than I have tried, I suppose that these people have preferred to use the *Topological Psychology* more in the way of a picture book, making their own text for the pictures, instead of using it for reading.

Or do they identify geometry with physics? Perhaps the idea of an empirical space which is not identical with the physical one runs so much counter to a firmly established metaphysical prejudice, that one should grant some time to become acquainted with it. Actually it means merely taking seriously the co-existence of a multitude of interdependent psychological facts and therefore using an "order of co-existence"—that is, a mathematical space—to represent them.

3. I have been accused of "ahistorical" thinking. It is true that I try to distinguish more sharply than is usually done between historical and ahistorical problems in psychology. However, that does not imply at all a neglect of the historical categories. As a matter of fact, anyone who defines stimuli in psychological rather than in physical terms, and does not forget about the social side of psychological phenomena, cannot possibly omit the historical aspect of every psychological datum.

It may be appropriate to add a word in regard to the geometrical problems discussed here. Recently, particularly since Einstein's theory of relativity, physics has been deeply interested in determining which geometry is fitted best to describe the "spatial" relations between the empirical physical data. The previous idea that the Euclidian geometry is a priori valid and the only one to be considered was abandoned. The problem of space in an empirical science was recognized to be one of "applied geometry": a geometry had to be found which could be used as mathematical framework to describe the "order of coexistent empirical data" in a way which facilitates an intelligible representation of their dynamic interrelations.

Psychology today has to face a similar problem, although in a much less developed condition. The behavior of an individual is determined by a "multitude of coexisting facts," the life space, containing the person and his psychological environment. To some degree the relative position of the various parts of this life space can be mathematically represented by means of the relatively recently developed topology (Princ.). However, this general "qualitative" geometry does not permit determination of direction and distance which are quantitative in nature. On the other hand, in handling dynamical problems psychology never has nor could have avoided using these geometrical quantitative concepts. To my knowledge, mathematics seems not to have developed a geometry, both sufficiently general and sufficiently specific, to satisfy these needs of psychology.

Under these circumstances, some years ago, I found myself

obliged to outline the simplest basic characteristics of a geometry (the hodological space) which would serve this purpose, although I am more than conscious of my shortcomings as a mathematician. I hope that in due time a competent mathematician, thoroughly trained in psychological problems, might become interested, and I would not be surprised if such an undertaking would be of definite value also to mathematics proper.

The more I applied, during the last years, the concepts of hodological space to various psychological problems, the more I became confident that what in the beginning seemed rather venturesome turned out to be a workable and realistic approach. The few basic assumptions of hodological space frequently led to conclusions surprisingly adequate to psychological facts. In this regard I might mention the following general points:

(1) Everyday language and also all scientific psychological language uses frequently such terms as direction and distance in a way which, when physically interpreted, becomes obviously absurd or meaningless (e.g., "social approach or withdrawal"). The geometry of hodological space gives to these terms a strictly scientific and fully intelligible meaning.

(2) Hodological space is a geometry which mirrors certain basic biological facts, particularly the fact that an organism consists of definite units (wholes of various order) in nearly all its properties.

(3) It permits an adequate representation of social problems.

(4) It permits the bringing together of the cognitive factors with the dynamical ones, an ancient but hardly solved and rather puzzling problem.

Getting thoughts into mathematical form is sometimes a laborious and tedious task, and one often wonders whether it really pays. The most gratifying experience I had in this attempt was the finding that the various schools of psychology show a surprisingly high degree of agreement if one forgets differences in terminology and tries to represent nothing else than the interrelation of facts: in other words, tries to use a mathematical language. This seems to be the only answer also to a second major task of psychology, namely, to analyze psychological data and still preserve the meaning of the event within its total (individual historical) psychological setting.

Psychology at the moment is rich with more or less new "general approaches." However, more important for psychology today than general approaches is the development of a type of "Theoretical Psychology" which has the same relation to "Experimental Psychology" as Theoretical Physics has to Experimental Physics. Theoretical Psychology then cannot be satisfied with generalities (however correct they might be) but has to supply specific means of solving the concrete problems of the laboratory and the clinic. I feel myself here in full agreement with the purpose of such an undertaking as that of Tolman or Hull. A reader who judges this monograph merely as a part of a "general approach" would miss the point.

I acknowledge with great appreciation the opportunity which Professor Chittenden gave me to go over the mathematical part of the problems (hodological space) with him, and I am grateful for his suggestions. Professor Hull obliged me by reading the representation of the goal-gradient hypothesis, and made suggestions which I was very glad to follow. On some points I have made use of valuable suggestions made by D. K. Adams. Several of my friends, particularly K. E. Zener, J. F. Brown, and R. Barker, were good enough to look over the manuscript. I am particularly grateful to R. Leeper, who was a very constructive critic and has read the galley proofs and has made many improvements.

K. L.

Iowa City, August 3, 1938.

CONTENTS

[5]

INTRODUCTION

The purpose of the following chapters is the discussion of one of the fundamental problems of psychological dynamics—namely, the problem of representing psychological forces conceptually. The headings under which these problems have been presented by different psychologists have been multifarious, including such headings as "instinct," "drive," "excitatory tendency," "force," "libido," "urge," "goal," and "motivation." In recent years some progress has been made in experimental studies in this field. However, relatively speaking, the progress of experimental research, especially with human beings, hardly corresponds with the deep and widespread interest which the problem of instinct and motivation always has enjoyed.

To my mind, it seems that much of the responsibility for this state of affairs can be traced to a lack of development of the conceptual tools which one needs for theoretical and experimental research in this field. The following chapters are devoted to a discussion of some of these conceptual problems which seem unavoidable in any research in this field, and which arise regardless of the terminology that one is accustomed to use. The discussion of the concept of psychological forces confronts us with these tasks: (1) to see the value and position of this concept within the framework of psychological concepts and theories; (2) to clarify the logical side of the concept (in which task one of the most difficult and important parts is the discussion of the "geometrical" problems involved in the "directedness" of forces); (3) to discuss the empirical laws which govern psychological forces and the methods of measuring psychological forces.

Those readers who regard the discussion of the second and third chapters, which deal with the geometry of the life space, as rather difficult might find it agreeable to turn from chapter one directly to chapters four and five, which have a closer contact with the experimental work. The geometrical problems discussed in chapters two and three might be referred to whenever needed.

I will not repeat here the explanation of certain concepts given in *Principles of Topological Psychology* (Lewin 1936).[1]

---

[1] Further references to *Principles of Topological Psychology* will be indicated by (Princ.).

I

THE POSITION OF THE CONSTRUCT OF FORCE IN PSYCHOLOGY

A. Directed Values in Psychological Explanations

1. The Necessity for Constructs (Intervening Concepts)

The task of psychology is that of conceptually represent ing and deriving psychological processes. Oddly enough such derivations (or, as one might say, explanations) are not possible if one attempts to link directly with other observable facts (B_2, B_3) the behavior (B) which has to be explained. It is becoming increasingly clear that it is necessary to intro duce between these groups of directly observable facts a num ber of concepts or "constructs" which one can call "inter vening concepts" (Tolman 1935 and 1937) or "conditional genetic concepts" (Lewin 1935, Brown 1936) or, briefly, "dy namic concepts."

One reason for this roundabout route in scientific thinking is that rather small apparent differences can be represent ative of important dynamical differences (and vice versa) and that a change of dynamical facts in one direction does not necessarily lead to a change in the same direction in the re sulting symptoms. For instance, a slight degree of anger might express itself openly with relative ease. However, an increase of intensity of anger usually leads, not to an increase of anger expressions, but to a quieting down. A further in crease might again lead to open expressions (Dembo 1931). Only in relatively rare cases is there a direct one-to-one re lationship between the directly observable phenomenological facts and dynamical facts. In these cases the observable facts can be used as symptoms and eventually as measuring instru ments for the dynamical facts.

Whatever the reason for the introduction of intermediate concepts, it must be recognized that any science which deals with questions of causation employs them. In physics, e.g., such terms as "force," "energy," "momentum," and "grav ity" are names for facts which cannot be directly perceived, but which are properties representing certain types of reaction or behavior. The existence of such states cannot be directly "seen," but must be demonstrated by "manipulation."

It is fair to say, I think, that there never has been a psychological school which did not make use of such intervening concepts. Concepts such as "association," "instinct," "libido," "drive," "Gestalt" (in the dynamic sense), "excitatory tendency," "conditioned reflex," and "intelligence," all represent dynamic facts the existence of which can be proved only indirectly by means of certain manipulations.[1] In popular speech we have many terms that refer to such inferred determinants of behavior—such terms as "forget," "want," and "fear." Science changes these dynamic concepts and provides definite methodological bases for them. However, it does not abandon this intervening type of concept altogether.

The introduction of dynamical facts involves theory. However, it is an illusion to believe that it is possible to develop on a purely empirical basis any science which deals with questions of interdependence and causation, if one understands by empiricism the exclusion of theories. None of the psychological systems thus far developed has been "empirical" in this sense. Consequently, instead of attempting to follow the mystical ideal of a "purely empirical" science of "facts" without theories or concepts, one may as well face openly and without disturbance the "fact" that dynamic constructs have been unavoidable in any worth-while psychology. Why not then introduce these concepts in a deliberate and orderly fashion, rather than permit them to slip in secretly and uncontrolled by the back door?

The danger of speculation lies not in the introduction of constructs, because they are unavoidable, but in the way they are introduced.

[1] It is rather difficult to state briefly the relations involved with a sufficient degree of accuracy. Koehler (1925), Heider (1927), and others have pointed out that dynamical facts might be perceived "directly" (without "thinking") through the medium of appearance. However, I trust that the difference between the two types of concepts and properties to which I refer is sufficiently clear.

2. The Empirical and Conceptual Properties of Constructs: Operational Definitions

The sole purpose of constructs is that of deriving scientifically the observable processes which one might want to explain or predict (Princ., p. 6). Such a scientific derivation is possible only if (1) the conceptual properties of the dynamical facts are clearly defined (i.e., if the logical-mathematical properties of these constructs are clear), (2) an empirical process or operation is defined which permits one to determine whether or not, in a concrete case, the dynamical fact exists.

The recently growing interest in "operational" definitions in psychology (Stevens 1935) has helped to emphasize the necessity of introducing concepts (constructs) beyond the level of directly observable phenomena, and has helped emphasize the necessity of linking these constructs in a definite way to concrete manipulations. Unfortunately, however, the emphasis on operational definitions seems to have led in some cases to a somewhat dangerous disregard of the conceptual side of constructs. Some workers seem to be satisfied with coordinating a conceptual "something" with some empirical operation even if the conceptual properties of this something are left so vague and unclear that one could hardly speak of it as a "concept."

The concept of intelligence, for instance, is today one of the best defined constructs as far as its coordinating definition to empirical operations is concerned. At least, this is the case if one accepts the widely used definition: "Intelligence is what is measured by intelligence tests." The operations which then define intelligence are most exactly and elaborately determined. If one accepts coordination with empirical operations as the criterion of a scientific construct, one would have to say, therefore, that the concept "intelligence" is probably as good and as exact a concept as can be had in psychology for quite a while to come.

On the other hand, one might well hold the position that the concept thus defined is entirely inexact, unclear, and vague. Because, there is nothing within this concept which permits any statement about its dynamical nature, except maybe that intelligence is not an energy or need (not something which can be treated as a source of action), and that it is merely an "ability" (leaving it rather open as to what logically is meant by "ability"). In other words, the conceptual side of the construct "intelligence" is so vague that it is hard to see how one could use such a concept within a frame of scientific derivations, if one understands by scientific derivations a strictly logical sequence of sentences.

No wonder, then, that very little conceptual relation exists between the symptoms (tests) used for measuring intelligence, and the construct itself; and that the question of the validity of a new test can be answered merely by finding whether it measures the same thing as did the previously developed tests. (This is not intended to be a criticism of intelligence tests. It rather implies that the conceptual side of intelligence needs consideration, if this construct is to contain its full value within the realm of psychological derivations.)

In a somewhat better position in this respect is the construct "association." As a coordinating definition one could use either the statement that an "association" between the experiences (or actions) A and B is built if A and B have been together repeatedly (or in close sequence), or one could use the tendency toward reproduction as an operational definition of association. The behavioral symptoms which are used for measuring associations are directly related to this definition.

In regard to the dynamical properties of the construct, one could say that association generally is viewed as a "tendency," as, e.g., in the classical definition of G. E. Müller (1913). This tendency is defined by him in a purely statistical sense, as the frequency of certain occurrences. However, such statistical characterization leaves the dynamical and conceptual properties of the construct rather open. The frequency could be due, for instance, to a link between A and B similar in nature to a link in a chain. Or it might be due to a directed force from A to B. Each of these possibilities (and there might be many more) would lead to different conclusions as to the effects of an association.

N. Ach (1910) in his measurement of the "strength of the will" used association as a directed force. Aside from his treatment, associationism has to my knowledge been rather evasive on this aspect of the problem. However, it is clear that unless one attributes definitely certain dynamic properties to associations, one could derive either everything or nothing from them.

As a whole, I think the methodological state of the psychological constructs of today is better in regard to their empirical coordinating definitions than in regard to the definition of their dynamic and conceptual properties. Psychology obviously has tried so hard in recent years to depart from speculative constructs and to confine itself to empirical ones that we seem to have forgotten about the conceptual requirements of scientific constructs.

I do not wish to be understood as meaning that I would like to see a slackening of this effort toward better empirical operational definitions. However, the neglect of the conceptual side of psychological constructs is nearly as dangerous for psychological research as is the neglect of the empirical side. What psychology needs is an equal emphasis of both.

Bridgman (1932) speaks of operational definitions in relation also to the conceptual side of constructs: Logical properties can be defined as something which permits certain conceptual operations, or as the effect of such operations. What is to be required from psychological constructs is then the clear definition of both the empirical manipulations and the logical operations permitted with the construct.

3. Definitions and Laws

One might distinguish in relation to every construct (or dynamical fact) three questions: (a) what are its conceptual properties? (b) what is its empirical coordinating definition? and (c) what are the laws governing its causes and effects? The questions (a) and (b) together can be viewed as dealing with the (conceptual and coordinating) definition of the construct.

Frequently the same logical (mathematical) concepts can be used for representing different empirical facts. For instance, the mathematical concept of vectors can be used for representing either physical locomotions or physical forces. On the other hand, a certain dynamical fact might be represented by different mathematical concepts without contradictions.

It has therefore been customary to view the conceptual and coordinating definition of constructs as a question of convention or convenience. We know, however, especially since the theory of relativity, that a similar freedom exists for assuming certain laws. On the other hand, it has become clear that such "liberty" of assumption exists only for constructs and laws separately, but not for them collectively.

In other words: *laws and definitions are a network of statements which only as a whole can be viewed as right or wrong.*

This means that also the definitions (questions (a) and (b)) should not be viewed as something which could be decided arbitrarily, but as something which should be determined in view of the laws and the empirical data involved.

It will be well for psychology to be conscious of these interrelations from the beginning and to remember that every construct in psychology has a certain position within the totality of its dynamical concepts. Therefore the first definitions involve especially difficult decisions and should be made in a tentative manner.

This cautiousness, however, cannot possibly imply that we must wait until we know all laws before developing the necessary constructs and before defining them accurately. Several "laws," for example, already have been proposed concerning psychological forces. But these laws, based only on empirically well-proved experimental data, do not suffice for the establishment of dynamical laws. For, as long as the conceptual properties of the constructs implied in a law are not clearly determined, the law cannot be said to be either right or wrong, because it lacks definite meaning.

One of the main purposes of this monograph is to emphasize this state of affairs and to point to the questions which must be settled before empirical laws regarding psychological dynamics can be stated in definite terms.

B. THE CONCEPT OF FORCE AS A DIRECTED ENTITY

1. Directed Entities as Causes of Behavior

The various psychological theories concerning the causes of behavior differ greatly. Yet, one characteristic seems to be common to most of them. The concept of "tendencies" in associationism and reflexology, the excitatory tendency (Hull 1932), the concept of propensities (McDougall 1932) or libido (Freud 1933), the different theories of drives, Tolman's theory of purposive behaviorism (1932), the Gestalt theoretical approach to the intelligent act (Koehler 1925) and to certain processes of perception, and any kind of theory which includes the concept of goal or of equilibrium—all of these include more or less consciously and persistently the thesis that behavior or any other kind of psychological change is caused by *directed* entities.

In mathematics, one distinguishes vectors and scalars. The latter have only magnitude, and may be represented by a single number. Vectors have both magnitude and direction. Accordingly, to represent a vector, one needs at least two numbers, one to represent the direction, the other to represent the magnitude of the vector.

One can then say that psychology derives changes from constructs (dynamical factors) which are of vectorial nature. We call these dynamical facts "psychological forces." In using this terminology we intend to stress merely that we have to deal with directed dynamical values, without committing ourselves to any more specific theory.

Considered in this way, the concept of psychological force is in no way new. It is merely a restatement of a concept included in nearly all psychological theories. It is intended, however, to be conceptually more definite and more empirical, because it disregards the more speculative or more far-reaching content implied in the terms mentioned above.

2. Can the Concept of Directed Entities as Causes of Change Be Eliminated?

All changes imply two positions: A change may be viewed as something *from* a first constellation *to* a second constellation. It may be that this is the logical justification for using directed factors as constructs for the derivation of change.

At any rate, since every psychological school uses some concept of force, it might be well to try to determine clearly the logical and empirical implications of this construct and to find how far one can get with it.

The conceptual properties of the construct force have to be viewed as an interrelated unit. This makes it rather difficult to defend the necessity or convenience of the various assumptions if regarded singly. Their *raison d'être* depends finally on their fruitfulness in research. In any attempt of this sort, I suppose, one has to ask the reader to be willing to suspend judgment until he can see a sufficient part of the network of concepts, theories, and facts.

Before making any decisions regarding the following definitions, I tried my best to survey all the possibilities. Often several possibilities presented themselves as almost equally valuable. Not infrequently the logical interrelations between quite distant statements have compelled certain assumptions.

The main objective of this paper is to bring into the open some of the basic concepts and assumptions which objectively are presupposed in practically all psychological research in this field. Often they are contained more in experimental technique than in theoretical statements and they are to a high degree independent of the more specific psychological theories.

On the whole, I have tried to make as few assumptions as possible and to be rather conservative. In fact, this monograph contains very little psychological theory which is not accepted by most psychologists and psychological schools. Only the treatment of the relation between need (tension) and goals (valences) is based on a more specific theory, although this theory is fortunately by no means exclusively mine.

When proceeding with this study I became increasingly impressed by the amount of conceptual agreement which exists in psychology when one disregards all differences of words, and looks only for actual content. And this, after all, has to be done if any discussion about theories or theoretical differences shall be meaningful.

The reader and critic should keep in mind therefore the following considerations: (1) The assumptions made must be without logical contradictions, of course. However, one should be careful not to presume that those mathematical axioms which hold for Euclidian space or for the spaces used in physics must necessarily be valid for those types of mathematical space which psychology may find most useful. (2) There is not much point in refusing an assumption (save on grounds of logical inconsistency) unless one gives a positive statement as to how the problem involved may be solved more adequately. (3) Psychology today can hardly undertake to find a theoretical framework which is absolutely correct, but must aim merely at that which is sufficiently correct. Accordingly, when one is comparing the values of different assumptions, he should ask himself how great the difference between the effects of the different assumptions would be. For, to use a saying of Herbert Feigl, differences which do not make differences are not differences.

II

THE GEOMETRY OF DIRECTION IN PSYCHOLOGY

1. Direction as a Property of Behavior and of Dynamic Factors

Direction is a property not only of certain dynamic constructs aiming to explain behavior, but also of behavior itself. Many, if not all, psychological activities show directedness (Lewin 1935)—especially every action toward a goal or away from a region. Therefore, the concept of direction is unavoidable in the description of behavior (Line 1937). This presupposes that one can distinguish and determine directions within the life space.

2. Geometrical and Dynamical Constructs

The concept of direction is a mathematical, and more specifically, a geometrical one. The determination of directions in psychology implies rather elaborate mathematical and psychological problems.

Among psychological constructs, one may distinguish geometrical and dynamical constructs. Examples of dynamical constructs in psychology are instinct, libido, force, tension. Dynamical constructs deal with causation, with the conditions of change. They are the main objects of interest in psychology. Examples of geometrical constructs are direction, distance, and position.

The geometrical constructs might be called "constructs of the first order" as compared with dynamical concepts as "constructs of the second order." The dynamical constructs are based partly upon the geometrical ones. The geometrical properties of behavior are at least to some degree directly observable. On the other hand, to some degree they imply constructs. We have to deal here with problems of applied mathematics. This involves (as with dynamic constructs) the necessity (1) of finding a type of geometry which can be applied in psychology and (2) of giving ''coordinating definitions'' (that is, the rules of how to apply those geometrical concepts in psychology).

I have tried elsewhere (Princ., pp. 41 ff.) to show that even if one could avoid the concept direction, the use of geometrical concepts would be unavoidable in psychology. For, even the part-whole relation is geometrical in nature. Many relations within the life space (for instance, the various types of connectedness and part-whole relations) can be defined by means of topology. The topological relations are basic also for the determination of direction in the life space; the concept of ''path,'' which, as we shall see, is basic for the definition of direction in psychology, is a topological one (Princ., pp. 90 ff.). The coordination between a mathematical path and a psychological locomotion in topological psychology can therefore be used also as the main coordinating definition in determining directions in the life space.

Moreover, although topological principles are necessary, in themselves they are not sufficient to determine directions. The reason for this is that, mathematically, direction is closely related to distance, and that topology does not distinguish differences in size.

3. The Discrepancy between Psychological and Physical Directions

It is important to remember that in an empirical science the kind of geometry chosen to represent the empirical data should fit the dynamical characteristics of these data (Reichenbach 1928).

Unfortunately, it is impossible to define directions in the life space by physical directions, except under very special circumstances. Many social locomotions (for instance, the passing of an examination, or the acquiring of a new position) clearly involve changes of position (Princ., pp. 46-50) and are directed actions. It would be inadequate to characterize these directions by the physical directions of the bodily movements involved.

Even in cases where the goal is the reaching of a physical object, the direction of this action does not need to be identical with the physical direction from the person to the goal. In cases of roundabout routes, the person (P) may have to go away from the goal, in terms of physical direction, even if psychologically the action clearly has the character of an action *towards* the goal. We are so accustomed to interpret the words "withdraw" and "approach" in a psychological meaningful way that we have lost sight of the fact that in physical terms an approach often includes increases of distance, even in such simple cases as a rat running through a maze. What happens in the "aha" experience (insight), which is characteristic of many solutions of such a roundabout problem, can be described partly as a change in the direction of a certain action: actions which previously had the character of being directed toward the goal now acquire the character of being directed away from the goal, and vice versa (Lewin 1933).

Consequently, if we are to speak of directions in psychology, we are faced with the necessity of developing a geometry adequate for the handling of these problems.

4. General Properties of Hodological Space

For representing directions in psychology, it seems to be possible to use a geometry which I have called "hodological space." Generally it is difficult to grasp the real meaning of a system of mathematical axioms. It will be well to state in advance, therefore, the main differences between hodological space on the one hand, and Euclidian and Riemannian space on the other:

1. The concept of direction in all three types of space is based on the concept of a "distinguished path." Euclidian and Riemannian space use as the distinguished path the shortest connection between two points. In hodological space, on the other hand, the character of the distinguished path varies according to the situation.

2. In hodological space, direction depends upon certain units (wholes) of paths. This does not hold in Euclidian space.

3. Direction in hodological space depends upon the degree of differentiation of the space into subregions and depends upon the structure of these subregions.

4. Direction in hodological space depends upon the properties of the field at large. In this respect, too, there is a marked difference from Euclidian space.

5. Hodological space distinguishes ''direction toward'' and ''direction away from.''

The properties of hodological space are such that Euclidian space may be viewed as a special case of hodological space. Hodological space is therefore one of those scientific generalizations which include previous steps as specific cases (Reichenbach 1928).

I may repeat that the purpose of hodological space is to find a type of geometry which permits the use of the concept of direction in a manner which will correspond essentially with the meaning that direction has in psychology. Any such mathematization implies, of course, that this relatively fluid, popular meaning will be restricted to a more definite meaning.

I have intended to characterize the properties of hodological space sufficiently. It is, however, not my intention to find the best way of ''axiomatizing'' this geometry. That could well be done later on by a more competent mathematician.

B. THE CONCEPT OF DIRECTION IN EUCLIDIAN SPACE

According to Hausdorf (1914), direction is a relation between two points, a and b (a bipolar relation). The direction a,b is not equal, but rather is opposed to the direction b,a.

The concept of direction is closely related to the concept of a straight line—it refers to the straight line which connects a with b (Figure 1). A difference in direction (i.e., an angle) is measured by the amount of discrepancy between two such beams.

In Riemannian space, direction refers to a straightest line, instead of to a straight line (Figure 2).

Both Euclidian and Riemannian space show the following characteristics:

1. Equality of direction is a transitive relation. That is, if two directions are equal to a third, they both are equal to each other.

2. The totality of points which lie, in relation to a given point, in the same direction are a one-dimensional manifold, namely, a half straight line in Euclidian space, a circle in Riemannian space.

C. HODOLOGICAL SPACE

1. The Life Space as Finitely Structured Space. Points in the Life Space

As I have discussed elsewhere (Princ., pp. 163 ff.), the life space is not indefinitely divisible into smaller and smaller subparts. At any given time it is composed of certain units or regions which should not be regarded as divided into subregions. We call such an undivided subregion a "cell," on the analogy that the cell is a small unit of structure in a plant or animal.

(1)   Definition: If A is a cell, no regions
a, b, ..., n (a $\neq$ b $\neq$ .... $\neq$ n) should be
distinguished such that a + b + ... + n = A.[2]

It is impossible to distinguish the position of different points within such units, even though these units may have more than one dimension. Therefore, as far as position is concerned, cells have the character of points within the life space.

We want to retain the basic idea of Euclidian space that a direction is a relation between two points. But, in accordance with the nature of the life space, we shall refer to cells (units of regions) rather than to points. Accordingly, by direction in hodological space we understand a certain relation between two regions A and B. We represent this relation

---

[2] + represents the topological sum (Princ., p. 87).

by the symbol $d_{A,B}$ (read: "direction at A toward B" or "direction AB"). As in Euclidian space, the direction $d_{A,B}$ should not be equal, but should be opposite to the direction $d_{B,A}$ ("direction BA").

2. Direction, Distance, and Distinguished Path

In Euclidian space, both distance and direction refer to a connection between two points. From the point of view of topology, this connection is to be considered a "path" from a to b (Princ., pp. 90 ff.). There are of course many paths $(w, w^1, w^2 \ldots)$ possible between a and b (Figure 1). One of these possible paths (w) is distinguished as the shortest path between a and b. The concept of direction refers to this distinguished, shortest path.

The *distance* a,b refers to the length of this distinguished path from a to b, i.e., it refers to a characteristic of the *total* path. Also the *direction* a,b refers to a characteristic of this distinguished path from a to b; however, it refers to a characteristic of this path *in the point a*.

The concept of direction in hodological space follows the same pattern. It also refers to a path between two regions A and B. Generally there are many paths (w, w_1, w_2) possible between two such regions (Figure 3) and it is necessary to select one path which will determine the direction $d_{A,B}$.

Since topology does not know differences of size, one cannot use shortness as a general principle for such a selection. It might be possible to substitute for the concept "shortest path" the idea of the minimum number of regions which might be crossed by a path from A to B. However, we shall not confine ourselves to this one method of selecting a distinguished path from the possible ones. The property which makes one path between two regions of the life space outstanding seems to vary considerably with the situation. Sometimes the fastest connection is outstanding; at other times it is the cheapest connection, or the most pleasant, or the least dangerous. So, all that we would like to assume is that there should be, in the given case, one outstanding path from

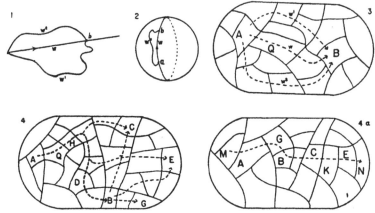

Fig. 1. Direction in Euclidian Space. w, straight line from A to B; w1 and w2, two other paths from A to B.

Fig. 2. Direction in Riemannian Space. w, straightest line from A to B; w1, another path from A to B.

Fig. 3. Direction in Hodological Space. w, distinguished path from region A to B; w1 and w2, two other paths from A to B.

Fig 4. Equality of Direction at the Same Point. $d_{A,B} = d_{A,C}$.

Fig. 4a. Equality of Direction within One Distinguished Path. $d_{A,B} = d_{C,E} = d_{G,K}$.

A to B. If there is only one path, this one, of course, can be viewed as outstanding.

The concept of direction in hodological space then is based on the "distinguished path" w from A to B. This may be written as $w_{A,B}$.

D. K. Adams has called my attention to a general principle which might hold for the determination of the distinguished path in psychology.

The task might be to select the distinguished path from A to B from among three paths. We designate the three paths as $w_{A,C,B}$, $w_{A,D,B}$, and $w_{A,E,B}$. C, D, and E represent the different means one would use (the different intermediate regions these paths cross). We can now compare the relative degree of attractiveness of these intermediate regions, C, D, and E as means, or to use a concept which we will discuss later, the "valence" Va(C), Va(D), and Va(E) of these intermediate regions. In psychology, that of the various paths seems to be the distinguished one for which the positive valence of the means (M) is a maximum.

(1a)   A distinguished path in psychology is probably determined by: $Va(M) = max$.

Which of the various possible means has the greatest valence would depend, according to what we will discuss later, upon the momentary circumstances, in particular, upon the nature of the path and the need of the individual at that time (see formula (31)). Besides, not the valence as such but the force corresponding to the valence has to be considered (21).

I am not entirely certain whether the formula (1a) is the only principle of selection for the distinguished path. However, I am persuaded that it covers at least most of the cases.

The *distance* $e_{A,B}$ between A and B should refer to the totality of the distinguished path $w_{A,B}$; the *direction* $d_{A,B}$ should refer to a certain property which the distinguished path has in A. One can express this characteristic by correlating direction to the beginning step of the distinguished path from A to B. This beginning step—see proposition (4) —would be functionally equivalent to a differential within an indefinitely divisible space. We can give, then, the following definition:

(2)   Definition: The direction at A toward B ($d_{A,B}$) is a relation between the regions A and B which is determined by the beginning step ($w_{A,Q}$) of the distinguished path ($w_{A,B}$) from the region A to B (with $w_{A,Q} \subset w_{A,B}$).[3]

There are cases in which more than one direction $d_{A,B}$ exists at region A toward region B. There might be, for instance, one direction for *looking* from A to B, and another for *walking* from A to B, another for *flying* from A to B, each corresponding to the distinguished path for one of these types of locomotion—to the best way of looking from A to

[3] The symbol $\subset$ is used in topology to mean "is included in," and the symbol $\supset$ to mean "includes." The reader is cautioned to distinguish between these symbols and the symbols $<$ and $>$, which mean respectively "is smaller than" and "is larger than." The term "step" is defined later (4).

B, the best way of walking from A to B, and the best way of flying from A to B. Therefore, one must remember that direction is related to the *type of locomotion in question.*

Quite a number of psychological conflicts are related to such discrepancies between the directions related to different types of locomotion. This is a typical situation, for instance, in many roundabout *(Umweg)* problems (Lewin 1933). We will refer first to cases in which only one distinguished path between two points exists, later on to cases with more than one distinguished path.

3. Equality of Direction at the Same Point

a. Definition of Equality of Direction at the Same Point.— One can derive from (2) the conditions under which two directions $d_{A,B}$ and $d_{A,C}$ (Figure 4) are equal.

(3) $d_{A,B} = d_{A,C}$ if there exists a $w_{A,H}$ such that $w_{A,H} \subset w_{A,B}$ and $w_{A,H} \subset w_{A,C}$.

In other words, two directions can be called equal if a beginning part of the two distinguished paths which determine these directions is identical. For then also the beginning step of both paths is identical.

From (3) there follows as a special case (Figure 4) the equality of direction if two distinguished paths with the same starting region stand in the relation of part and whole:

(3a) $d_{A,B} = d_{A,D}$ if $w_{A,D} \subset w_{A,B}$ *or* $w_{A,D} \supset w_{A,B}$.

We have mentioned that hodological space, as every geometry, has a certain amount of liberty concerning what sentences should be used as the basic axioms. Instead of defining equality of directions in the same point (3), one can start by defining at first equality of directions in different points of one whole path (proposition 6 or 6a). This would have the advantage of determining from the beginning a certain relation between equality of direction and unity of path, which we will find rather important for all relations within hodological space.

The dependence of direction in hodological space upon the unity of paths, and upon the amount to which the paths in question are parts of or are not parts of one whole path, changes even to some degree the meaning of "equality of direction": One of the basic characteristics of equality in general is considered to be transitivity. However, we will see later that equality of direction is transitive only under certain conditions. One might prefer, therefore, to speak of *"partly equal"* instead of equal directions in many cases which conform to (3).

b. Segmented and Unsegmented Paths.—The life space contains regions which are not subdivisible at a given time. Also an action might contain part actions. However, these part actions might not be divisible into smaller and smaller subparts indefinitely, at least if it be required that psychologically these subparts themselves should have the meaning of actions.

As an example, I have discussed elsewhere (Princ., p. 163) the fact that eating an agreeable food generally contains fewer psychologically distinguishable subactions than eating a disliked food. In the latter case, taking the hand to the spoon, putting food on the spoon, taking it half way to the mouth, putting it into the mouth, and chewing might be psychologically well-separated units, whereas in the case of an agreeable food the taking of a bite might be one undivided unit of action.

It might have good psychological meaning to divide a speech into subparts, but it might not have any psychological meaning to divide the spoken word into subparts and treat these subparts as separate actions. The same holds for any or at least most of directed actions toward a goal. A locomotion from A to B might be done in one sweep without any interruption, or it might be done in definite steps.

As an empirical criterion for a unit or subunit of action one can often use the fact that such a unit has been started by a separate intention, decision, or other special initiation. A second, similar way to determine the subunits of a more inclusive action is to determine which stage of this action can be viewed as a subgoal with a certain amount of separate psychological existence.

The units of actions are closely related to the units of regions which determine the cognitive structure of the life space at that time. We will call an undivided subpart of an action a "step." One can correlate steps and cells in the life space in the following way:

(4)   Definition: $w_{M,N}$ is a "step" within $w_{A,B}$
        if $w_{A,B} \supset w_{M,N}$ and if $w_{M,N}$ has common
        parts with no other cells than M and N.

(4a)   Definition: A path is called "segmented,"
        if it contains more than one step.

A segmented path involves, therefore, at least three regions: the starting, the end, and one (or more) intermediate regions which are crossed by the path.

The way actions are segmented is very important with regard to equality of direction. A person (P) wants to go from the room A to B to get a glass of water. Another time, while being in A, he wishes to bring wood from the cellar C. To do this he has to pass through the room B. Does the person in both cases start out in the same direction? In other words, is $d_{A,B} = d_{A,C}$?

Two persons are taking the train from Iowa City (I) to Chicago. The one wants to go to Detroit (D), the second by way of New York to Europe (E). Do both go in the same direction? Is $d_{I,D} = d_{I,E}$?

In such cases one can argue as strongly for as against the right to call both directions equal. In passing through the room B to bring up the wood from C, the person P might not feel at all that he is doing something in the same direction as when he goes to B to drink a glass of water ($d_{A,B} \neq d_{A,C}$). On the other hand, if the door (R) to the room B is closed and the key has been lost, or if some other obstacle makes it difficult to enter B, the person P might feel very strongly that by overcoming this obstacle he would be able to get both the water as well as the wood. The locomotions he has to make to both goals will then very clearly appear to him to start in the same direction ($d_{A,B} = d_{A,C}$).

This rather annoying problem can be clarified if one goes back to the definition of equality (3) in hodological space. Figure 5 represents a situation where either getting to the water($w_{A,B}$) or getting to the wood ($w_{A,C}$) is accomplished as one unsegmented action. Therefore each of these paths has to be considered as one indivisible unit, as one step. It follows that there does not exist a region Q so that $w_{A,Q} \subset w_{A,B}$ and $w_{A,Q} \subset w_{A,C}$. Therefore, according to the definition (3), we will have to say that $d_{A,B} \neq d_{A,C}$, in spite of the fact that, to some extent, P must pass the same geographic regions in going to either goal.

This situation is different if the same obstacle hinders P from reaching B and C. If the obstacle (R) is strong enough to break the action into psychologically meaningful subactions $w_{A,R}$, $w_{R,B}$, and $w_{A,R}$, $w_{R,C}$ respectively (Figure 6)— as in our example of the locked door—one can say that $d_{A,B} = d_{A,C}$. This is in line with the definition (3) because there exists a subpath $w_{A,R}$ such that $w_{A,R} \subset w_{A,B}$ and $w_{A,R} \subset w_{A,C}$.

These derivations from the concept of equality of direction in hodological space seem to fit very well the needs of psychology. They show that the determination of direction depends upon the way in which the life space is structured into cells. If the unity of actions is so definite that no subactions can be distinguished, the direction of any such action is different from that of any other action. Only if common steps are distinguishable within two actions (or if the one action is a subpart of the other) might the two actions have the same direction.

This leads us to a third case. We have seen that the equality of direction $d_{A,B} = d_{A,C}$ presupposes that $w_{A,B}$ and $w_{A,C}$ are not undifferentiated units, but segmented paths (or that one of two distinguished paths is itself a part of the other). However, if the degree increases to which the steps $w_{A,R}$ and $w_{R,B}$ within the whole path $w_{A,B}$ are separated, and to which the steps $w_{A,R}$ and $w_{R,C}$ within the path $w_{A,C}$ are separated, a state finally would be reached where $w_{A,R}$

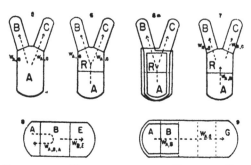

EQUALITY OF DIRECTION AND THE UNITY OF PATH

Fig. 5. $w_{A,B}$ and $w_{A,C}$ are unsegmented paths. $d_{A,B} \neq d_{A,C}$.

Fig. 6. $w_{A,B}$ and $w_{A,C}$ are segmented and have a common part $w_{A,R}$ · $d_{A,B} = d_{A,C}$.

Fig. 6a. The constellation of Figure 6 viewed as overlapping of three situations: one containing the regions A,R, the second containing the regions A,R,B, the third containing the regions A,R,C.

Fig. 7. $w_{A,R}$, $w_{R,B}$, and $w_{R,C}$ are entirely separated actions. $d_{A,R} \neq d_{R,B}$: $d_{A,R} \neq d_{R,C}$.

Fig. 8. $w_{A,B,A}$ and $w_{B,E}$ are separated actions.

Fig. 9. $w_{A,B}$ is to some degree an independent part of $w_{A,G}$. This can be represented as an overlapping of two situations: one consisting of the regions A and B, and the other of the regions A,B, . . , G.

$w_{R,B}$, and $w_{R,C}$ are themselves entirely separated units of action. In this case we would be dealing again with a number of unsegmented actions. One would have to say that $d_{A,B} \neq d_{A,C}$ (because the conditions of (3) are not fulfilled); or, rather, that the directions $d_{A,B}$ and $d_{A,C}$ are undefined. For, the question would be left open as to what the distinguished paths $w_{A,B}$ and $w_{A,C}$ would be, and especially whether or not $w_{A,R}$ would be a part of either of those paths.

In case $w_{A,R}$, $w_{R,B}$, and $w_{R,C}$ become entirely separated actions, we will represent these actions as unconnected paths, as in Figure 7.

It might be appropriate to give an example of such a situation. A person might go from the place A to the place B to visit a friend. At this visit he learns of an occupational opening (E) which was unknown to him before. He makes up his mind to accept the position.

Under these circumstances it would not be proper to say that the person went in the direction $d_{A,E}$ when he started his trip to B. Visiting his friend B was not a subgoal of entering the position E. Therefore it is not $w_{A,B} \subset w_{A,E}$. As a matter of fact, the path $w_{A,B}$ was originally included in a path $w_{A,B,A}$ (Figure 8) because the person was planning to go back to A after visiting his friend in B. Therefore the locomotion from B to E in this case has to be viewed as a change in direction $(d_{B,E} \neq d_{A,B})$. $w_{B,E}$ is a new separate unit and $w_{B,E}$ and $w_{A,B}$ are not parts of one action.

It is of course possible that the cognitive structure of the situation may change for the person afterwards so that the paths $w_{A,B}$ and $w_{B,E}$ will appear to have been parts of one segmented path $w_{A,E}$.

In summary, we distinguished three cases: (a) both $w_{A,B}$ and $w_{A,C}$ are unsegmented paths (undifferentiated units); (b) $w_{A,B}$ and $w_{A,C}$ are segmented paths; (c) $w_{A,R}$, $w_{R,B}$, and $w_{R,C}$ are fully separated units, independent whole paths. Only in the second case (b) might an equality of directions be established. In other words, equality of direction in hodological space refers to segmented paths which show a certain degree of unity as wholes, and the "degree of equality" is influenced by this degree of unity. It is an important question as to how such differences of unity can be defined and represented.

c. The Degree of Unity of a Path.—One could attempt to define the wholeness of a path in the same way as one defines a dynamical Gestalt, namely, by the property that a change of any part of a Gestalt changes any other part (Koehler 1929 and Princ., p. 173).

This definition seems to be quite adequate if one thinks of the effect which a change in an earlier step has on the later steps of the same path: a later step depends highly on every previous one. However, this criterion does not hold for the effect of the later on the earlier steps. For instance a person who has finished the first two steps w^1 and w^2 of a path w might be influenced by an unexpected happening to use another third step w^3 than he had contemplated. Such a change will not be able to affect the steps w^1 and w^2, because these steps are already a matter of the past and therefore cannot be changed (Princ., pp. 36 ff.).

Of course the *cognitive structure* which the whole path w has for P will be changed by every step. The change resulting from the third step w^3 might well include the cognitive structure of the steps w^1 and w^2 which are history. The criterion of a dynamic Gestalt might, therefore, hold for the cognitive structure of the path (w). It is, however, not applicable to the unity of a path as a process.

It is not our purpose to discuss here the rather difficult problem of "time-Gestalt." We prefer to offer instead a positive technique which permits us to handle the problem of the degree of unity of a path satisfactorily (there might of course be other ways).

We have mentioned that the regions B, C, . . . which are reached by the steps $w_{A,B}$, $w_{B,C}$ . . . of a path $w_{A,G}$ can be viewed as subgoals. We can conceive, therefore, of the person at a given moment as being in two overlapping situations, namely, the situation which includes the whole path $w_{A,G}$ and the second situation which includes the momentary step, for instance $w_{A,B}$ (Figure 9). We understand under potency (Po) the relative weight of one of two or more overlapping situations (Princ., p. 138).[4]

We can make the following proposition:

(5)   The degree of unity of a path w is greater the more Po (w) > Po (w^x).

Under w we understand the path as a whole; under w^x that step in which the person is involved at the given time.

This proposition covers the following points: (a) in case the potency of the path w as a whole becomes fully dominant ($Po(w^x) = 0$), the path w ceases to be segmented. (b) In case the step becomes alone dominant (Po (w) = 0), again the path is not segmented. A segmented path exists, therefore,

---

[4] If one distinguished, arbitrarily, eleven degrees of relative potency (0, 0.1, 0.2, . . . , 1), the sum of the potencies of overlapping situations at a given time should equal one. If the potency of a single situation equals one it is the only situation present.

only if both Po $(w) \neq 0$ and Po $(w^x) \neq 0$. Only in those cases may the question of equality of direction come up. The representation of the case illustrated in Figure 6 is therefore not complete. It has to include statements about the relative unity of the paths $w_{A,C}$ and $w_{A,B}$. One may say that $d_{A,B} = d_{A,C}$ only if the potency $Po(w_{A,B}) > 0$, Po $(w_{A,C}) > 0$, and Po $(w_{A,R}) > 0$ (Figure 6a).

This definition of the degree of unity of a path leads to a number of conclusions which seem to be in line with the psychological facts:

(a) The degree of unity of the path does not need to be constant during the whole locomotion. It can be different in every step and might even change during the completion of a step.

(b) With the approach to the main goal, the unity of the remaining paths seems generally to increase. This is in accordance with the fact that the potency of the main goal generally increases if one comes closer to it.

(c) The unity of the path depends upon the intensity of the need related to the goal in question. Again, the increase of the need generally increases the relative potency of the situation containing the main goal.

(d) The development of automatisms during learning decreases the relative potency of the single steps. A routine path shows, therefore, a relatively high degree of unity.

One can probably say that the more the unity of the path as a whole increases, the more the single steps take on the character of merely a "means" to an "end."

d. Partly Equal Directions.—The degree to which a whole path is a unit is obviously of importance for the problem of equality of directions. The existence of various degrees of independence of the steps within a whole path involves the necessity of distinguishing different "degrees of equality" of two directions. (That should not be confused with different angles.) In hodological space one can speak of "partly equal" directions. This relation might be written as

(5a) $$d_{A,B} (=) d_{A,C}.$$

We will discuss later the problem of equality of direction within one path. It is probably fair to assume that the degree of equality of direction within one path increases with the degree of unity of the path as a whole.

However, if one compares two paths from one point to different goals, we have seen that the degree of equality of direction at the starting point approaches zero if each of these paths shows a very high degree of unity (unsegmented path) as well as if each shows a very low degree of unity (independent sub-paths).—If the first step becomes an independent whole, one can, of course, speak of identical directions in regard to the two performances of the first step.—The optimum of equality of direction of two different paths lies therefore in a degree of unity somewhere between both extremes for each of the paths.

In all cases of segmented paths every step will be to some degree a dependent and to some degree an independent part of the whole path. Therefore all of the previous and later representations should be represented in a fashion similar to Figure 6a, namely, by overlapping regions and by attributing a certain relative potency to the overlapping regions. As this, however, would complicate the figures too much, we generally merely indicate the regions which the path crosses, trusting that the reader will always keep in mind that a necessary condition of our conclusions is a certain part-whole relation between the single steps and the whole path.

For the same reason our formulas will contain the term for "equal" directions rather than for "partly equal" directions even when we have in mind only partly equal directions. In all cases of applications, however, and in considering the results of experimental work, the problems of the degree of equality of direction should be kept in mind.

4. The Totality of Points Lying in the Same Direction Viewed from one Point

a. *Semi-Euclidian Space.*—We have mentioned that in Euclidian and Riemannian space the totality of points x which lie in the same direction with reference to a point a represents a one-dimentional space (Figures 1 and 2). This does not hold for hodological space:

Let us assume a hodological space with the following properties: (a) its regions are infinitely structured (an infinitely structured space can be conceived of as a boundary case of a finitely structured space); (b) the shortest path between two points should be regarded as the distinguished path; (c) the space should be homogeneous with regard to the ease of locomotion.

Under these circumstances hodological space becomes rather similar to Euclidian space. For instance, the totality of points 1, 2, 3, etc., which lie to the point A in the same direction, is a one-dimensional space, namely, a half straight line (Figure 10; $d_{A,1} = d_{A,2} = d_{A,3}$).

We will call a hodological space, for which the conditions (a), (b), and (c) hold, a "semi-Euclidian space." In psychology such conditions might be fulfilled approximately within the physical surroundings if a locomotion can be made with the same degree of difficulty in every point and in every direction and if the person is well acquainted with these surroundings. They are fulfilled to some degree in the space of vision if one considers looking as a connecting path (Princ., p. 128).

Semi-Euclidian space is still a hodological and not a Euclidian space. The differences will become clear in the later discussion.

b. Homogeneous Fields with Impassable Barriers.—Let us introduce into a semi-Euclidian space a barrier B which should be impassable (Figure 10). The direction from A to the points 5 and 6 "behind the barrier" would be equal to each other and to the direction to the point 7: $d \quad = d_{A,6} = d_{A,7}$ according to (3), because $w_{A,7} \subset w_{A,5}$ and $w_{A,7} \subset w_{A,6}$.

The totality of the points X to which $d_{A,X} = d_{A,5}$ is not a one-dimensional but a two-dimensional region which includes all points within the area H. Certain other points "behind the barrier" like point 8 are lying in the direction $d_{A,10}$ ($d_{A,8} = d_{A,9} = d_{A,10}$), namely, all points of the area K.

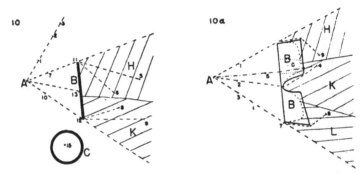

Fig. 10.   Semi-Euclidian Space with Impassable Barrier.   B, impassable barrier; C, impassable barrier; $d_{A,1} = d_{A,2} = d_{A,3}$. H, totality of points which lie in the same direction from A as 7; $d_{A,5} = d_{A,6} = d_{A,7}$; K, totality of points which lie in the same direction from A as 10; $d_{A,8} = d_{A,9} = d_{A,10}$; $d_{11,5} \neq d_{11,6}$.

Fig. 10a.   Inhomogeneous Semi-Euclidian Space.   B, region with increased difficulty of locomotion; $d_{A,2} = d_{A,4}$; $d_{A,1} = d_{A,9}$; H, totality of points which lie in the same direction from A as 1; K, totality of points which lie in the same direction from A as 2; L, totality of points lying in the same direction from A as 3.

If we would have to deal with a three-dimensional instead of a two-dimensional space, the totality of points X lying to A in the same direction $d_{A,X}$ behind the barrier would be a three-dimensional manifold.

In Euclidian space a continuous shift from a point n to a point m corresponds to a continuous change in direction from $d_{a,n}$ to $d_{a,m}$. In a hodological space such is not necessarily the case: for instance, if one shifts a point N gradually from the point 6 to 8, the direction $d_{A,N}$ at first remains constant ($d_{A,N} = d_{A,7}$). When N crosses the boundary between the area H and K, the direction $d_{A,N}$ suddenly jumps and becomes equal to $d_{A,10}$ ($d_{A,N} = d_{A,10}$).

If a point 15 is so enclosed by an impassable barrier C that it can in no way be reached from A the direction $d_{A,15}$ is undetermined (there exists of course the direction $d_{A,C}$).

   c. *Inhomogeneous Fields.*—If we introduce in a semi-Euclidian space a barrier B which is passable, but less easily passable than other parts of the field, and if the path of least effort is the distinguished one, a situation results like that presented in Figure 10a. In our examples three areas H, K, and L lie behind the region B, the points of which have to A the direction of $d_{A,1}$, $d_{A,2}$ and $d_{A,3}$ respectively (for details see Lewin 1934).

The number and shape of these areas depend upon the form of the barrier B and the amount of difficulty the various parts of the barrier offer to locomotion. For instance, if the thickness of the middle part of the barrier should increase, the area K would decrease, because some points previously located in K would be more easily accessible by going around the barrier than by crossing it.

d. The Unity of the Hodological Field as a Whole.—It might be stressed especially that the direction $d_{A,N}$ from a point A to a point N in hodological space does not depend only upon the circumstances along the distinguished path $w_{A,N}$. That holds true for the situation represented in Figure 10 as well as that in Figure 10a. For instance, a shortening of the barrier B (Figure 10) from the point 12 to the point 13 would change the direction $d_{A,6}$ so that $d_{A,6} = d_{A,13}$ instead of $d_{A,6} = d_{A,11}$. Increase in resistance of the barrier B in Figure 10a would finally make $d_{A,4} = d_{A,1}$ instead of $d_{A,4} = d_{A,2}$. That might not be surprising, because such a change directly affects the path $w_{A,2,4}$. However, the direction $d_{A,4}$ might be altered by a change of any subpart of B. For instance a decrease of resistance of the subregion C might change the distinguished path $w_{A,2,4}$ into $w_{A,5,4}$.

This dependence of direction in hodological space on the properties of the totality of the field reminds one of certain characteristics of physical paths. The path of light, for instance, follows the principle of "minimum of action." Similarly, a stable equilibrium can be defined as a state in which the potential energy shows a minimum. Such a statement includes the dependence of the distinguished path or distinguished position upon the characteristics of the surrounding field.

There is, however, a decisive difference between such cases and that in hodological space. The minimum in these physical examples has to be calculated by taking into account the immediate surroundings and only the immediate surroundings. It is a minimum relatively to the possibility of *differential, "microscopic" changes.* It would be wrong to determine the minimum for the physical field at large instead of for the immediate surroundings. *Direction in hodological space, however, depends not only on the state of the immediate surroundings of the distinguished path, but upon the field at large.*

5. Equality of Direction in Different Points

a. *Definition.*—

$$(6) \qquad d_{A,B} = d_{H,D} \text{ if } w_{A,B} \supset w_{H,D} \quad \text{(Figure 4)}$$

In other words, all directions $d_{X,Y}$ from any point (subregion) X of a distinguished path $w_{A,B}$ to any other point (subregion) Y of this path, are equal. The points X,Y and H,D, respectively, have to be counted in the order they are met by the locomotion from A to B. Like a straight line in Euclidian space, a distinguished path in hodological space does not change its direction at its various points.

A special case of (6) is given if both paths have the same end-points in addition to standing in the relation of part and whole:

$$(6a) \qquad d_{A,B} = d_{D,B} \text{ if } w_{A,B} \supset w_{D,B}$$

Our definition implies that $d_{A,5} = d_{7,5}$ (Figure 10) and that in Figure 10a $d_{A,8} = d_{7,8}$.

One might think of calling all locomotions *to the same goal* equal in direction regardless of where they start. For, in everyday language we often use the term direction in this way. In this case one would have to say that, for instance, in Figure 11, $d_{A,B} = d_{C,B} = d_{E,B}$. Hodological space does not use such a proposition. Instead we speak of "the same goal," but of different "directions" $d_{X,B}$ and $d_{Y,B}$ if the regions X and Y are not crossed by the same path ($d_{A,B} \neq d_{C,B} \neq d_{E,B}$). Such a treatment is more in line with the concept of direction in Euclidian space.

However, if the goal B dominates the situation to a high degree, the situation can be said to contain mainly two regions B and Non-B (Figure 11a). In this case the main psychological characteristic of the regions A and C outside B is the fact that they are parts of Non-B (A $\subset$ Non-B; C $\subset$ Non-B). According to the principles of hodological space, the direction from any part of Non-B to B would be $d_{Non-B,B}$. Therefore, the directions from two different regions to the same region B can be considered more nearly identical the more the two regions become undifferentiated parts of one region Non-B. We will come back to this when we discuss the relation between equality of directions and the structure of the space.

b. The Problem of Transitivity of the Equality of Direction. Equality of Direction as Symmetrical Relation.—We have already mentioned that equality of direction is a transitive relation in Euclidian space. That is, if $d^1 = d^2$ and $d^2 = d^3$ then $d^1 = d^3$.

One can ask whether this transitivity holds for hodological space, too. The answer has to be negative.

In the example of Figure 10, for instance, one can state that $d_{11,5} = d_{A,11}$ and that $d_{A,11} = d_{11,6}$ according to (6). If equality of direction would be transitive for hodological space, it should follow that $d_{11,5} = d_{11,6}$. That, however, is not the case, because $w_{11,5}$ and $w_{11,6}$ have no common parts and the condition of (3) is therefore not fulfilled.

The lack of transitivity in this example is only another expression of a characteristic of hodological space which we have mentioned above: for a person making a locomotion along the path $w_{A,11}$ to approach the point 5 (Figure 10) the whole region H behind the barrier B is undifferentiated as far as the direction of its points is concerned. However, the moment the person goes around the corner of the barrier, the direction of the various points of H become differentiated (about details see Lewin 1934).

This characteristic of hodological space corresponds nicely with certain psychological facts. It represents adequately what happens if a person goes around a corner of a physical barrier. It describes as well certain situations of social locomotions. A student, for instance, who wishes to take his

Ph.D. might work for years in the same direction, namely, toward this examination, without having made up his mind what to do afterward. After reaching his goal he sees himself suddenly confronted with a variety of possibilities all of which lie in different directions. He then has to make up his mind in which of these previously undifferentiated directions he wishes to proceed.

Under two conditions the equality of direction is transitive in hodological space too. (a) It is transitive if the starting region of all three directions is the same and the correlated three paths have a common beginning part (Figure 4).

(7)   If $d_{A,B} = d_{A,C}$ and $d_{A,C} = d_{A,E}$ then $d_{A,B} = d_{A,E}$, in case there exists a $w_{A,Q}$ such that $w_{A,Q} \subset w_{A,B}$, $w_{A,Q} \subset w_{A,C}$ and $w_{A,Q} \subset w_{A,E}$.

(7) follows from (3). We will see later that the identity of the starting region alone does not suffice to secure transitivity. (b) Equality of direction, furthermore, is transitive if all three directions refer to parts of one distinguished path (Figure 4a).

(7a)   If $d_{A,B} = d_{C,E}$ and $d_{C,E} = d_{G,K}$ then $d_{A,B} = d_{G,K}$ in case there exists a $w_{M,N}$ so that $w_{M,N} \supset w_{A,B}$, $w_{M,N} \supset w_{C,E}$ and $w_{M,N} \supset w_{G,K}$.

The correctness of this proposition follows immediately from (6).

It is generally considered one of the basic characteristics of equality that it is a transitive relation. One might therefore criticize the use of the term "equality of direction" in hodological space. We have mentioned that other reasons speak for the use of the term "partly equal direction." What one will have to realize, independent of terminology, is the fact that the restriction in regard to the transitivity of equality of direction points to a rather basic difference between hodological and Euclidian space. *Euclidian space disregards the question of unity of paths, whereas hodological space does not.* That is one of the reasons why equality of direction is always transitive in Euclidian space, but is transitive only under special conditions in hodological space.

Equality of direction is in hodological space, as well as in Euclidian space, a "symmetrical" relation. That is:

$$(8) \qquad d_{A,B} = d_{C,D} \quad \text{if} \quad d_{C,D} = d_{A,B}$$

c. Equality of Direction in the End Point of a Path.—In Euclidian and Riemannian space it has a definite meaning to say: "Proceed in the same direction at the end point of the path." In other words, if the points a and b are given, the request to proceed in a direction $d_{b,x}$ so that $d_{b,x} = d_{a,b}$ determines fully the direction $d_{b,x}$. Is such determination possible in hodological space?

It is clear from what we have discussed that this is possible only under specific circumstances. After reaching the end region B of a path $w_{A,B}$ there might be a number of possibilities for going ahead. For instance, in Figure 4 one might go from the region B to E or to G or to C. Under what conditions is $d_{B,X} = d_{A,B}$?

If a person after getting his Ph.D. goes ahead with research, one might say he is going in the same direction. If he begins to prepare for an M.D., is he still going in the same direction? Does he change his direction if he enters business? After all it might have been his purpose from the beginning to get his Ph.D. to be better able to promote the business of his father.

In hodological space, a direction $d_{B,X}$ which is equal to $d_{A,B}$ is defined only under the following circumstances:

$$(9) \qquad d_{B,X} = d_{A,B} \quad \text{if} \quad w_{A,X} = w_{A,B} + w_{B,X}.[5]$$

It means that one can determine direction beyond the end of a path only if this end is the end of a *part* of a more inclusive distinguished path. In other words, only if X represents a goal, for which B has the position of a means or a subgoal, is $d_{B,X} = d_{A,B}$. (9) follows from (6). In case B is the end

[5] See p. 45, note.

of the total path, there is no way to determine the direction beyond the end.

6. The Direction of Two Different Paths between Two Regions

a. Conditions of Equality and Inequality of Direction of Such Paths.—We have mentioned that sometimes more than one distinguished path leads from A to B. In a roundabout problem, for instance, the path for locomotion might differ from that for looking. In other cases, one path might be distinguished as the quickest, the other as the cheapest.

We can indicate two paths from A to B by referring to an intermediate region which is crossed by the path concerned. In Figure 12, for instance, the one path from A to B can be called $w_{A,E,B}$, the second, $w_{A,H,B}$. Correspondingly, we can speak about the directions $d_{A,E,B}$ and $d_{A,H,B}$.

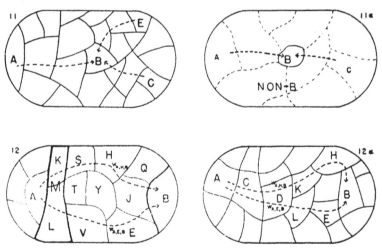

Fig. 11. Paths from Different Beginnings (A, E, and C) to the Same End Region (B). $d_{A,B} \neq d_{C,B} \neq d_{E,B}$.

Fig. 11a. Paths from Different Sub-parts (A and C) of One Region (Non-B) to the Same Region (B).

Fig. 12. Various Paths between Two Regions (from A to B). $d_{A,H,B} \neq d_{A,E,B}$.

Fig. 12a. Two Paths between Two Regions (from A to B). Equal in Direction. $d_{A,H,B} = d_{A,E,B}$.

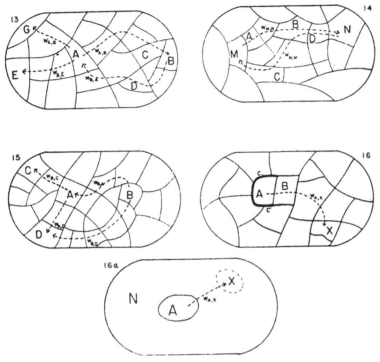

Fig. 13. Opposite Directions. $w_{A,B}$, distinguished path from A to B; $w_{B,A}$, distinguished path from B to A; $d_{A,B} = d_{B,A}$.

Fig. 14. Opposite Directions. $w_{M,N}$, distinguished path from M to N; $w_{N,M}$, distinguished path from N to M; $d_{A,B} = d_{D,C}$.

Fig. 15. Direction Away From. The distance $e_{B,C} > e_{B,A}$, and $e_{B,D} > e_{B,A}$; $d_{A,-B} = d_{A,C}$; $d_{A,-B} = d_{A,D}$.

Fig. 16. Case where Direction Away From Is Equal Direction Toward. C, impassable barrier; $d_{A,-B} = d_{A,X} = d_{A,B}$.

Fig. 16a. Direction within a Region (A) Away From It, and Direction Toward that Region. $d_{X,A} = d_{A,-A}$.

The fact that these two paths are different can be expressed by saying that each of the paths does include at least one of the regions not crossed by the other path ($w_{A,E,B} \cdot H = 0$ and $w_{A,H,B} \cdot E = 0$).[5]

[5] The sign $\cdot$ refers to the topological intersection, the sign $+$ to the topological sum (Princ., p. 87).

We will have to ask whether the direction from A to B along the two different paths is to be considered equal or unequal.

Figure 12 represents a situation in which these directions are to be considered unequal according to the definitions of hodological space. For, the beginning step of the two distinguished paths is not the same.

(10) $d_{A,E,B} \neq d_{A,H,B}$ if no path $w_{A,X}$ exists such that $w_{A,X} \subset w_{A,E,B}$ and $w_{A,X} \subset w_{A,H,B}$.

In other words, the direction at a region A toward a region B is different for two paths if the two paths do not contain a common beginning part. (10) is in line with (3).

The inequality of direction holds true, of course, if both paths have no common steps whatever. However, even if both paths have later steps in common (in Figure 12, $w_{J,B}$ is part of both paths) the direction $d_{A,E,B}$ and $d_{A,H,B}$ might, nevertheless, be different.

If both paths have a common beginning part as in Figure 12a, the direction becomes equal in A in spite of later differences between the paths.

(10a) $d_{A,E,B} = d_{A,H,B}$ if there is a $w_{A,X}$ such that $w_{A,X} \subset w_{A,E,B}$ and $w_{A,X} \subset w_{A,H,B}$.

(10a) is in line with (3). In Figure 12a, $w_{A,D}$ is such a common part of both paths.

   b. Many-Valued Directions.—In case of more than one distinguished path from A to B the direction $d_{A,B}$ is what one might term "many valued." In our example (Figure 12) $d_{A,B} = d_{A,K}$ and also $d_{A,B} = d_{A,L}$ in spite of $d_{A,K} \neq d_{A,L}$. $d_{A,B}$ is under these circumstances two-valued, like, e.g., $\sqrt{1}$. (A many-valued direction is somewhat similar to an equation with more than one solution.)

The fact that $d_{A,B} = d_{A,K}$ and $d_{A,B} = d_{A,L}$ in spite of $d_{A,K} \neq d_{A,L}$ shows again that equality of direction is not necessarily transitive in hodological space.

   c. Equality of Direction and the Structure of the Space.—Under certain circumstances two different paths from a region A to a region B can be considered equal in direction, even if these paths are as much separated as in Figure 12. We have seen that paths from different starts to the same end can be regarded as equal in direction if the starting regions are relatively undifferentiated parts of the same more inclusive region. A similar consideration can be made in regard to regions which represent means. One can consider in Figure 12 $d_{A,E,B} = d_{A,H,B}$ if the regions K and L can be viewed as parts of one undifferentiated region M. Namely, in this case both paths have a common beginning step $(w_{A,M} \subset w_{A,E,B}$ and $w_{A,M} \subset w_{A,H,B})$ and the correlated directions are equal according to (3).

This makes it understandable why the direction from one region along different paths to the same goal appears psychologically often as the same direction. It is to a certain degree possible to regard as one region the totality of regions corresponding to "means" which one has to apply to get to the same "end." This region has topologically the position of a boundary region (intermediate region (Princ., pp. 120, 139)) between the starting region A and the end region B. In Figure 12, for instance, the totality of the regions K,L,S,T,V,H, Y,Q,J,E can be viewed as one boundary region between A and B.

In psychology we often deal with a situation where such a barrier region is neither entirely undifferentiated nor consists of entirely separated part regions. Such cases can be represented by using overlapping situations in a fashion similar to that employed for handling the problem of the unity of paths (see above). One of the overlapping situations would correspond to a state where the barrier region consists of fully independent subparts (that would include in Figure 12 that $d_{A,H,B} \neq d_{A,E,B}$). The second situation would correspond to an undifferentiated barrier region (this would include that $d_{A,H,B} = d_{A,E,B}$ because H and E are undifferentiated parts of the same region). One can represent the degree to which the one or the other statement is correct by attributing a different relative potency to each of the overlapping situations.

This problem is rather important for the question of conflicts in regard to the choice between two paths to the same goal. Such a choice is generally considered the easier the more the two paths are different. This is in line with certain results of experiments with animals (Maier and Schneirla 1935).

If our considerations are correct it would follow that, in addition, the process of decision is determined by the importance (relative weight) which the means (paths) have relative to the end. In case of two paths to the same goal a decrease in importance of the means should decrease the intensity of the conflict, because it decreases the relative potency of that situation in which the conflict exists. (This factor might have influenced the outcome of certain experiments of Hull and Leeper, which we discuss later in Chapter V.)

7. Opposite Directions

a. *Definition.*—We have mentioned that the basic characteristic of a direction is to be a relation between two points (regions) A and B, and that the direction from A to B is not equal but opposed to that from B to A.

(11)   Definition: $d_{A,B} = \overline{d_{B,A}}$[6]

This formula should be read as "$d_{A,B}$ is opposite to $d_{B,A}$."

This definition compares two directions in different points, namely, the direction in the beginning point of the path toward the end point with the direction in the end point of the path toward the beginning point. Definition (11) presupposes that there exists not only a distinguished path $w_{A,B}$ but also a distinguished path $w_{B,A}$. The second condition does not necessarily follow from the first. A maze with one-way doors might permit a locomotion from A to B but there might be no path back.

Furthermore, in cases where such a distinguished return path $w_{B,A}$ exists, this path $w_{B,A}$ might not pass through the same regions as $w_{A,B}$ (Figure 13). For instance, the most comfortable path uphill is usually different from the most comfortable path downhill. According to (11) the direction $d_{B,A}$ which is correlated to the beginning step of the path

---

[6] We could have indicated opposition of directions by a minus sign ($-d_{B,A}$). However, we will use the minus later to indicate the "direction away from." To indicate opposition of directions we place the minus sign above the d.

$w_{B,A}$ will be called opposite to $d_{A,B}$ even if this step of $w_{B,A}$ is not a part of $w_{A,B}$. In the example of Figure 13, for instance, $d_{A,B} = d_{B,D}$.

The relation "of being opposed to" is symmetrical:

$$(11a) \qquad d_{B,A} = d_{A,B} \text{ if } d_{A,B} = d_{B,A}$$

If $d_{A,B} = d_{B,A}$ it follows that there exists a distinguished path both from A to B and from B to A; therefore $d_{B,A} = d_{A,B}$ according to (11).

b. Opposite Directions Within One Path To and From.

$$(12) \quad d_{A,B} = d_{D,C} \text{ if a } w_{M,N} \text{ and } w_{N,M} \text{ exist such that } w_{M,N} \supset w_{A,B} \text{ and } w_{N,M} \supset w_{D,C}$$

(The regions A,B and D,C (Figure 14) should be counted in the order in which they are met by the path $w_{M,N}$ and $w_{N,M}$ respectively.) (12) follows from (11) in connection with (6). (12) means that the direction of any step within one distinguished path is opposite to the direction of any step of the distinguished path back.

c. Opposite Directions at the Same Point.—In view of the problem of equilibrium and of conflict of forces it is important to define opposite directions in the same point. The definition (11) and the statement (12) do not suffice for determining this. To determine, for instance, in Figure 13 the direction $d_{A,B}$ in A, one should know whether the path $w_{A,E}$ or the path $w_{A,G}$ is an extension of $w_{B,A}$. $d_{A,B}$ is related to a definite path only under the following conditions:

$$(13) \qquad d_{A,X} = d_{A,B} \text{ if } w_{X,B} \supset w_{A,B} \text{ or if } w_{B,X} \supset w_{B,A}$$

For instance, in Figure 13, $d_{A,G} = d_{A,B}$ only if the distinguished path $w_{G,B}$ (or $w_{B,G}$) leads through the region A ($w_{G,B} \supset w_{A,B}$ or $w_{B,G} \supset w_{B,A}$).

It is possible that two distinguished paths to B are crossing A, for instance the path $w_{G,B}$ from G to B and the paths $w_{E,B}$ from E to B ($w_{G,B} \supset w_{A,B}$ and $w_{E,B} \supset w_{A,B}$). In this case it is $d_{A,G} = d_{A,B}$ as well as $d_{A,E} = d_{A,B}$. In

other words, two or more different directions can be opposite
to a given direction in the same point.

(13a)   It can be $d_{A,G} = d_{A,B}$ and $d_{A,E} = d_{A,B}$
      in spite of $d_{A,G} \neq d_{A,E}$.

An opposing direction can therefore be many-valued.

(13a) refers again to a case where equality of direction is
not transitive.

8. Differences of Distance

We have mentioned that not only direction but also distance (e) is a relation between two regions. Distance refers
to the totality of a distinguished path rather than to the property of this path at a given point (as direction does).

(14)   Definition: $e_{A,B} > e_{H,D}$ if $w_{A,B} \supset w_{H,D}$
      and $w_{A,B} \cdot w_{H,D} \neq w_{A,B}$ (Figure 4)

We will read $e_{A,B}$ as "distance between the regions A and
B." (The symbol "$\cdot$" means "topological intersection of
two regions"; the symbol "$>$" means "larger than" in the
usual meaning of this term.)

Definition (14) bases the comparisons of distances upon
a part-whole relation of two distinguished paths. However,
in psychology one also has to compare distances under conditions where this topological relation does not hold. One
could think of a number of possible means of comparing distances under such conditions, for instance, by correlating the
distance to the time necessary for carrying out a locomotion
along a given path. Tolman (1932) has discussed several possibilities. We will merely make the following statement:

(14a) $e_{A,B} > e_{H,D}$ shall not imply that
       $w_{A,B} \supset w_{H,D}$

In other words, the topological relation part-whole of two
distinguished paths shall always permit a conclusion concerning the difference of distance (14) but a difference of
distance shall in itself not imply the part-whole relation of the
paths concerned.

In Euclidian space the so-called "triangle-axiom" is considered to be the basic axiom concerning distances. A triangle axiom holds also in hodological space, as I tried to show elsewhere (Lewin 1934).

9. Direction "Away From"

a. *Definition.*—The concept of direction in hodological space is related to wholes of paths. Therefore aside from the direction at "A toward B" ($d_{A,B}$) we will have to distinguish the direction at "A away from B." We will write this direction $d_{A,-B}$.

(15)   Definition: $d_{A,-B} = d_{A,X}$ if $e_{B,X} > e_{B,A}$.

The direction at A "away from B" is therefore defined as a direction toward a region X which is farther away from B than A is.

b. *Direction Away as a Many-Valued Direction.*—There exists generally more than one region X for which (15) holds, and these regions X do not need to lie on one distinguished path. For instance, it might be $e_{B,C} > e_{B,A}$ (Figure 15) and also $e_{B,D} > e_{B,A}$. In this case it would be $d_{A,-B} = d_{A,C}$ and at the same time $d_{A,-B} = d_{A,D}$ in spite of $d_{A,C} \neq d_{A,D}$. In other words, a direction in A away from B can be many-valued.

10. Direction Away From and Opposite Direction

We would like to mention specificially that the direction "away from" should not be confused with the "opposite direction."

One cannot say that the direction in A away from B is always the same as the direction in A opposite the direction toward B; neither is the direction in A toward B always opposite to the direction in A away from B. In other words, it might be that $d_{A,B} \neq d_{A,-B}$ and that $d_{A,B} \neq d_{A,-B}$.

That this statement is correct can be proved in the following way:

According to (15) $d_{A,X} = d_{A,-B}$ if $e_{B,X} > e_{B,A}$; furthermore, it is according to (13) $d_{A,X} = d_{A,B}$ if $w_{X,A} \supset w_{B,A}$. In other words, the relation of opposing directions implies that the distinguished path from X to B (or from B to X) must pass through A. We have seen above that this does not necessarily follow from $e_{B,X} > e_{B,A}$ (15). Therefore the direction in A away from B is not necessarily opposed to the direction in A toward B.

In other words, either of the following propositions can be true:

(15a) $d_{A,-B} = d_{A,B}$ or $d_{A,-B} \neq d_{A,B}$

There are even cases in which the direction in A away from B is equal to the direction in A toward B $(d_{A,-B} = d_{A,B})$. This rather paradoxical equation arises in situations where one can reach a greater distance from B only by first passing through B. Figure 16 represents a situation where the region A is surrounded by an impassable barrier C so that only a path through the region B is left open. In this case any path $w_{A,X}$ to a region X for which $e_{B,X} > e_{B,A}$ must go through B $(w_{A,X} \supset w_{A,B})$. Therefore $d_{A,-B} = d_{A,X} = d_{A,B}$. The so-called "flight forward," that is, the attempt in desperate situations to break through in the direction towards the enemy, is an example of such a constellation.

In semi-Euclidian space (in which the whole field is homogeneous with respect to ease of locomotion and in which the shortest path is the distinguished one) the direction $d_{A,B}$ becomes a one-valued one. The direction $d_{A,-B}$ would still be many-valued because any paths which increase the distance from B determine a direction $d_{A,-B}$. Even in semi-Euclidian space therefore could be $d_{A,-B} \neq d_{A,B}$. However, there would exist one path away from B which would represent the quickest increase of distance to B. In semi-Euclidian space this "optimum direction away from" would be the same as the opposite direction $(d_{A,-B} = d_{A,B})$.

11. Directions Toward and Away from the Present Region

a. Direction Away from the Present Region.—There is no objection to applying the concept "direction away from" also to cases where one wants to go away from the region in which one is at present. This is the direction "in A away from A" $(d_{A,-A})$. One can say, namely:

(15b) $d_{A,-A} = d_{A,X}$ if $A \cdot X = 0$

In other words, the direction in A away from A is defined as the direction in A toward a region which is Non-A.

One can derive this proposition in the following way: from (15) it follows that $d_{A,-A} = d_{A,X}$ if $e_{X,A} > e_{A,A}$. It seems reasonable to call:

(16) $e_{A,A} = 0$

From any region X which is not identical with A (i.e., for which $X \cdot A = 0$) one has to make at least one step to get to A. Therefore $e_{X,A} > 0$. This implies that (15b) is correct.

The direction $d_{A,-A}$ does not involve any conceptual difficulties. Although only one region (A) seems to be mentioned, two regions in fact are involved, namely A and X (or non-A). The basic concept that direction is a relation between two regions is therefore not violated. (Topologically, every region A within a space S defines, according to Menger (1928), a region S-A which can be viewed as identical with the totality of our regions X.)

In psychology, the direction $d_{A,-A}$ is especially important in representing a situation where a person wishes to leave a region because this region is disagreeable (has a negative valence).

b. *The Direction Away from a Present Region as Opposed to the Direction from Outside toward That Region.*—We have seen that the direction in A away from B is not necessarily opposed to the direction in A toward B. It is, however, important for the measurement of psychological forces that the direction in a region *away from itself* is necessarily opposed to the direction from the outside towards that region. In other words:

(15c) $d_{A,-A} = d_{X,A}$ for any $X \cdot A = 0$

One could try to demonstrate the correctness of this statement in the following way: $d_{A,-A} = d_{A,X}$ for any $X \cdot A = 0$ according to (15b); furthermore: $d_{A,X} = d_{X,A}$ according to (11); therefore $d_{A,-A} = d_{X,A}$. Such a procedure might be criticized on the ground that equality of direction is not necessarily transitive in the hodological space. However, in our case we can point to the following fact: As mentioned before, the direction $d_{A,-A}$ refers to a division of a total space S into two parts, namely, the region B and the rest of the space N (S–A = N; Figure 16a). Any specific region X for which X · A = 0 can be viewed therefore as a subpart of N (X ⊂ N), because any path $w_{A,X}$ determines one of the solutions of the many-valued direction $d_{A,-A}$ ($d_{A,X} = d_{A,-A}$) according to (15b). On the other hand, for this given path we have the right to say that $d_{X,A} = d_{A,X}$ according to (11). Therefore $d_{X,A} = d_{A,-A}$ according to (7a). In other words, the transitivity of equality is correct because we have to deal with one distinguished path only.

c. Direction Towards the Present Region.—One can ask what direction one has to deal with if a person wants to remain within the region in which he is, for instance, because this region has a positive valence for him. In other words, what is the meaning of the direction $d_{A,A}$?

This problem is rather important for certain dynamical questions. For reasons which will be understood later, we will use the following definition:

$$(17) \qquad d_{A,A} = d_{A,-A}$$

This definition determines the direction "to stay in a region" as the direction "opposed to leaving this region." In this way we comply with the necessity of referring to two regions, namely to A and non-A. This definition implies that the direction $d_{A,A}$ is at least as many-valued as $d_{A,-A}$.

12. Hodological Space as One of the Geometries Applicable in Psychology

In terminating our discussion of hodological space, I wish to emphasize that hodological space is not necessarily the only space which might be useful in defining directions in psychology. This problem is one of "applied mathematics" or, more specifically, of "applied geometry." We know that in any empirical science more than one kind of geometry might be adequate to represent the empirical data.

COMPARISON BETWEEN SOME PROPERTIES OF HODOLOGICAL AND EUCLIDIAN SPACE

	Euclidian Space	Hodological Space
Direction is a relation between two:	points	regions
Connection determining direction is a:	straight line (no reference to unity of path)	distinguished path (reference to unity of path)
Types of direction	toward $(d_{a,b})$	a) toward $(d_{A,B})$ b) away from $(d_{A,-B})$
Relation between two directions	angle (a continuity of degrees is distinguished with: equality $= 0°$; opposition $= 180°$)	One can distinguish: a) equality $(d_{A,B} = d_{C,D})$ b) inequality $(d_{A,B} \neq d_{C,D})$ with the special case: b¹) Opposition $(d_{A,B} = d_{B,A})$ In case of a semi-Euclidian space a continuity of angles might be distinguished.
The relation "equality of direction" is:	transitive	not transitive
The totality of points lying from one point in the same direction determines:	a one-dimensional region (straight line)	usually a poly-dimensional region
Which path is the distinguished one depends upon:	the immediate neighborhood of the path	the total field and its cognitive structure

It might be possible, for instance, for psychology to use a geometry in which the concept of distance plays a more fundamental role than it has in hodological space. One could think of defining the "direction in A toward B" as the direction to any kind of region which is "nearer" to B than A. Such a definition would lead to a geometry which is quite similar to but not identical with hodological space.

At present the question as to which of the possible geometries will be the most adequate for psychology is rather premature. The important task, as I see it, is to find some kind of geometry which is sufficiently adequate. To my mind, hodological space is such a geometry.

III

PSYCHOLOGICAL EXAMPLES ILLUSTRATING THE APPLICATION OF HODOLOGICAL SPACE

It might be appropriate to give a few examples of the use of hodological space for determining directions in the life space.

A. DIRECTION IN A MAZE

Figure 17 represents the physical set-up of a maze with A as the starting place and G the place where food is contained. Psychologically, direction can be defined in this maze only by referring to the cognitive structure which this maze has for the individual concerned at the time in question. I would like to discuss two different cases:

1. *Direction in a Maze Familiar to the Individual*

Let us assume: 1.) The animal or person knows the maze well in so far as he is familiar with the way in which the different parts of the maze are connected. He does not need to know the exact geographical position of every part in relation to every other. 2.) The animal wants to approach G by the shortest path possible, perhaps because he is hungry and expects food at G. 3.) The maze should not be so familiar to the animal that the passing of many of the blind alleys would be one undifferentiated step; rather, every intersection should be considered psychologically as one region and any part of the maze between two intersections as another region.

Under these circumstances we can make the following statements.

(Ex. 1)[1] $$d_{A,G} = d_{A,B}$$

In other words, the direction in A to the goal G points to the region B in spite of the fact that this direction is not the direction to G from the point of view of physics. The correctness of (Ex. 1) follows from (3) because $w_{A,G} \supset w_{A,B}$.

(Ex. 2) $d_{A,G} = d_{C,D} = d_{E,T}$ etc. according to (6).

[1] The formulas marked by (Ex.) characterize the specific situation of an example. They do not refer to ''general propositions'' (laws) like the previous formulas which are indicated by a number only.

In other words, as long as the individual follows the path $w_{A,G}$ he proceeds psychologically always in the same direction.

(Ex. 3) $d_{C,G} \neq d_{C,L}$ according to (3) because $w_{C,G}$ does not include $w_{C,L}$.

In other words, if the individual enters from C the blind alley L he locomotes in a direction different from the direction to G.

These conclusions (Ex. 1), (Ex. 2), and (Ex. 3) merely indicate that the definitions given in hodological space represent adequately the psychological meaning of the situation.

If the running through the maze becomes more of a routine, the regions which have the position of cells (1) become more inclusive and therefore the steps (4) become also more inclusive.

The knowledge of spatial relations in the physical space might enable the animal or person to learn something of the physical positions of the different parts of the maze. Especially might that be the case when visual connection between the regions A and G is possible. Under these circumstances the life space will acquire to some degree the properties of a semi-Euclidian space, and the directions will become similar to the physical directions. One might expect that this would lead to a tendency of the animal to prefer those blind alleys which are physically in the direction toward the goal.

The result of experiments about this problem (Dashiell 1937) are somewhat controversial. Indeed, as long as the maze is not equivalent to an open homogeneous field, the life space will be characterized by the overlapping of two situations: the direction in the one is determined by the quickest locomotion as the distinguished path; the direction in the other as in semi-Euclidian space. How great the relative potency of either of these overlapping situations is depends upon the circumstances, for instance, upon the clearness of the physical (visual) direction and upon the intelligence of the individual. I would expect, however, that generally the direction defined by the quickest locomotion to the goal will be dominant and will become more dominant the more the individual gets familiar with the maze.

2. Direction in a Maze Unfamiliar to the Individual

The psychological directions in a maze generally are different from its physical directions. However, the topology of the well-known maze is as a whole in line with the topology of its physical structure. That is not the case if the maze is not well known to the individual.

Let us assume that the individual knows that a region G is accessible somewhere within the maze, but does not know how actually to reach G when he is placed in region A. Let us assume he had passed the region B in search of the food and is now located at C. Under these circumstances, what is the direction $d_{C,G}$?

The individual "knows." his path to the region G in a maze if he can distinguish for every subregion (1) whether it is G or not G, (2) which of the adjacent regions is connected (co) with the region G and which is not connected (n) with the region G. (Princ., p. 133; Tolman 1932). If the indi-

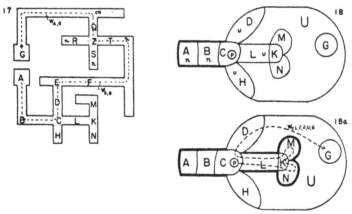

Fig. 17. Direction in a Maze Familiar to the Individual (Physical Constellation). A, starting region; G, goal; psychological directions are not determined by the physical ones, but by the distinguished path $w_{A,G}$; $d_{A,G} = d_{A,B} = d_{C,E}$.

Fig. 18. Topology of the Same Maze for an Individual Unfamiliar with It. P, the individual located in C; G, the goal. He knows that A and B are not connected (n) with G; U, cognitively undetermined region; H, L, and D, part of U; $d_{C,G} = d_{C,U} = d_{C,L}$.

Fig. 18a. Change in Topology after the Discovery that L is a Blind Alley. $d_{C,G} \neq d_{C,L}$.

vidual is, for instance, in the region Z (Figure 17) he should know that R, S, and T are not connected with G (viewed from the region Z), but that Q is connected with G (i.e., $R \subset n$; $S \subset n$; $T \subset n$; $Q \subset co$).

For our individual (P) who does not know the maze and has proceeded from A to C the cognitive structure of the situation is represented in Figure 18. He knows that the regions A and B are not connected with G ($A \subset n$; $B \subset n$). Between him and the goal G lies a region the structure of which is cognitively undetermined. We have discussed elsewhere (Princ., pp. 130 ff.) some of the characteristics of such cognitively undetermined regions (U) and their properties as barriers.

We have assumed that in our case the individual knows that somewhere in the maze the goal-region G exists. The region U separates C and G in such a way that every path, including the distinguished path $w_{C,G}$, has to cross U ($w_{C,G} \supset w_{C,U}$).

From this there follows according to (3) that

(Ex. 4) $$d_{C,G} = d_{C,U}$$

In other words, the direction from C to the goal is determined as the direction from C into the undetermined region U. Therefore:

(Ex. 4a) $$d_{C,L} = d_{C,G} \text{ as long as } L \subset U.$$

(We will remember that when the maze is known $d_{C,L} \neq d_{C,G}$ according to (Ex. 3).) Entering L means therefore an action in the direction to G.

When the individual enters L he might find that the food is not contained in L—in other words, that $L \cdot G = 0$. This, however, is not enough to change the character of L from U to n. The individual has, as we have stated, not only to find out that L is not G, but also that L is not connected with G in respect to possible locomotions from C to G—in other words, that $L \subset n$. That implies he has to prove the existence of an impassable boundary between the region L and U (Princ., pp. 140-144). To determine whether or not such a boundary exists one has to investigate all regions (K, N and M) connected with L. In our case one finds that these regions taken as a whole are surrounded by a boundary against U with the opening only in C. In this way the cognitive character of L changes from being a part of U into being a part of n ($L \subset n$). This involves a change in direction: instead of $d_{C,L} = d_{C,G}$ corresponding to (Ex. 4a) it now is true that $d_{C,L} \neq d_{C,G}$ corresponding to (Ex. 3).

In other words, the progress in knowledge leads to a change in direction. This might be viewed as an example of the general fact that *directions in the life space depend upon its cognitive structure.*

It is important for the understanding of behavior and of the learning process that a change of the cognitive structure of the situation is a condition for the change of the direction of action: If entering L did not really change the character of L from U to n, then after the individual returns to C there would still be $d_{C,L} = d_{C,G}$ because L is still a part of U. Therefore the individual might enter the same blind alley L again in trying to locomote toward the goal G. Such "repeated errors" are not infrequently observed in the early stage of maze learning. It shows that entering L did not suffice to change the cognitive structure of the field permanently so that L became a part of n instead of U. Even if the exploration of the blind alley sufficed to change the character of L and to make $d_{C,L} \neq d_{C,G}$ for the time being, the new cognitive structure might not be very stable. In this case the individual might on the next run enter the same blind alley again. However, later, one exploration or even a short entrance might suffice to make the individual recognize again that L is a part of n.

The animal does not know how to reach the goal as long as a gap (consisting of unstructured regions U) exists between the cognitively structured regions connected with the starting point and whatever cognitively determined regions might for him be connected with the goal. It knows a path to the goal as soon as this gap is closed by a "bridge" of cognitively determined regions (it is interesting to consider Koffka's (1928) Theory of Closure from this point of view). Later on, the animal may find a second bridge through U which might be preferable to the first one.

The degree to which the change of structure resulting from the exploration is stable is one of the main factors which determines the velocity of learning in mazes.

3. Mazes with One-Way Doors

The possibility for the individual to go back from L to C is rather important. In case of a one-way door between C and L which permits entering L but not going back to C the situation would be different.

Without the one-way door, the path $w_{C,L}$ into a blind alley can be viewed as a part of a path $w_{C,L,C,D,U,G}$ (Figure 18a). This path does not lead "directly" to G, but it leads to G by a roundabout route which goes first back to C. Without a one-way door the individual has to choose between two or more different paths. However, his decision is not too important because it involves merely the chance of using a longer instead of a shorter path.

In case a one-way door prevents the individual's return to C after he enters L, his choice will no longer mean the difference between a shorter and longer path, but between reaching and not reaching the goal. In other words, it will be definitely true either $d_{C,L} = d_{C,G}$ in accordance with (Ex. 4a) or that $d_{C,L} \neq d_{C,G}$ in accordance with (Ex. 3).

4. The Nature of Orientation and Search

The situation represented in Figure 18 is characteristic for any situation of exploration or search. Basic for this situation is that two regions can be distinguished: one region that is cognitively determined (S) and another which is cognitively undetermined (U), either in respect to its geographical properties or in respect to the location of a certain region (object) within U. In the first case one generally speaks of "orientation," in the second of "search."

In both cases one can speak of a goal G, if one understands under G an activity or a state of the individual rather than a geographical position. (It is possible to represent as region of the life space not only geographical areas and social groups but also activities and states (Princ., pp. 93, 215).) Region G would correspond to the solution of the problem, the region A to the present state of the individual.

In case of orientation and of search, a change in cognitive structure is attempted: namely, the learning of the geography of the place, or the finding of an object. The goal G is separated from the present position of the individual in A by a region U. It is characteristic for the cases of orientation and search that the individual is located in a cognitively structured region (S), i.e., that $A \subset S$ and that he has to locomote from this cognitively structured region (S) to an undetermined one (U).

(Ex. 5) $$d_{A,G} = d_{S,U}$$

This locomotion will generally change the character of a part of the region U from U to S. But as long as the person is exploring, he will always leave the determined region S for a new subregion of U and again this subregion after it has changed its character from U to S.

This tendency always to leave the already determined region S can be viewed as tendency in S away from S ($d_{S,-S}$) according to (15b), i.e.,

(Ex. 5a) $$d_{A,G} = d_{S,-S}$$

5. *Exploration and Restless Movements*

This points to a striking similarity between search and restless movements. Also, the restless movements imply (as we will see later) the tendency to leave the region A, which corresponds to the present state of the individual, for another one and that region again for another one and so on. It is a locomotion in the direction

(Ex. 6) $d_{A,-A}$

This similarity between search and restless movements is, I think, well in line with psychological facts. (The theory of learning through insight has emphasized directed search, whereas the theory of trial and error emphasized random locomotions which are similar to restless movements.) There are, however, certain differences between restless movements and search: in search the direction $d_{A,G}$ toward the goal G is dominant and the leaving of S is only a means to an end; in the case of restless movements, the direction $d_{A,-A}$ away from the present situation is dominant.

Moreover, in orientation and search the leaving of a region for another one is based on a cognitive difference between the region S and U and involves a change of the cognitive character of the present region from U to S. In case of pure restless movements, the question of cognitive restructuring is not necessarily involved. The individual tries to leave the region of his present state A and to enter another one X (X·A = 0). The new region X does not need to be an unstructured one (U), nor does the next step of the restless movement necessarily involve a change of the cognitive structure of the region X from being an undetermined to a determined one. In a case of restlessness, therefore, the individual might enter the same region again and again. He might run in circles.

A pure case of orientation, on the other hand, can be a very systematic goal-seeking behavior. In this case the same region would not be entered more often than is necessary for discovering its cognitive structure (to change from U to S).

There are many transitions and some interesting cases of overlapping between restlessness and orientation which should be studied in detail.

B. THE INSANE ASYLUM. (DEGREE OF DIFFERENTIATION OF THE LIFE SPACE, AND THE DETERMINATION OF DIRECTIONS.)

Dembo and Hanfmann (1935) discussed the situation of a patient newly admitted to an insane asylum. For the patient there exists essentially two regions, the hospital H (Figure 19) and the region of freedom G outside the hospital. These regions H and G are separated by a barrier B which topologically has the character of a Jordan curve (Princ., p. 90). Outstanding parts of this barrier are doors T, nurses N, doctors D. A group of primitive patients P try to leave the hospital H for freedom G by approaching every door, nurse, and physician. Indeed, it holds in accordance with (3) and our discussion on page 46:

(Ex. 7) $d_{H,G} = d_{H,N}$; $d_{H,G} = d_{H,T}$; and $d_{H,G} = d_{H,D}$

Such patients often change their behavior decidedly after understanding that they will not be able to get out in this way. They start to follow all regulations of the hospital and attempt to become "good" patients. Dembo and Hanfmann described this behavior as a complete reversal of the direction of action. Instead of actions in the direction toward the barrier B, actions toward the "inner life of the hospital" become dominant.

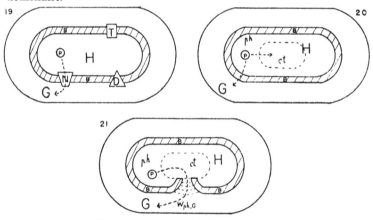

TOPOLOGY OF THE INSANE ASYLUM

Fig. 19. Topology for a Newly Admitted Simple-Minded Patient. H, the hospital; P, the individual; B, the barrier separating H from freedom G; T, doors; N, nurse; D, physician; $d_{H,G} = d_{H,N}$; $d_{H,G} = d_{H,T}$.

Fig. 20. The Same Situation, but Distinguishing a Peripheral Zone (ph) of Hospital Life, and a Central Zone (ct). The direction to freedom appears to be opposite to participation in hospital life ($d_{ph,G} \neq d_{ph,ct}$).

Fig. 21. Situation after Patient Understood that He Has to Fulfill the Requirements of Hospital Life if He Wishes to Be Discharged. $w_{ph,G}$, the distinguished path to G, leads through ct; $d_{ph,G} = d_{ph,ct}$.

We might ask how to represent this change in direction. It is impossible to represent the new direction by merely drawing the arrow on the region P representing the patient with a different angle, because any such arrow can be viewed as an arrow toward the barrier B. One can represent the new direction only by differentiating the region H into subregions. One must distinguish within the hospital life H an area ct corresponding to the "central life" of the hospital and an area ph corresponding to the periphery of hospital life (Figure 20). Then one can say that the attempt of the patient P to leave the peripheral region ph in the direction to G is different and even opposite to his attempt to participate in the inner life:

(Ex. 7a) $$d_{ph,G} \neq d_{ph,ct}$$

according to (3) and $d_{ph,G} = d_{ph,ct}$ according to (13) as long as the topology of the situation corresponds to Figure 20.

In reality, however, the situation is not entirely such as represented in Figure 20. It corresponds more closely to that in Figure 21: the patient recognizes that he will be permitted to leave the hospital only by showing that he is able to fulfill the requirements of the hospital and by proving in this way that he is normal. In other words, the action towards the inner life becomes for him a part of the distinguished, namely, the only way to freedom. Therefore,

(Ex. 7b) $$d_{ph,G} = d_{ph,ct}$$

according to (3) because $w_{ph,ct} \subset w_{ph,G}$

This change in behavior of the patient is another example of the effect which the cognitive structure and the degree of differentiation of the environment has upon the determination of directions in the life space.

C. THE ROUNDABOUT ROUTE

We have already mentioned that the problem of the roundabout route is closely related to that of direction in the life space. Later we will come back to the problem of conflict and of forces in situations involving roundabout routes; here we will discuss more in detail the determination of directions in such cases.

A canary P is in a cage E with the wire wall B (Figure 22). A person G is beckoning to it. The canary is accustomed to fly to his shoulder. The door R of the cage is open. Nevertheless, this canary will come out only if the person stands at the position 2 or some other place physically not too much opposed to the direction to the door R.

What are the psychological directions for the canary P if the person G stands physically opposite to the door in region C?

In this case the canary generally will come to a region A ($A \subset E$). The bird is in visual communication with its goal, the person G. It wants to fly over to G. The hodological directions in question are therefore those for looking and for bodily locomotion.

In case the door R were closed the region B would have the character of a Jordan curve surrounding E as the "inner region" (Princ., p. 91). C is a part of the "outer region"; A is part of E; therefore every path $w_{A,G}$ would have to cross B according to a basic axiom of topology (Princ., p. 91). In other words, $w_{A,G} \subset w_{A,B}$. From this it follows, according to (3), that for every kind of bodily communication

(Ex. 8) $d_{A,G} = d_{A,B}.$

Even if the door R were physically open, the situation would not be different psychologically as long as the fact that R is open is not present cognitively for the animal at that time. If, for instance, the opening is relatively small or the animal did not notice that the door was open, R can be considered for the time being as a part of B.

Past experience of the animal and the visual communication along the path $w_{A,G}$ ($\equiv w_{A,B,C,G}$; Figure 22) give its surroundings the character of a semi-Euclidian space at least to some degree. As far as this is true we can state:

(Ex. 8a) $d_{A,R} = d_{A,-G}$

according to (15) because $e_{R,G} > e_{A,G}$. In other words, the direction to the door R has for the animal not the character toward but away from its goal G. In the constellation of Figure 22 we could even say that both directions are opposite: $d_{A,R} = d_{A,G}$ (see Chapter II C).

As long as the psychological situation is such that (Ex. 8a) holds true, the animal will not fly to the door to reach his goal.

The animal will find the solution only if the cognitive structure of the field changes so that

(Ex. 9) $d_{A,R} = d_{A,G}$

In other words, the direction to the door has to acquire the character of "toward the goal G" instead of "away from G." That is the case only if $w_{A,G} \supset w_{A,R}$, for instance if the cognitive structure of the situation changed into that given in Figure 22a. In this case the regions A and C are no longer separated by the Region B, but A and C become part of one connected region. The distinguished path from A to G will not be $w_{A,B,C,G}$ as in Figure 22, but $w_{A,E,R,H,C,G}$.

The conditions for the solution are therefore: 1.) There is a split of the distinguished path $w_{A,G}$ into two paths, namely, (a) a path for looking (1) at G $(w^l_{A,G} \equiv w^l_{A,B,C,G})$; in relation to this path the directions to the door and to the goal are opposite $(d^l_{A,R} = d^l_{A,G})$, and (b) a path for bodily (b) locomotion $(w^b_{A,G} \equiv w^b_{A,E,R,H,C,G})$. For this path both directions are equal $(d^b_{A,R} = d^b_{A,G})$. 2.) The direction for flying (instead of for looking) should be sufficiently dominant in the situation to determine the actual behavior.

This permits certain conclusions in regard to the factors which determine the degree of ease of the solution of a round-about problem. *Ceteris paribus*, the problem is the more difficult:

(a) The more B has a character of a closed curve. This would involve such factors as the size and the visual significance and presence of the opening; in case of a U-shaped barrier the solution should be the easier the more open the U gets.

(b) The more $e_{R,G} > e_{A,G}$. Namely, if $e_{R,G} = e_{A,G}$ the direction from A to the door R will no longer be a direction away from G (it will be $d_{A,R} \neq d_{A,-G}$).

(c) The more the visual field dominates the situation. For, in this case, the differentiation of the direction from the present place A to the goal G into a visual direction and one for bodily locomotion will be more difficult. In an emotional state the person generally shows a higher degree of unity; therefore, the solution then generally will be more difficult. The same reason holds for the fact that the younger child will find such a problem more difficult.

(d) The less the path for bodily locomotion $w_{A,E,R,H,C,G}$ can be seen as a unit. This accounts for the fact that the solution is often facilitated after one has increased one's distance from the situation. The restructuring of the field can occur only if the psychological field is wide enough to include, for instance, the door R and the area H.

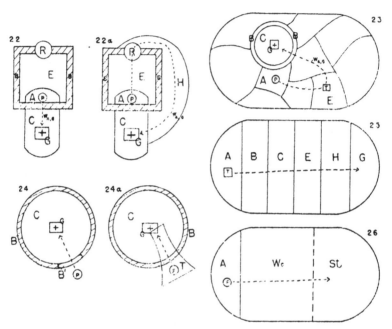

Fig. 22. The Round-About-Route Problem. Physical setting and psychological situation before understanding the round-about-route. P, canary; B, wall of cage; R, open door; G, goal; $w_{A,G}$, distinguished path for looking from A to G; $d_{A,G} = d_{A,B} \neq d_{A,R}$.

Fig. 22a. Topology of the Psychological Situation after Understanding the Possibility of a Round-About-Route. $w_{A,G}$, the distinguished path from A to G; $d_{A,G} = d_{A,R}$.

Fig. 23. Use of Tools. P, person; G, goal; B, barrier separating A and C; T, tool, the use of which would make B passable; $d_{A,G} = d_{A,T}$.

Fig. 24. Change in Situation Brought About by Use of Tool. The sector B_1 of the barrier B is made passable by the use of the tool, T.

Fig. 24a. A Slightly Different Representation of the Same Situation. The tool, T, serves as a bridge connecting A with G.

Figs. 25 and 26. Well Defined and Vague Goals. A toy train, T, (Fig. 25) has to pass from A, through the regions B, C, E, H, which are clearly distinguishable, to the region G. A person P (Figure 26) has to proceed from pressing a bulb weakly (We) to strong pressure (St). These regions are not clearly distinguishable.

As far as I can see, the experimental results are in line with our conclusions.

D. THE USE OF TOOLS

One can view the use of tools as an example of a round-about route. A goal G might be separated from the individual P by a barrier B. The barrier B might be passable only by using certain tools T. The person P might be located in the region A (Figure 23), the tool T in E, the goal G in C. If the person knows that he can pass the barrier B by using the tool T the following statement would be correct, independent of the physical positions of P, T, B and G:

(Ex. 10) $d_{A,G} = d_{A,T}$

according to (3) because $w_{A,G} \supset w_{A,T}$.

Generally, the use of a tool implies an actual change in the structure of the situation after the individual reached the tool and starts to apply it. If the barrier were a physical obstacle and T a tool to destroy the obstacle, the application of T would involve a change of a sector B^1 of B (Figure 24) in such a way that B^1 will become passable for P. In other cases T is used like a bridge which permits communication between P and G (Figure 24a). Similarly, if an individual gets help from a second person the situation is restructured so that the barrier B becomes passable in the way of Figure 24 or 24a.

E. WELL-DEFINED AND VAGUE GOALS

Chase (1935) has tried to compare the effect which reward and punishment have on the efforts of a child. She found that the child's efforts when expecting a reward are considerable greater than without such expectation. This might be the case. However, her experiments seem to involve a second difference which might be sufficient to account for her results.

In both cases the child has to press a bulb. In the reward situation the child by pressing the bulb pushes a hand representing, for instance, a train T along a scale (Figure 25). A bell rings if the train reaches a certain point G at the end of the scale. The child can observe the locomotion of the train from the point A of the scale through the regions B,C,E,H to G. In the case without reward, however, the child does not see a moving hand on a scale. He is supposed merely to press as hard as he can.

The goal of the child is that T should enter G. There exists only one path for the train. One can say therefore that $e_{A,G} > e_{B,G} > \cdot \cdot > e_{H,C}$ according to (14) because $w_{A,G}$

$\supset w_{B,G} \cdots \supset w_{H,G}.$ The direction $d_{A,G} = d_{A,B} = d_{B,C} = \cdots = d_{H,G}$ according to (6).

It is always easy for the child to determine the position of T. The distance $e_{T,G}$ is therefore always well defined. Especially is it always clear whether or not T is already in G.

In the non-reward situation, however, the effect of pressing the bulb is not visible. In this case, too, the child tries to press as hard as possible. The cognitive structure of the field, however, is much less clearly differentiated in respect to the effect of the pressing, because the child has to rely on his tactile and kinesthetic impressions of the strength of his pressing rather than on the visual control by way of the scale. Under these circumstances the child might be able to distinguish only two regions: a region We representing weak pressing, and a region St representing strong pressing (Figure 26). The field as a whole is certainly less differentiated into subregions than when the child can see the scale.

Just as in the reward situation the child wants to enter the region of highest pressure. However, the region St is less differentiated than the previous regions (E,H,G,); the child will be less able to distinguish clearly what part of St he has reached. In other words, the "cells" determining the field are in the second situation larger and have less clearly defined boundaries than in the first case.

From this it should follow that the child might be satisfied more easily in the second situation and might show a greater variability in behavior. This difference of the structure of the situation might suffice theoretically to account for the results of Chase. The effect of reward could be seen only if the structure of the situation would be kept sufficiently constant.

These considerations are well in line with results of Kounin (1936) in respect to the work output on the ergograph. He compared situations: (a) without visible work record, (b) with visible work record, (c) with visible work record plus a visible goal. He found that the visibility of the work record improves the output clearly and that visibility of record plus goal (a situation which corresponds to Figure 25) nearly doubles the output.[2] The comparison of Crawley (1926) of such output under competition with and without goal visible also shows the effectiveness of these factors.

[2] The goal in case (c) was somewhat changed relative to (b). Therefore the difference between (b) and (c) is not only that of giving a definite position to the goal.

IV

THE DETERMINATION OF PSYCHOLOGICAL FORCES

One of the properties of psychological forces, that is, of those dynamic facts which are commonly assumed as "causes" of change, is their directedness. The geometry of direction in the life space can be determined by the axioms of hodological space. Forces, however, are not geometrical but dynamical constructs: they have to be coordinated to certain psychological processes; they depend upon other dynamical facts— for instance, upon tension; they possess, aside from directedness, strength and a point of application.

Before we enter a more systematic presentation of the many rather complicated problems involved, it might be well to discuss one experimental example of measurement of forces. This will supply a more concrete point of reference.

I will use as this example one of the classical measurements of "motivations" in animal psychology, namely, the "obstruction box" (Warden 1931).

A. THE PSYCHOLOGICAL GEOMETRY AND DYNAMICS OF THE OBSTRUCTION BOX

1. The Physical Set-up

Figure 27 is a simplified schematic representation of the physical set-up. The animal P is located in region A. The goal G, for instance food, is located in region C. Between A and C is a region B consisting of an electric grill.

2. Purpose of the Obstruction Box. The Measuring of One Force by Another

The purpose of this set-up is to measure the same drive of the animal P under different circumstances—for instance, the drive for food in different stages of hunger, or to compare the hunger, the sex drive, and the maternal drive by placing different kinds of goals beyond the grill. The electric shock applied by the grill might be kept either constant or changed in a certain way (Warden 1931; Syzmanski 1918).

If we are permitted to use the term *force* as a directed dynamical entity, we might well say that the purpose of the

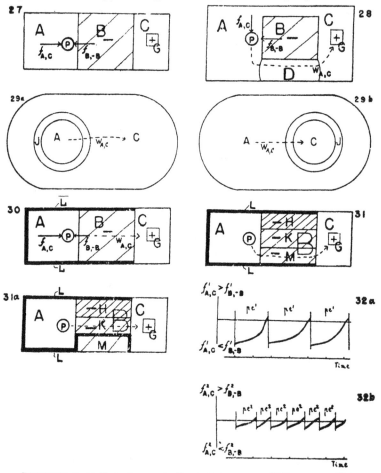

Psychological Geometry and Dynamics of the Obstruction Box

Fig. 27. Schematic Representation of the Physical Setup. P, the animal located in A; G, the goal located in C; B, the electrical grille; $f_{A,C}$, force acting on P in the direction from A to C; $f_{B,-B}$, force acting on P in the direction of not entering B.

obstruction box is to measure forces. The basic idea of the obstruction box is to measure one force, namely, the tendency to go to G, by another force, namely, by the tendency to avoid entering B. The food possesses what we call a "positive valence" (in the Figures indicated by "$+$"), that is, it corresponds to a region which the individual wants to enter. The grill B corresponds to a "negative valence" (indicated by "$-$"), that is, to a region the individual does not like to enter. The individual, therefore, is influenced by two forces: namely, a force, which we will write as $f_{A,C}$, in the direction $d_{A,C}$, and, secondly, a force not to enter B which has the direction $d_{B,-B}$ and which we will write $f_{B,-B}$.

The experimenter observes whether or not (and how often) the animal is willing to cross B to reach G. We will indicate the strength of a force (for instance, of $f_{A,C}$) by two perpendicular lines (for instance, $|f_{A,C}|$). We then can state that the basic idea of the obstruction box is to find out whether under certain circumstances

(Ex. 11) $$|f_{A,C}| > |f_{B,-B}|$$

By using the obstruction box one assumes implicitly that only if the drive to G is greater than the dislike of B would the animal cross B.

Fig. 28. Constellation if the grille were to lie physically between the individual P and the goal G, but without further restriction. $w_{A,C}$, distinguished path from A to C; the force $f_{A,C}$ is not opposite to entering the grille B ($f_{B,-B}$) but has a direction to D.

Figs. 29a and 29b. The two ways in which two regions A and C can be separated. J, Jordan Zone.

Fig. 30. The grille B together with the physical walls L constitute a physical Jordan zone surrounding A such that the distinguished path from A to G ($w_{A,C}$) has to cross the physical area B.

Fig. 31. It might still be possible for the rat P to cross the physical area B by the activity "jumping" (M).

Fig. 31a. The physical setup prohibits the use of the activity jumping (M) for crossing B. It still permits running of different speeds, K, H.

Figs. 32a and 32b. The frequency with which the animal crosses the grille (B) within a given time depends upon the time necessary to change the state of the individual in which the force to the goal $f_{A,C}$ is smaller than the force away from entering B ($f_{A,C} < f_{B,-B}$), into the opposite constellation ($f_{A,C} > f_{B,-B}$). This period (pe) is relatively long in figure 32a and short in 32b.

The idea of measuring one force by its overcoming or not overcoming another force is entirely legitimate. Such measurement, however, presupposes that both forces are opposite in direction. To make these forces opposite, the obstruction box places the negative valence "between" the individual and the goal. It is illuminating to discuss more in detail how the set-up guarantees that the directions of these forces are psychologically opposite.

3. Excursus Concerning Symbolizing Forces

One might wonder why we coordinate to the negative valence of the grill B a force $f_{B,-B}$ instead of a force $f_{A,-B}$. The latter would be correct in case something dangerous were located at B and the animal would try to run away from B. However, in our situation there is generally no tendency or at least no marked tendency to increase the distance from B, aside from the tendency not to enter B.

One could ask whether the force toward the goal should not be indicated by $f_{P,G}$ rather than by $f_{A,C}$. Indeed, such a representation would be fully adequate. In our case $d_{P,G} = d_{A,C}$ because P is located in A $(A \supset P)$ and G in C $(C \supset G)$ in such a way that $w_{P,G}$ necessarily crosses A and C. One could use both formulas referring either to the individual P and his goal G, or to the regions in which P and G are located. We could write, furthermore: $f_{A,G}$, because in our case $f_{P,G}$, $f_{A,G}$ and $f_{A,C}$ would be expressions of the same force.

However, one should keep in mind that the force $f_{A,C}$ is in our case not acting on the region A but on the region P. In other words, P and not A shows a tendency to move to the goal. We will say that P is in our case the "point of application" of the force $f_{A,C}$. If we wish to indicate specifically the point of application we will write: $f_{A,C}^{P}$ where A represents the region where the force exists, $d_{A,C}$ the direction of the force and P the point of application. We will not indicate specifically in our formulas the point of application when the meaning is clear.

One could argue that the behavior of an individual who is located at A can be affected only by forces at A, i.e., by forces like $f_{A,B}$ or $f_{A,-B}$ but not by a force $f_{B,-B}$ which refers to a force at the region B. The statement that a force can influence the behavior of an individual only in regions where the force exists is correct. However, the regions A and B have a common boundary and, according to (15b), the force $f_{B,-B}$ corresponds to the tendency to locomote from B to a region X outside B, for instance to A. The force $f_{B,-B}$ exists, therefore, at least at the common boundary of A and B.

This is particularly clear if we refer to regions of activities rather than to regions corresponding to physical areas: the activity "entering B" has a negative valence on account of B being a grill. The correspondent force away from that region of activity becomes effective whenever the individual considers going into it; that is, during his being located at A. Therefore the force away from the activity "entering B" exists at A (during the contemplation of this action) and can therefore counteract the force $f_{A,C}$ at A.

These remarks might suffice to justify our indicating the forces which are acting on the individual P in A by $f_{A,C}$ and $f_{B,-B}$.

When we wish to refer to the strength of a force independent of its direction we will write $|f_{A,C}|$.

4. The Cognitive Structure of the Situation

When using the obstruction box, it does not suffice to locate the animal in the region A physically without the animal's knowing the set-up. If the animal, for instance, does not know that a goal is in G or if it does not know the specific character of this goal (for instance, food, sex object, or litter) the forces acting on him will be different and might not have at all a direction to C. In other words, the cognitive structure which the situation has for the individual at a given time is one of the factors which determines $f_{A,C}$. Similarly, the force $f_{B,-B}$ away from B will be different if the individual knows or does not know the character of B.

Indeed, the first procedure in these experiments is to structure the set-up cognitively for the individual to a sufficient degree: the experimenter pushes the animal from A to B. He makes it experience B and gives it time to find out about the existence and the type of goal G in C before the actual experiment starts. Only if this knowledge is established can one speak of a force $f_{A,C}$ and $f_{B,-B}$.

5. The Conditions under Which the Force to the Goal and That away from the Grill Are Opposite in Direction

The measurement of the force towards the goal by the force away from the grill has meaning only if both forces are opposed to each other. If the psychological directions were identical with the physical (geographical) ones, it would suffice to create a situation in which the grill B is located physically between P and G. That is, however, not sufficient psychologically. For, if the field were otherwise unrestricted (Figure 28) the animal would choose a roundabout route to G, for instance, through the region D. Namely, under this condition the distinguished path $w_{A,C}$ would not pass B but D ($w_{A,C} \equiv w_{A,D,C}$). Therefore it would be, according to (3), the direction $d_{A,C} = d_{A,D}$ and, according to (12) and (15b),

(Ex. 12) $$d_{A,C} \neq d_{B,-B}$$

In other words, the forces $f_{A,C}$ and $f_{B,-B}$ would not be opposed to each other. Therefore, the one force could not be measured by its overcoming the other.

To make both directions opposed to each other psychologically, it is necessary to create a set-up in which the regions A and C are separated by a boundary zone in a *topological* sense. There are, as I have discussed elsewhere (Princ., pp. 140 ff.), only two principal ways for accomplishing that: the barrier should encircle the region A as a Jordan zone J (Figure 29a) or the region C as a Jordan zone J (Figure 29b). Under both circumstances, any path, and therefore also the distinguished path $w_{A,C}$, has to cross the zone J. Only if the region B has topologically the position of a Jordan zone J can we say that $d_{A,C} = d_{A,B}$ according to (3) and

(Ex. 13) $d_{A,C} = d_{B,-B}$ according to (15c).

Only under those circumstances, therefore, is it meaningful to measure the force $f_{A,C}$ by the force $f_{B,-B}$.

Indeed, the set-up of the obstruction box surrounds the region A by a barrier B^1 (Figure 30), which has the character of a Jordan zone: it consists of the impassable physical walls L and the grill B $(B^1 = L + B)$. Under these circumstances every path $w_{A,C}$ has to cross the region B.

This set-up now fulfills geographically the conditions required by the axioms of hodological space to make the measured and the measuring force opposite in direction. However, it is still not sufficient psychologically.

Psychologically, the region B should not be characterized merely by its geographical properties, but rather by the possible activities related to it. The crossing of the grill B can mean a variety of different activities. It could mean walking very slowly, or running as fast as possible across B, or jumping over B. In other words, psychologically B is not a homogeneous region in spite of its physical homogeneity. It consists rather of a number of sub-regions H,K,M (Figure 31) which correspond to the different methods of crossing (B = H + K + M). Each of these methods has a different negative valence. In other words, $|f_{H,-H}| \neq |f_{K,-K}| \neq |f_{M,-M}|$. The animal P will probably choose those paths to C for which the negative valence of the subregion of B is the smallest.

Thus, one can speak of a definite force $f_{B,-B}$ only if the type of activity used in crossing the barrier is sufficiently determined. In other words, the obstruction box can be used as a measuring device only if the individual P has to cross a definite subregion of B, for instance, K.

Warden took care of this necessity by introducing, after his preliminary experiments, a low ceiling above B. In other words, he erected an impassable barrier around the region of jumping which corresponds to region M in Figure 31a. There are still different velocities possible in crossing B, and therefore different subregions (H,K, etc.) might be distinguished within B. However, the animal probably will choose that subregion of B which corresponds to the activity of the least negative valence (probably a rather fast locomotion). As far as one could trust that this activity K would be about the same for different individuals and different trials of the same individual, the region B as a measuring stick could be said to be sufficiently determined.

In summary, the measurement of the strength of the force $|f_{A,C}|$ by the force $|f_{B,-B}|$ presupposes the opposition of the direction of both forces and a sufficient determination of the strength of $f_{B,-B}$. This implies that the region B should correspond to a sufficiently determined region of activity and that the path $w_{A,C}$ should lead through B ($w_{A,B} \subset w_{A,C}$).

6. The Measurement of the Strength of the Force to the Goal

We have discussed thus far the geometrical side of the problem of measurement in the obstruction box; furthermore, whether or not the force to the goal is stronger than the opposing forces. We will now discuss the criterion for the amount of difference between the strength of both forces.

a. Directed Locomotion as Criterion for Inequality of the Opposing Forces.—The fundamental assumption which underlies the set-up is the following: the animal P will not cross B if the force $|f_{A,C}| < |f_{B,-B}|$. However, he will cross the grill if $|f_{A,C}| > |f_{B,-B}|$. We will indicate a locomotion from A in the direction $d_{A,C}$ by saying that the velocity $v_{A,C} > 0$. We can then state as the basic assumption of the obstruction box that

(Ex. 14) $$v_{A,C} > 0 \text{ if } |f_{A,C}| > |f_{B,-B}|$$

There will be no locomotion in the direction A,C, in other words $v_{A,C} = 0$ if $|f_{A,C}| \overline{\lessgtr} |f_{B,-B}|$. This means, for instance, that if the animal is not hungry enough he might not be willing to cross the grill, but if he becomes hungrier he will be willing to do this.

One should keep in mind this assumption (Ex. 14). We will see later that a similar assumption can be used as the basic coordinating definition of the concept of force in psychology.

b. The Frequency of Crossing as a Criterion of the Difference between Forces.—Crossing the grill indicates that

$|f_{A,C}| > |f_{B,-B}|$. However, it does not tell how great the difference in strength is.

To find out this, one could decrease or increase the negative valence of B until one has determined the limit of the negative valence where the animal still crosses. This type of procedure was attempted by Moss (1924). It is technically much more difficult than might be expected. Generally, experimenters have used a different criterion for the amount of difference between the strength of $f_{A,C}$ and $f_{B,-B}$—namely, the number of crossings of the grill within a given time. To determine this the animal always is put back into A when it has crossed the grill. The details of this procedure vary; for instance, the animal may or may not be permitted to consume a little bit of G before being returned. Some investigators add as a second criterion of the strength of the force the frequency with which the animal touches the grill B without crossing it. It might suffice here to discuss the major procedure.

The measurement of the strength of the force by the frequency of crossing the grill implies two assumptions. The first is related to crossing or not crossing (Ex. 14), and the second to the frequency of crossing. These assumptions should be rather clearly distinguished because the first does not necessarily involve the second.

The frequency of crossing is a rather complicated symptom. One could view it as a direct criterion of the velocity of locomotion, because the faster the animal crosses the barrier the more frequently might he cross it within a given time.

However, such a view does not represent the situation fairly. The difference in frequency is less due to different speeds in crossing the grill than to differences in the time the animal spends in A before it makes a new attempt to cross B.

Generally, the animal will not attempt to cross B immediately again after being put back into A. That involves, according to (Ex. 14), that for a certain period it will be: $|f_{A,C}| \leqq |f_{B,-B}|$. After a while a change in the relation of the strength of the two forces might occur so that finally $|f_{A,C}| > |f_{B,-B}|$. The animal then crosses the grill a second time.

We will call the time from the return of the animal to A until the next attempt to cross B the period pe. Figures 32a and 32b represent schematically the change in the relative strength of the two forces in a case where this period pe is long (Figure 32a) and where it is short (Figure 32 b). The line zero represents the state where $|f_{A,C}| = |f_{B,-B}|$; above this line is $|f_{A,C}| > |f_{B,-B}|$ below is $|f_{A,C}| < |f_{B,-B}|$. The vertical line in the curve indicates the moment when the animal is put back into A; the distance between two vertical lines represents the length of the period pe.

In the case represented in Figure 32b the strength of the force $f_{A,G}$ is supposed to be greater than in the case represented in Figure 32a.

If one uses in this way the frequency of crossing as a measuring stick for the relative strength of $f_{A,C}$ one makes the following assumption:

(Ex. 15) $|f^2{}_{A,C}| > |f^1{}_{A,C}|$ if $pe^2 < pe^1$, in case
$|f_{B,-B}| = $ constant

In other words, the strength of the force $f_{A,C}$ is assumed to be an inverse function of pe.

(Ex. 15a) $|f_{A,C}| = F\left(\dfrac{1}{pe}\right)$ whereby F means a

constantly increasing function.

The assumption (Ex. 15a) might seem plausible. However, the problems involved are rather complicated. For instance, one might ask the following question: Since the first crossing of the grill has proved that $|f_{A,C}| > |f_{B,-B}|$, why does the force $f_{A,C}$ not remain constantly greater than $f_{B,-B}$? I will enumerate some of the possible reasons for the periodical shift of the relative strength of both forces:

a. One could refer to the general instability of a psychological situation, e.g., to *chance* variations. From this assumption it would be plausible that if "basically" $|f^2{}_{A,C}| > |f^1{}_{A,C}|$ the probability is that $pe^2 < pe^1$.

b. The explanation given in (a) presupposes that $|f_{B,-B}|$ is constant. That, however, cannot be assumed. On the contrary, it is most probable that the crossing of the grill accentuates the negative valence of the *grill*. One could explain the difference between pe[1] and pe[2] by assuming that the force $|f_{A,C}|$ is rather constant in each case and that the animal needs a certain time after his first crossing to "forget" the disagreeableness of the crossing before he makes a new attempt, that is, before $|f_{B,-B}|$ decreases to its previous level. Also under this assumption the greater force $|f_{A,C}|$ could be expected to go hand in hand with a shorter pe.

c. A third assumption would be that the animal has lost so much "*energy*" by the crossing of B that he needs time for "invigoration."

d. Considering *adaptation*, the crossing of the grill could be assumed as making the next crossing less disagreeable. However, one could argue as well the other way and say that each new crossing will be experienced as more painful.

e. One could make a periodic change of the *cognitive* structure of the situation responsible for the periods. The animal learns after his first crossing that the path $w_{A,C}$ does after all not lead to G, because the animal is not permitted to satisfy his need. In other words, it has experienced that $d_{A,G} \neq d_{A,B}$. That would mean that even if $|f_{A,G}|$ and $|f_{B,-B}|$ were constant $f_{A,G}$ would no longer have the direction $d_{A,B}$. Therefore, no action in this direction would occur. It might well be that immediately after the animal's return to A the cognitive structure of its life space is in line with this new experience. After some time the older cognitive structure might become dominant again and therefore the force $f_{A,G}$ will again acquire the direction $d_{A,B}$. The explanation of the different length of the period pe would in this case be based on the velocity of change of the cognitive structure rather than on a change in the relative strength of the valences and forces.

It is not necessary here to discuss which of these assumptions might be correct and which not. It might suffice to draw but one conclusion: the use of the number of crossings as a measuring stick for the relative strength of two forces refers to a "historical" process (Princ., pp. 30 ff.) which involves the velocity of a periodical change of the cognitive structure and of the constellation of forces within a physically determined situation. It is clear that this process depends directly upon a great number of variables including the sensitivity, the intelligence, and the flexibility of the individual. One might expect, therefore, some statistical regularity, but the value of the procedure as a measuring instrument of the amount of difference between both forces in an individual case seems rather limited.

In this respect this measurement is quite different from that discussed under 1. If we coordinate locomotion and force, we can definitely say that $|f_{A,C}| > |f_{B,-B}|$ in the concrete individual case whenever the animal crosses B. This statement is independent of any assumption regarding historical processes or problems of origin.

B. THE DEFINITION OF PSYCHOLOGICAL FORCE

The discussion of the obstruction box as an example might suffice to make understandable the following definition of psychological force. A justification of this definition can be seen ultimately only in its usefulness for research. We will discuss several general aspects of this definition after we have first given it.

The definition of force has to contain (a) the conceptual properties of the construct and (b) its coordinating definition:

1. The Conceptual Properties of Force

We have emphasized in the beginning the directedness of force. We have discussed later on its strength. We have implicitly assumed, in discussing the obstruction box, that the force has in addition a point of application. We will not assume that the point of application of a force is always that region in a life space which stands for the individual whose life space is represented. The point of application can be also another region of the life space. (This fact is rather important. However, we will not make much use of it in this study, in which we will discuss relatively simple problems of forces.)

The conceptual properties of the construct "force" in psychology are then the following:

A force has:
1. Direction
2. Strength
3. Point of Application

The properties 1 and 2 together can be represented mathematically as a vector. Graphically, we will represent the direction of the force by the direction of an arrow; its strength by the length of the arrow; the point of application by that region which is touched by the point of the arrow.

In writing we refer to these properties, as mentioned before, in the following manner: the direction of $f_{A,B}$ is $d_{A,B}$; the strength $|f_{A,B}|$ refers to $f_{A,B}$ regardless of direction; by $f_{A,B}^{P}$ is meant a force in A, which has the direction $d_{A,B}$ and P as point of application. Generally, it suffices to write in this case either $f_{A,B}$ or $f_{P,B}$.

2. Forces and Resultants of Forces

It is one of the basic conceptions behind the construct force that force should be linked with locomotion. The relation between locomotion and force has been emphasized already in (Ex. 14) and will come up again and again.

However, the obstruction box shows clearly, and the later examples will confirm this, that one cannot correlate an actual locomotion to a single force existing at a given time. For instance, there might well exist a force in the direction to the goal on the other side of the grill ($f_{A,C} > 0$). But if the opposing force of the grill ($f_{B,-B}$) is great enough there will be no locomotion in the direction of $f_{A,G}$.

That means that an *actual locomotion can be related only to the totality of forces acting on a given region at a given time;* in other words, to a "resultant" of forces.

It might seem adventurous to introduce the concept of resultant of forces into psychology. Can we speak of a resultant if we do not know the laws which determine the direction and the strength of the resultant force of two given forces? Can we assume that the principle of the parallelogram of forces which holds in physics holds in psychology too?

We obviously cannot make the latter assumption without proof. As a matter of fact, everything seems to indicate that this principle does not hold in psychology. This principle presupposes the definition of angles. Angles might under certain circumstances be determinable in the life space. However, the geometry of hodological space prevents a simple transfer of the principle of the parallelogram of forces from Euclidian space. Besides, the empirical laws governing the determination of resultants might be different in psychology and in physics.

Nevertheless, there seems to be no way in psychology to avoid the concept of resultants. That is shown by the following consideration: The construct force has no scientific value if one is not able to coordinate the existence of a force to observable facts, such as locomotions. It is impossible to assume that at a given time only one force exists. As a rule, one will have to assume that always a group of forces are acting on the person. Therefore, any kind of coordination between force and observable events can link these events only to the resultant of forces existing at that time.

These considerations show a peculiar difficulty. On the one hand, the concept of resultant of forces is conceptually more complicated than the concept of a single force; it presupposes certain principles of resultance. On the other hand, the resultant of forces is less complicated as far as observation is concerned. The only way open seems to be to coordinate the observable event (e.g., locomotions) to the resultant of forces and to consider both the determining of a single force and the finding of the laws governing resultants as the later tasks of research. (We will come back to the problem of resultants later.)

Such a procedure seems less objectionable when one realizes that any psychological school using the concept of equilibrium (in other words, practically every school) assumes for itself the right to presuppose the concept of resultant forces, for an equilibrium is a constellation of forces with the resultant zero.

3. The Coordinating Definition of Force

$f_{A,B} + f_{A,C} + f_{A,D}$ should mean the resultant of the three forces $f_{A,B}$, $f_{A,C}$, and $f_{A,D}$ in A. The totality of all forces in A shall be written as $\Sigma f_{A,X}$:

(18) Definition: $\Sigma f_{A,X} \equiv f_{A,B} + f_{A,C} + \cdots + f_{A,N}$.

The resultant of a group of forces can have the same direction as one force of the group. To distinguish both forces, we will characterize the resultant as f*. For instance, it might

be that $\Sigma f_{A,X} \equiv f_{A,B} + f_{A,C} + \cdots + f_{A,N} = \overset{*}{f}_{A,B}$.

We will now give tentatively the following coordinating definition of psychological force.

> Definition: If the resultant of psychological forces acting on a region is greater than zero, there will be a locomotion in the direction of the resultant force, or the structure of the situation will change so that the change is equivalent to such a locomotion.

In formulas:

(19)   Definition: If $\Sigma f_{A,X} = f^*_{A,B}$ and

$|f^*_{A,B}| > 0$, then $v_{A,B} > 0$.

The term $v_{A,B}$ in this formula should refer either to a locomotion or to a restructuring of the field equivalent to such locomotion. We refer here not only to locomotions but also to restructurings because both are closely related. As a matter of fact, one can view a locomotion (that is, a change in position) as one type of restructuring (Princ.) and might therefore regard the restructuring as the more general type of process.

An unpublished paper by J. Frank on social pressure has convinced me that it is necessary from the beginning to include restructuring as equivalent to locomotion, in the definition of force. To my mind this implication proves very useful for the whole problem of cognitive change and seems to be well in line with certain ideas underlying Koehler's (1929) treatment of intellectual problems.

Every coordinating definition should be reversible if possible (Princ., p. 93). The reversal of the above definition holds also: Every psychological locomotion (or change of structure equivalent to such locomotion) is due to a resultant of forces in its direction.

(19a)   Definition: If $v_{A,B} > 0$ then a resultant

$$f^*_{A,B} = \Sigma f_{A,X} \text{ exists such that } |f^*_{A,B}| > 0.$$

This reversal should refer only to changes which are due to psychological forces. There are cases in which the life space is changed by non-psychological factors, like the falling of a stone, the opening of a door, or some social event which enters the life space of an individual "from outside" without being subject to the laws governing this life space (Princ., p. 70). The question might be left open as to how psychology has to deal with these "alien" or imposed changes.

The coordinating definition determines:

1. The direction of forces
2. The strength of forces insofar as it determines under what condition the resultant force is greater than zero.

However, it does not permit comparison of different strengths of forces above zero. Such a comparison would imply an additional definition coordinating the strength of the force to the speed or to the acceleration of locomotion, or to some other observable facts. We will discuss this question later and try to clear up some more general problems first.

C. THE POSITION OF THE CONCEPT OF FORCE WITHIN THE SYSTEM OF DYNAMICAL CONCEPTS AND LAWS

1. The Reality of Psychological Forces

The operational definition of psychological force coordinates this construct to psychological processes. It should be definitely recognized, therefore, that a psychological force is a psychological construct independent from any construct of physics. The laws governing psychological forces might be very different from those governing forces in physics. Perhaps it would have been better to use different terms. However, the logical position of these constructs within the network of explanatory concepts in the two sciences seem to be sufficiently equivalent to justify the use of the same term.

Under certain conditions bodily forces might be representative of psychological ones.

It is often asked whether a psychological force is something "real" or only an "analogy." The problem of the reality of a dynamic construct is a peculiar one in any science (Princ.). It will suffice here to emphasize that a psychological force is as real as any other kind of dynamical construct in psychology and certainly as real as a physical force.

The situation is not merely one in which the person *appears* to locomote in the direction to a goal. A change in the position of the goal easily proves that the dynamical interrelation between person and goal expressed in the term force is a real one: the person will change the direction of his action if the position of the goal is changed.

In case one should prefer to speak of "physiological" forces rather than psychological ones we would not mind such terminology, although it might be misleading. The reality of the psychological forces is the same as that of the "biological forces governing the brain." But it seems impossible to determine directions of locomotions without referring to the structure of psychological life space and the hodological directions in it.

2. Valence and Force

a. Definition of Valence.—In the example of the obstruction box the forces in the region A were due partly to the fact that the animal wanted to reach the goal-object G ($f_{A,G}$) and partly to the fact that he wanted to avoid the grill B ($f_{B,-B}$). They were not due to the property of the region A as such, aside from the fact that A did not contain the possibilities for satisfying the individual's need.

Both the region G and the region B in the obstruction box are examples of regions which have what we call a valence. (For convenience, we will often speak of regions as being and not merely as having a valence, just as one speaks of an object's not only having but being a Gestalt.)

Definition: A region G which has a valence ($Va(G)$) is defined as a region within the life space of an individual P which attracts or repulses this individual. In other words:

(20)   Definition of positive valence: If
$$Va(G) > 0, \text{ then } |f_{P,G}| > 0.$$

In our diagrams we will indicate a positive valence by a plus sign within the region representing the valence. If the valence G is located within the region C and the individual P in A we can write $|f_{A,C}^{P}| > 0$ instead of $|f_{P,G}| > 0$.

(20) defines the case where G attracts the individual P. In this case we will speak of a positive valence. If the individual is repulsed by the region G, or, in other words, if G has a negative valence ($Va(G) < 0$), the following would hold:

(20a)   Definition of negative valence: If
$$Va(G) < 0 \text{ then } |f_{P,-G}| > 0.$$

In our diagrams we will indicate a negative valence by a minus sign. If G is located in C and P in A we can write $|f_{A,-C}^{P}| > 0$ instead of $|f_{P,-G}| > 0$.

The concept of valence as defined in (20) and (20a) does not imply any specific statement concerning the origin of the attractiveness or the repulsiveness of the valence. The valence might be due to a state of hunger, to emotional attachment, or to a social constellation. The final goal related to a valence might be a consumption like eating a cake; it might be the joy of watching a performance at a theater; a negative valence might be based on the fear of being defeated in a competition. The statement that a certain region of the life space has a positive or negative valence merely indicates that, for whatever reason, at the present time and for this specific individual a tendency exists to act in the direction toward this region or away from it.

b. Valence, Force, and Force Field.—The definitions (20) and (20a) relate the concept of valence to that of force. However, a valence is not identical with a force.

If the valence of a region decreases or increases because of a change of the intensity of the need the forces corresponding to the valence also will decrease or increase. However, the strength of the force $f_{P,G}$ does not depend only upon the strength of the valence, but besides, for instance, upon the relative position of P and G. By P's coming closer to a goal, the force in the direction to the goal might increase; or by P's increasing the distance from a dangerous region the strength of the force away from this region might decrease.

The strength of the force is a function at least of two factors, namely, the strength of the valence (Va) of G and the distance (e) between the person P and the valence. In other words,

$$(21) \qquad |f_{P,G}| = F\left(\frac{Va(G)}{e_{P,G}}\right)$$

Since the force increases with the strength of the valence but often decreases with the distance, we might be tempted to say:

$$(21a) \qquad |f_{P,G}| = \frac{Va(G)}{e_{P,G}}$$

However, such a statement would imply an exact inverse proportionality of strength of force and distance, and this is probably not correct.

Also the direction of the force $f_{P,G}$ will generally be different for different positions of P. If, for instance, P is located in A and the valence G in C (Figure 33) the force $f_{A,C}$ correspondent to the valence $Va(G)$ has the direction $d_{A,C} = d_{A,D}$ in accordance with (3) because $w_{A,C} \supset w_{A,D}$. However, if P is located in L the same valence $Va(G)$ will correspond to a force $f_{L,C}$ which has the direction $d_{L,E}$ and both directions might well be different $(d_{A,D} \neq d_{L,E})$.

Thus a valence $Va(G)$ does not correspond to only one force but to a variety of forces $f_{X,G}$ from different regions X to G. These forces will be different in strength and direction.

One can proceed to determine systematically for every region X of the life space what the direction and strength of the force $f_{X,G}$ would be in this particular region. The totality of these forces we will call a "force field."

One can define a force field in the following way:

(22)   Definition: A force field correlates to every region of a field the strength and direction of the force which would act on the individual if the individual were in that region.

The concept of force field does not imply that a force is acting on an individual in a region without that individual being within this region. In other words, one can say that, as in physics, the forces of a force field are only conditional ones; they are those forces which *would* exist in a region if the individual should be located in this region.

We can then change our definition of valence (20) and (20a) slightly by saying:

(20b)   A positive valence corresponds to a force field where all forces are directed toward the same region. (This region is said to have a positive valence.)[1]

(20c)   A negative valence corresponds to a force field where all forces have the direction away from the same region. (This region is said to have a negative valence.)

We call a force field of the first type (Figure 33) a "positive central field." In such a field it holds for every region X that $f_{X,Y}$ has the form $f_{X,G}$.

(23)   Definition: A positive central field is a field in which for every region X a force towards the same region G exists ($f_{X,Y} = f_{X,G}$).

In case of a negative valence (Figure 33a) all forces $f_{X,Y}$ within the field have the form $f_{X,-G}$.

---

[1] The term "corresponds to" means "is equivalent to" or "is dynamically the same as," or, "as far as dynamics are concerned, amounts to the same as."

(24) Definition: A negative central field is a field in which for every region X a force away from the same region G exists $(f_{X,Y} = f_{X,-G})$.

We can then state our formulas (20b) and (20c) in the following form (Figure 33) and (Figure 33a):

(20d) A positive valence $(Va(G) > 0)$ corresponds to a positive central field $(f_{X,Y} = f_{X,G})$

(20e) A negative valence $(Va(G) < 0)$ corresponds to a negative central field $(f_{X,Y} = f_{X,-G})$.

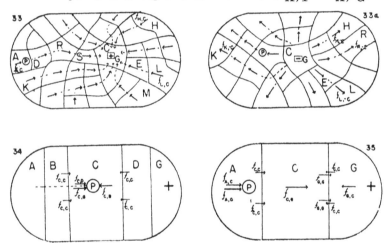

POSITIVE AND NEGATIVE VALENCES. SIMPLE FORCE FIELDS

Fig. 33. Positive central force field corresponding to a positive valence $(Va > 0)$.

G, region of positive valence $(Va(G) > 0)$, located in C; P, person; the forces $f_{A,C}$, $f_{H,C}$, or $f_{L,C}$ correspond to $Va(G)$ in case P is located at A, H, or L, respectively; $f_{X,Y} = f_{X,G}$.

Fig. 33a. Negative central field corresponding to a negative valence $(Va > 0)$.

G, region of negative valence $(Va(G) < 0)$ located at C; P, person; forces $f_{H,-C}$, $f_{K,-C}$, or $f_{L,-C}$, correspond to $Va(G)$ in case P is located at H, K, or L, respectively; $f_{X,Y} = f_{X,-G}$.

Figs. 34 and 35. Means and Ends. Cases are represented where the activity region C which is a means of reaching the goal G $(Va(G) > 0)$ has in addition a positive valence of its own $(Va(C) > 0)$. See text.

In summarizing we can say there is a close relation between valence and force. A valence corresponds to a force field. However, the valence is not a force. It has no direction, but merely strength. Therefore it is not a vector but a scalar.

There are, of course, great differences in the quality of valences or, as one might say, in the content of the activity or the status which is represented by the valence and which the individual wishes to enter. These qualitative differences can be represented by the character of the topological region within the life space, for instance, by coordinating the region of the valence to those activities.

c. Forces within a Region Which Has a Positive or Negative Valence.—The definition of valence includes the possibility of speaking of a positive or negative valence of a region in which the person is located. A person might be, for instance, involved in an occupation A which he dislikes. The force corresponding to the negative valence $Va(A)$ will be in this case $f_{A,-A}$ which has the direction $d_{A,-A}$ in line with (15b).

A person may be located in a region A in which he feels himself comfortable, and which he does not like to leave. The positive valence $Va(A)$ corresponds in this case to a force $f_{A,A}$ which has the direction $d_{A,A}$ in line with (17).

d. Means and Ends.—The individual P might be located in A (Figure 33), and the region G might have a positive valence and might be located in C. The distinguished path $w_{A,G}$ might cross the regions D,R,S. Therefore the force $f_{A,G}$ would have the direction $d_{A,G} = d_{A,D}$. Could one not say under these circumstances that the regions D,R and S have positive valences for P?

To state our problem in more general terms: one can say that the regions D, R, and S in Figure 33 represent activities which have psychologically the character of means to the end of reaching ‘G. Can one attribute to such means positive valences?

James (1890) and others have correctly emphasized that means may become ends. Social institutions which have been created as means toward a goal might finally acquire a positive valence themselves and might retain it even if they do not longer serve the end. This problem is related to that of "conditioned reflex," "association," or other cases where the character of a previously neutral region might get a positive or negative valence by becoming connected with a region G which has a positive or negative valence.

It is, however, important to recognize that the means-end relation does not necessarily imply that the means acquire a positive valence. If this were the case it would follow:

An individual P follows the force $f_{A,G}$ toward the positive valence G. He has started from the region A (Figure 34), passed through the region B, and is now in C. The force corresponding to the valence G would be $f_{C,G}$. However, if the means would have acquired a positive valence there should be aside from $f_{C,G}$ the forces $f_{C,B}$, $f_{C,C}$ and $f_{C,D}$ corresponding to the positive valences of B, C, and D. $f_{C,D}$ would be equal, $f_{C,B}$ would be opposite in direction to $f_{C,G}$. The force $f_{C,C}$ would tend to keep P in C.

In other words, the more regions the individual has ahead of him, the stronger would be force in the direction towards the goal. The greater is the part of the path which the individual had already crossed the stronger would be the force which would hinder his going ahead.

One can argue that a means after it has been used loses its character as a means, just as an object loses its valence by consumption. However, it would still hold that the forces acting on an individual in the direction to a goal should be the stronger the more means lying between him and it. This is usually not the case.

One can avoid this dilemma only by assuming that in case a means has the character of a sub-goal, the life space is composed of two overlapping situations, one containing the goal, the other the sub-goal. Then the increase of the potency of one of the two overlapping situations necessarily involves a decrease of the relative potency of the other. In this way one avoids the paradoxical conclusion that a force in the direction to the goal is increased by the number of activities one has to go through to reach it.

These considerations show that one should not confuse the valence of a means with the valence of an end. A force in the direction toward a means can exist without the valence of this means as a region in itself being different from zero.

Of course, a region of activities representing a means might have in itself a positive or a negative valence, aside from its being a means. The obstruction box is an example of a negative valence of an intermediate region. In other cases, the intermediate region might well have a positive valence in itself: one can have a pleasant trip to a pleasant goal. In such cases we have to deal with more than one valence in the field and therefore with an overlapping of several fields of forces.

Figure 35 represents a simple example of such a case: G represents a positive valence. The individual P is located in A and has to pass through the region C to reach G. There exist, therefore, the forces $f_{A,G}$, $f_{C,G}$ and $f_{G,G}$ in the regions A, C, and G respectively as the result of $Va(G) > 0$. The region C, which might be a pleasant drive, should, however, have a positive valence in itself $(Va(C) > 0)$. To this valence would correspond the forces $f_{A,C}$, $f_{C,C}$ and $f_{G,C}$ in the regions A,C and G respectively. The individual P is very eager to start the locomotion in C because both forces $f_{A,G}$ and $f_{A,C}$ are acting in the same direction $d_{A,C}$. However, he will like to remain in the region C, extending his trip, for instance, more than necessary, especially if the force $f_{C,C}$ is relatively great compared with $f_{C,G}$. In case $f_{C,C} > f_{C,G}$ the person would try to remain in C rather than enter G. Many prolonged actions which one can observe in the eating of good things by children are related to such situations.

Later we will come back to the question of the overlapping of more than one force field.

e. Measurement of Strength of Valence. Strength of Force and Distance in a Force Field.—From formula (21) it follows that it is possible to measure the strength of a valence if one is able to measure the strength of forces corresponding to it. However, the comparison of the strength of two valences presupposes that the forces compared should have the same relative position within both fields of forces corresponding to the valences. Otherwise, the measurement of the strength of a valence would presuppose detailed knowledge about the relation between the force $|f_{P,G}|$ and the distance $e_{P,G}$ in the formula (21a).

Lewin (1935) and Hull (1932) have pointed out that the strength of a force $f_{X,-G}$ corresponding to a negative valence G often decreases faster with distance than the strength of the force $f_{X,G}$ corresponding to a positive valence G. We will come back to this problem later.

Under certain circumstances the force corresponding to a valence does not decrease but increases with distance. Experiments with animals (Hull, 1932) and observation on children indicate that the force in the direction to a positive valence might decrease as soon as the goal comes "within reach." Sometimes also very great distance seems to make things more attractive (e.g., faraway countries).

f. Valence Affecting a Person "Through a Distance."— The fact that the valence corresponds to a central field which spreads over more regions than those neighboring the valence means that a valence can be said to affect the person "through a distance." We do not wish to enter here the complicated problems of dynamical effects through "contact" and "through a distance" which have worried physics for a long time.

3. Tension and Force

a. Force and the Mechanisms of Locomotion.—In our discussion of forces thus far no statement has been made as to the specific "mechanisms of the locomotion" resulting from the force. It is not shown "why" the force in the direction to a goal leads, for instance, to certain movements of the limbs. Instead the person thus far has been treated as one whole in regard to locomotions.

One could object to such a procedure because doubtless also the technical side of a locomotion is important for behavior. The person P does not roll like a ball to the goal. He walks, climbs, drives, or talks. Every type of locomotion presupposes a certain set-up concerning the mechanics of the body of the person or of his vehicle for locomotion. It presupposes a certain state of maturity of the person, certain experiences and abilities. The velocity of the locomotion is very essentially influenced by those technical possibilities.

Psychological forces, at least generally, do not affect directly the "motoric system" (M) of the person, but what one can call the "inner-personal" regions (I, Figure 36) (Princ., p. 177). In other words, psychological forces do not carry a person forward mechanically but generally by way of "motivation."

Nevertheless, when handling problems of bodily or social locomotion we consider it entirely legitimate to regard the person at first approximation as one dynamical unit (Princ., p. 166). Even in physics the concept of force of gravity would not have been permissible if the knowledge of the "mechanics" which makes the bodies move would have been required. Furthermore, a great number of experiments (Lashley 1934) have proved that relatively extensive damage or other changes to muscular organs and even certain changes in the connection between nerves and muscles do not prevent the individual as a whole from moving in the direction of the force.

Whether such "macroscopic" treatment is possible in psychology is an empirical question. One might, however, point to the fact that directed movements are observable even in organisms which do not have specialized organs for locomotion (Maier and Schneirla 1935).

On the other hand, one has to emphasize that the problem of the "mechanics" of the effect of a psychological force is an important problem and certainly not a simple one. It is important both for social and for bodily locomotions. Language defects, self-consciousness, a broken leg, will influence greatly the effect of a psychological force on locomotion.

In summary, the effect of a force depends partly upon the specific properties of the motoric system (the "executive" in the terminology of Koffka 1935) of the person, and partly upon the relation between the motoric system and the inner-personal regions. This is one of the reasons why the proper treatment of problems of force in psychology makes it necessary to consider not only the structure and the properties of the environment, but also those of the person.

b. The Structure of the Person. Tension Systems.—The basic idea of the field-theoretical approach is that every behavior Be is a function of the total life space (L) which includes both the person P and the environment E (Princ., pp. 12, 30):

(25) $$Be = F \ (L) = F \ (P,E).$$

The person P and the psychological environment E are not independent factors.

Among the dynamical factors basic for the environment, we have considered thus far:

1. The cognitive structure of the environment
2. Valences
3. Forces

Among the factors basic for that part of the life space which represents the person within the environment we wish to mention here: 1.) The structure of the person; and 2.) Tension.

1.) A person can be considered as a system of dynamically more or less inter-dependent sub-systems .(Princ., pp. 168, 177). An individual can show a different degree of differentiation; for instance, an adult is more highly differentiated into subregions than a child. One can distinguish typical layers of systems within the person, for instance, the motoric-perceptual region (M) (Figure 36), and the inner-personal region (I). Within the inner-personal region one can distinguish more peripheral and more central layers of systems (S). There are great individual differences, not only in the degree of differentiation, but also in the type of structure.

2.) One of the outstanding dynamic characteristics of such a system is its tension (t). The concept of tension is closely related to that of need. One can correlate to a need in the state of hunger a system in a state of tension (Zeigarnik 1927, Ovsiankina 1928, Lewin 1935). The satisfaction of the need corresponds to a release of the tension within this system.

The arising of goals or other valences is closely related to needs and changes of their state. We can therefore say that the force $f_{P,G}$ which might lead to a locomotion of the individual P is a function of the tension (t) in P.

(26) $f_{P,G} = F(t)$ aside from other factors

To understand the interrelation of forces and tension, it is necessary to consider the concept of tension more closely.

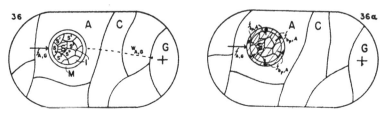

RELATION BETWEEN A FORCE FOR LOCOMOTION ACTING ON THE PERSON
AS A WHOLE AND THE TENSION IN INNER PERSONAL SYSTEMS

Fig. 36. The person P, consisting of the totality I of the inner personal systems (S, S^1, S^2, S^3, S^4, S^5, . . .) and the motoric-sensoric M; P is located at A, a force $f_{A,G}$ exists for the person as a whole in the direction of the path $w_{A,G}$ to the goal G; the system S is supposed to be in tension (t) corresponding to a need which is related to G.

Fig. 36a illustrates that the force $f_{A,G}$ to the goal cannot be directly derived from the tension (need) $t(S)$ or from the spreading of this tension over the whole person. $f_{A,G}$ force in direction to G; $f_{bP,A}$, forces on the boundary of P resulting from spread of tension.

c. The Concept of Tension.—Every dynamical construct in psychology needs a definition of its conceptual properties and a coordinating definition.

The concept of tension as used here refers to a *state* of a system of an individual. Tension has, besides others, the following properties:

(a) It is a state of a system S which tries to change itself in such a way that it becomes equal to the state of its surrounding systems S^1, S^2, . . . , S^6 (Figure 36).

(b) It involves forces at the boundary of the system S in tension.

One can formulate these statements in the following way indicating the boundary of a system S by b_S and the tension of a system S by $t(S)$:

(27)   If $t(S) \neq t(S^1)$ and $b_S \cdot b_S^1 \neq 0$, a
          tendency exists to change t so that
          $t(S) = t(S^1)$.

This statement indicates that the tension in a system S has to be determined always relative to the tension of its neighboring systems.

(28)   If $t(S) > t(S^1)$ and $b_S \cdot b_S{}^1 \neq 0$ there
exists forces $f_{b_S,S^1} > 0$.

(The term f_{b_S,S^1} will indicate a force working on the boundary b of S in the direction of the neighboring system S^1). (27) and (28) correspond to the statements (a) and (b) and express the main *conceptual* properties of the concept of tension.

As the *coordinating* definition of tension one can use the following statement:

(29)   Hypothesis: Whenever a psychological need exists, a system in a state of tension exists within the individual.

This hypothesis includes also "quasi-needs" (Lewin 1935) resulting from intentions.

The empirical facts to which this statement refers, are those acts or behavior which generally are recognized as a syndrome indicating a need; it refers, furthermore, to the after-effect of an intention.

I am speaking about the syndrome indicating a need because the term need itself can hardly be recognized as a concept in the strict sense. It is a term of the same type, as, for instance, learning, which probably will have to be eliminated in time. In other words, in formula (29) the term "need" will have to be replaced by more precise behavioral symptoms for tension.

The hypothesis (29) linking intention with tension (quasineed) has been made in opposition to a previous theory which coordinates the effect of an intention to an association (or to a *Determinierende Tendenz* in the sense of Ach 1910) between the image of the occasion and the image of the intended action. An association is from a dynamic point of view, as we have mentioned before, equivalent to the joining of two links of a chain or perhaps to a certain force, but it does not imply the properties (27) and (28) of a tension system.

The following derivations of the statement (29) combined with (27) have been made, and more or less proved:

1.) Tendency to resumption of interrupted tasks (Ovsiankina 1928, Lissner 1933, Mahler 1933);

2.) A tendency of a tension to spread over the whole person, especially if the tension is high and if the individual shows a relatively great fluidity (Dembo 1931, Birenbaum 1930, Zeigarnik 1927, Allport 1933);

3.) Communication between two systems as a condition of substitute value. The communication is facilitated by similar content and type of transition (Lissner 1933, Mahler 1933);

4.) Breaking of the walls of the systems and release of the tension by sudden changes of the general tension within the person (Zeigarnik 1927);

5.) Diffuse release of tension in time (Zeigarnik 1927, Brown 1932);

6.) Dependence of velocity of diffuse release upon the fluidity of the system (Brown 1932).

d. Force and Tension of the Whole Person.—We have stated above that the force for locomotion of the person is a function of the intensity of the need and therefore of the tension (26). We will have to ask whether this force $f_{P,G}$ (Figure 36) in the direction to the goal G can logically be derived from the tension (t) of a system S within the person P.

The force $f_{P,G}$ refers to a locomotion of P within the environment, for instance, from the region A through the region C. There is no direct way to derive the force $f_{P,G}$ conceptually from the tension in S. The forces derivable from the tension are concerned with the boundary of S. One can derive from the tension in S that this tension eventually might spread over all systems of P. It could seem as if in this way one would be able to derive some forces existing for P in relation to the environment E. However, the forces resulting from this tension of P ($t(P) > 0$; Figure 36a) would have according to (29) the boundary of the region P as point of application $f_{bP,A} > 0$. They would imply pressure on the "skin" of the person, but this would not conceptually involve a tendency for the person to move from A to G.

In other words, $f_{P,G}$ can not be derived from $t(S)$ even if the tension spreads over the whole person.

e. *Tension in the Inner-Personal Region and in the Motoric.*—A second attempt to derive locomotion from tension could refer to the motoric region: One can imagine that a tension in an inner-personal region might affect the motoric in such a way that a locomotion would take place.

Such a consideration would be in line with the common type of thinking in psychology and physiology. The more central processes in the brain are supposed to influence the motoric nerves, and these in turn the muscles. It is probably fair to say that this is a classical and widely accepted type of explanation of behavior.

We do not at all object to interpreting the inner-personal systems as representing certain brain regions. The motoric region in our representation correlates at least partly with the muscular system. However, it is important to see that one can derive conceptually tension of the motoric from tension in an inner-personal system but that one can not derive directed actions.

The relation between tension and motoric action is a wide field which of course cannot be treated adequately here. However, it might be necessary to mention briefly some of the problems which seem to be fundamental in this connection.

The motoric region is one subregion of the person. Its functioning will therefore depend upon the specific structure of the person as a whole and the specific functional interrelation of his parts. Indeed, the relation between the motoric and the other personal regions might vary greatly both in the ontogenetic and in the phylogenetic development. Both developments show certain "differentiation," not only in relation to the number of the subparts of the person, but also in regard to type of the functional interrelation between the various sub-parts. It seems to be necessary to distinguish, besides the mere spreading of tension which corresponds to (27), a different type of interrelation between different systems: a dominant system "uses" a subordinate system as its "tool."

1) Spreading of Tension from Inner-Personal Regions into the Motoric.—An illustration may make the point clear. If an adult is doing a delicate piece of work he will be careful to do it with light movements and not to apply strong pressure, even if he is very eager to do it. On the other hand, he might use much bodily force and muscular tension in lifting a heavy load, even if his need for this action is weak or very peripheral. Such examples show that for the adult there is no fixed relation between the intensity of his need and the tension in his muscular system. If we indicate the tension of an inner-personal system related to a need by $t(I)$ and the tension of a motoric system as $t(M)$, we have to say that for an adult $t(M) \neq F(t(I))$; for an increase or decrease of inner-personal tension does not necessarily lead to an increase or decrease of motoric tension. At least one has to say that, aside from $t(I)$, other factors (N) are dominant in determining the muscular tension in *adults:*

$$(30) \qquad t(M) = F\ (t(I),\ N)$$

The relation between inner-personal and motoric tension seems to be different in young children at least to some degree. The muscular system of the *young child* is much more likely to increase its tension (muscular tonus) whenever the tension in the inner-personal region increases. He is, therefore, likely to be "too tense" if he is very eager to do a piece of work. If he wants two blocks to stick together he will press them forcibly.

$$(30a) \qquad t(M) = F\ (t(I))$$

The adult under the same circumstances would see whether pressing would help or whether other actions would be the proper means to his end. Of course, even for an adult there is a tendency to get too tense if he is too eager. This is in line with formula (30).

The dependence of muscular and inner-personal tension is in line with (27) and can be viewed at least partly as a spreading of tension from one part of the person to another.

2) Induction of the Motoric by Inner-Personal Regions.—
The individual, especially the adult, makes use of his motoric
in a "purposeful" way. He uses the motoric as a "tool."
This involves a high degree of independence of the inner-
personal tension $t(I)$ and the motoric tension $t(M)$.

In this respect the infant is quite different from the adult.
The infant is not able "to make use" of his limbs for a directed action. However, tension and change of tension are
already clearly observable. The general muscular tension
seems to increase with the increase in hunger in line with
(30a) and leads to a greater amount of random movements
(Irwin 1932). With satiation during drinking a decrease
of the tonus of the limbs, culminating finally in sleep, can
readily be observed. Very soon, however, the motoric of the
infant becomes partly useful for directed actions. The
mouth, and after some weeks the eyes, have functionally the
position of "tools" for directed behavior. The further development makes this function of the motoric as a tool more and
more dominant.

One will have to ask: what is the nature of the dynamic
interrelation between the motoric and the inner-personal
region in case the one is used as a "tool" for the other?

To characterize the motoric as a tool might sound as a
mechanistic theory of *l'homme machine.* Of course, such a
theory is out of question. However, here as usual, a wrong
theory might still point to a rather important and correct
question. Since this problem is merely a side line in our discussion, we will try only to circumscribe its conceptual place.

By characterizing the motoric as a tool for the inner-
personal region we coordinate its dynamical nature with the
interrelation between the person as a whole and a real tool for
action. We have discussed briefly some of the topological
problems and problems of direction connected with the use
of tools (p. 69). Indeed, one's own motoric can serve as
"bridge" like any other tool. Koehler (1925) has approached
the dynamic problems by pointing to the "goal-directed character" which an object acquires if it becomes a tool in a concrete situation.

It seems to me that the movement of tools and particularly the movement of the motoric as a tool can be represented by referring to a dynamic field which is similar in nature to certain social fields. It is similar to a "power field" (Lewin 1935) which corresponds to the influence which one person has on another. The basic dynamical fact is that the structure of one field of forces is "induced" by an "inducing" field of somewhat different nature, namely, by the power field of another person. The difference between a power field and a field of forces of the type that we have treated thus far is quite important. For instance, a conflict where one of the opposing forces is induced is essentially different from a conflict where both opposing forces correspond to the person's own needs.

We shall limit our discussion to this brief remark and merely point to the fact that the concept of inducing and induced fields has been widely used in physics and for quite a time in a more vague sense also in biology to express a logically similar interrelation. A more exact way of applying the concept of inducing and induced field to the relation between inner-personal regions and motoric might be of considerable help for understanding the relative independence of the locomotion of the person as a whole from the state of particular muscular organs.

3) The Motoric as a Medium.—The induction of the processes in the motoric by inner-personal regions becomes increasingly important (relative to a mere spreading of tension) during development. This development becomes more understandable if one refers to the concept of "thing" and "medium" as used by Heider (1927). In the case of perception through a distance, a medium transfers certain effects of the perceived "thing" through the distance so that the structure of the thing becomes visible by means of its effects on the medium. Heider has pointed out that a basic characteristic of every medium is that it consists of a great number of "microscopic" parts which can be changed relatively independently of each other. He has shown that this independence of the parts of the medium is instrumental in transferring the structure of the thing through the medium.

Heider speaks also of a medium for expression and for actions. The properties of a medium for actions are similar to those mentioned above. For instance, the possibility of the use of written and spoken language for self-expression and understanding is based upon a vast number of constellations of letters or words.

In general, the variety of constellations which can be set up by different combinations of relatively independent parts of the motoric is very essential for the possibility of specific expressions or purposeful actions.

It is important that the growth from infancy to adulthood involves high differentiation, not only within the inner-personal region (I), but also within the motoric region (M). The motor development increases the relative independence of the different sub-parts of the muscular system (Allport 1933). It increasingly gives to the motoric the character of a medium. This enables the motoric more and more to be "integrated" for a special purpose in a specific way, i.e., to be used as a "tool" to serve a special purpose or need. In other words, *the tension of certain inner-personal regions t(I) induces specific constellations and changes in the motoric (M). These changes (actions) tend to lead to a reduction of the tension in these inner-personal regions (in line with (27)) not by merely spreading tension from I to M, but mainly by having the person reach certain goals.*

In older children and adults the relation of an inducing and an induced field holds not only between the inner-personal region and the motoric, but to some degree between central and peripheral inner-personal systems. A central need may set up a peripheral "quasi-need" as a tool for its fulfillment. Again, a sufficient degree of differentiation within the inner-personal region seems to be the condition for the development of this relation of thing and medium.

In summary, there seem to be at least two rather different relations between the motoric (M) and the inner-personal region (I) of the person P. The one is characterized by the interrelation between the tensions of these regions (such as spreading of tension). This type of interrelation can be logically derived from the concept of tension. Besides, the motoric can have the position of a tool for the inner-personal systems. In other words, between the inner-personal region and the motoric there exists the relation of an inducing thing to an induced field, or of thing and medium. The second type of interrelation seems to increase in importance from infancy to adulthood.

f. Two General Theories about the Relation between Tension and Force.—We might sum up our discussion of the relation of force and tension by comparing two types of theories. The one which we might call the traditional theory is not set up as a straw man but represents, I think, a rather widely used and rather natural view, although it may not often have been defended in such radical form as we describe it.

This first theory explains behavior as a result of the inner state of the person including the "inner stimuli" (which in turn might be due to stimuli from outside). The tendency of this theory is to explain the behavior by studying more in detail the way the motoric depends upon the other regions of the person (brain). This view is characteristic of many of the so-called physiological theories. It involves, aside from other things, a derivation of behavior including directed locomotions (forces) from the state of inner-personal regions. (One rather important difficulty of this view is the relative independence of the direction of locomotion from the state of the single motoric organs; see Hilgard 1936.)

The second theory holds that such an explanation of behavior is not possible. The dependence between the inner state of the person and behavior is recognized, but viewed at least as partly indirect. We have to emphasize especially the following points:

1.) Forces for locomotions cannot be derived logically from tension in the person.

2.) There exists a relation between certain tensions of the inner-personal regions of the person and certain valences in the environment: with a state of hunger the strength of the valence will change $Va(G) = F$ (t). However, the existence and the strength of the valence does not depend only upon the tension of the person but also upon certain non-psychological "alien" factors (Princ., p. 70). Whether within the environment food exists, what type of food, and at what place is not a result, or at least not alone the result of psychological factors. More specifically, the valence $Va(G)$ which an object of activity G possesses for a person at a given time depends upon the character and state of the person P, and upon the perceived nature of the object or activity G;[1]

(31) $Va(G) = F$ (t,G)

3.) In the same indirect way tension and forces for locomotion are related. The existence of a valence is equivalent to the existence of a force field (20d and 20e). According to (21) the force $f_{P,G}$ is a function of the valence (G) and of the relative position of P and G $(f_{P,G} = F \left(\dfrac{Va(G)}{e_{P,G}} \right))$ From (21) and (31) follows that:

(32) $f_{P,G} = F\left(\dfrac{t}{e_{P,G}}, G \right)$

In other words, the force for a locomotion depends on the need or the tension of the person; on those non-psychological factors which affect the existence of the valence; and on the relative position of the person and the valence.

The second theory, then, does not try to derive forces from tension logically. Instead, it is based on *two rather independent hypotheses*. Hypothesis I correlates a need to a tension in the inner-personal regions of the person P in line with (29). A second independent hypothesis II correlates this state of the person to certain properties of the environment E in line with (31). In particular, a tension might be related

---

[1] It might be necessary to insert such an alien factor also in other formulas. However, by introducing it into formula (31) it is indirectly introduced into all formulas making use of (31); in other words, into every formula which directly or indirectly refers to the concept of valence.

to a positive valence corresponding to a goal and to a negative valence of the situation in which the individual is at present. However, the existence of the valence does not depend only on the state of the person, but on non-psychological factors as well.

We could, therefore, not state that: wherever a need exists there exists a region with a positive valence. This statement might be correct if one includes planes of irreality of the environment, although in cases of vague needs, it might be difficult to determine this region. It is, therefore, advisable at present to state the hypothesis of the interrelation between the state of the person and the character of the environment in the more cautious way expressed in (31), which means: wherever a negative or positive valence in the environment exists there exists a system in tension within the person. In some cases of negative valences, e.g., in case of fear, it is doubtful whether this tension has the usual characteristics of a need.)

This hypothesis includes a rather far-reaching statement concerning the dependence of forces for locomotion upon the state of the person (or in more popular terms it relates forces to needs, corresponding to (32)). However, this relation between force and tension is not a direct one as in the first theory. *Instead of linking the need directly to the motoric, the need is linked with certain properties of the environment. The environment then determines the motoric.*

This theory obviously separates need and directed actions much more than did the previous theories. Only after determining the environmental situation can one make any definite conclusions from a need to behavior. This indirect connection might seem to be of disadvantage. To my mind it has many advantages. Psychology has proved increasingly that a given need might lead to a great variety of different or even contradictory actions in accordance with the specific environment. It might lead to restless movements, to conflicts, to directed actions toward phenotypically quite different goals. Every change in the potency of the situation or in the barriers separating person and goal or in the cognitive structure of the field will change the occurrences resulting from the need.

One can express the second theory by saying that the motoric region is viewed as much as a part of the psychological environment as a part of the person.

Frequently the attempt has been made to represent a need by a concept which has the property both of a tension and of a force. The psychoanalytical concept of libido is often used as such "directed tension," and other schools seem to develop somewhat similar concepts (Murray 1936, McDougall 1932). To combine the concept of tension, which is mathematically a scalar, with the concept of force, mathematically a vector, is logically quite adventurous. It is still more important that such a theory tries to link need and action in a too direct way: instead of introducing the environment as well as the person right at the start and instead of deriving the behavior B according to the formula (25) $B = F(P,E)$, it derives B from P and recognizes only somewhat later that E also is important.

I may mention one more specific advantage of the second theory. We have mentioned that the effect of a force can be either: (a) a locomotion in the direction of the force, or (b) a change in the cognitive structure of the environment equivalent to such locomotion. Theoretically, it is somewhat difficult to understand how a force acting on a person in a certain direction can produce a change in the structure of the environment. However, if one links force with need and sees the primary effect of a need in the change of certain psychological environment (valence), it is understandable that a need may result in a structural change of the environment as naturally as it may result in locomotion. As we have mentioned, the tendency to change the structure of the environment thus appears even as a more fundamental and more general effect of a need: the need leads to a change of the environment either by a cognitive restructuring or by a change of structure through locomotion.

D. THE FORMAL CONDITIONS FOR MEASURING FORCES

If one wishes to measure forces one has to fulfill certain general conditions of measurement.

One might distinguish four different types of functional interrelation between constructs (dynamical facts) and observable facts, namely: (a) logical interdependence of constructs; (b) empirical interdependence of constructs; (c) measurement of constructs by observable facts; and (d) functional interrelation between observable facts.

All of these interrelations can be mathematically expressed by equations in which one value X appears as a function F of the other value Y, i.e., $X = F(Y)$. The various meanings which an equation might have seem sometimes to cause a confusion, and the recent discussion about operational definition (Stevens 1935) seems not to have decreased this confusion. It is, however, rather important to be clear about the widely different meanings which functional interdependence can have.

1. Conceptual Interdependence of Constructs

One dynamical fact might be a function of another because the one can be *logically* derived from the other. The possibility of such derivation depends of course upon the definition of those constructs.

For instance, if one accepts the definitions we have given one can say: a force on the boundary of a system in tension can logically be derived from the concept of tension; a force $f_{P,G}$ can logically be derived from a positive valence G.

The functional interdependence in this case is not an empirical problem but a purely logical derivation of one concept from another.

2. Empirical Interdependence of Constructs. Empirical Law

The relation between tension and the forces concerning locomotion or between tension and valences are examples of the second type of functional interdependence of dynamical facts.

In these cases there is no purely conceptual way to derive one dynamical fact from the other. Their interdependence has to be proved empirically, e.g., by experimentation, unlike the conceptual interdependence which does not need empirical proof.

The concept of "empirical law" points exactly to this type of functional interdependence. Every law presupposes at least two different constructs. The interdependence expressed by an empirical law should not be conceptual in nature. To prove a law it must be possible to measure these dynamical facts independently. If one, for instance, wishes to establish an empirical law about the interrelation of forces for locomotion and tension, one will have to have separate measurements for tension and for forces.

Philosophers have pointed to the fact that empirical laws frequently establish functional interdependence between entities which seem conceptually very divergent, as for example, velocity and weight, and which could not be compared directly. Indeed, the functional interdependence expressed in a law is often established in a peculiar indirect manner without comparing the two types of constructs involved:

One measures the same dynamic fact (construct) under two conditions. For instance, the intensity of tension (need) would be determined under two circumstances. One then compares the intensity of the second construct, force, under the same two conditions. The law then states how the intensity of the one dynamic factor (force) changes if the intensity of the second factor (tension) changes. In this way, the one construct (tension) is never directly compared with the other (force), but always forces with forces and tension with tension. This procedure permits the establishment of functional interdependence between two logically very different constructs on an empirical basis.

Sometimes an empirical law is used later on as a definition for one of the constructs. This definition, of course, changes the meaning of the mathematical equation. The functional interdependence then loses the character of an empirical law and acquires the character of a conceptual interdependence. *The mathematical formula as such does not tell whether we have to deal with a definition or with an empirical law.* This is a difference which can be determined only by examining the total procedure used in the system of propositions. The meaning of an equation might change during the development of a science, e.g., from that of a law to that of a definition. It remains, however, rather important to be conscious at a given time of whether one is dealing with empirical laws or definitions. Otherwise one might find himself easily drawn into a meaningless circle of argumentation.

3. Measurement of Constructs

Both the conceptual interdependence and the empirical law deal with the relation between two constructs. Measurement to my mind is different in this respect: it relates one construct (or certain properties of one construct) to observable facts. In other words, it correlates "symptoms" with dynamical facts.

With the development of science, measurement tends to become rather indirect and necessarily is interwoven both with laws and with conceptual interdependencies. However, the essence of measurement still is the correlation of dynamical facts and "symptoms."

In physics, for instance, to measure temperature one can use a great variety of methods which are more or less crude and more or less dependent. One can use a mercury thermometer, or an alcohol thermometer, or the shape of a solid body consisting of two different materials, or a change in electrical current of certain set-ups, or the color of some material. Whether or not those symptoms are indicative of the temperature which one would like to measure depends upon rather specific circumstances. The color, for instance, can be used only for temperatures which are high enough. The mercury thermometer is indicative only within a certain range of not too high and not too low temperatures. Whether the thermometer really measures the temperature depends, furthermore, very much on how this instrument is applied. It would, for instance, not suffice to measure the temperature of a solid body by letting the thermometer touch this body.

Every measurement thus refers to certain observable symptoms which are changes of what one calls an "instrument." However, whether these symptoms are indicative of the dynamic fact which should be measured depends upon the concrete circumstances and the creation of what is generally called the "standard measuring situation."

If symptoms are to be used for measurement they must conform to the following requirements (according to Helmholtz 1921, Carnap 1926, Blumberg and Feigl 1931):

1.) They should build a so-called "topological series." That is, the symptoms should build an order so that the next is always included in (or includes) all previous ones.

2.) There should be a definition of what "equal" means— in other words, under what conditions two symptoms should get the same position within the order.

Those two conditions suffice to have the symptoms used for measuring in the sense of a rank order. They do not suffice for so-called quantitative measuring. For quantitative measurement the symptoms have to conform besides to the following requirements:

3.) A unit must be defined within the measuring stick (e.g., centimeter or meter).

4.) It is necessary to define what are equal units in different points of the series.

5.) An "absolute" zero point must be established.

From this it might be clear that the problem of exactness is rather secondary for the problem of measurement. In the beginning, rather crude measuring methods might suffice because the question of exactness of measurement should be treated in direct relation to the specific problem concerned. Many different types of measurement might be available for the same dynamical fact, and it depends on the concrete circumstances which kind of measurement might be the best.

In the beginning one might choose symptoms for the measurement of a construct on a rather arbitrary basis. The main task then is to find any kind of observable symptoms which are in line with the formal requirements and which are sufficiently dependent and which are easily enough applicable. In the long run, of course, one will try to use only such symptoms as have also a definite conceptual relation to the construct which they measure (Brown 1934). In other words, one will use only those instruments the theory of which is clear. Gradually the measuring instruments and the measuring situations become more and more related to the definitions and the empirical laws of the total field concerned, and the measuring becomes rather indirect.

4. The Relation between Conceptual Interdependence, Empirical Law, and Measurement—Exemplified by the Obstruction Box

The mathematical form of an equation which represents the functional dependence characteristic for measurement is not different from that of an equation which represents a logical interdependence or an empirical law. As far as the content is concerned, the variables on *both sides* of the equation refer to *constructs* in the case of logical interdependence and in the case of empirical law; but in the case of measurement the variables in the equation refer to a *construct* on the one hand and an *observable fact* on the other hand. However, by indirect measurements it very often happens that one construct is measured by another construct, the measurement of which is already known. Therefore, the formula itself does not tell what we are dealing with. The meaning of the formula can be found out only by an inquiry into the specific scientific situation.

It might be worth while to examine from this point of view, for instance, the obstruction box.

The purpose of the obstruction box is obviously not to establish *logical* interdependence. However, the procedure used is based on the coordinating definition between force and locomotion, namely, that a locomotion occurs in the direction of a resultant of forces if this resultant is greater than zero (Ex. 14) and (19). So far the procedure of the obstruction box can be viewed as an expression of this definition of force.

The main purpose of the obstruction box is either to establish certain laws or to measure the strength of certain dynamical facts. Historically it is probably fair to say that at least one of the original purposes was to solve certain problems of *measurement*, namely, to compare the strength of different types of drives (hunger, maternal, sex). Previously it has been possible to compare the different strengths of the hunger drive by using as a measuring stick the period of starvation since the last feeding. To use the period of starvation as a crude measurement of the intensity of the drive (need) is probably sufficiently adequate if one compares different states within the same individual and within an otherwise "normal" situation (with regular feeding on a constant diet, and if the period of starvation is not too long). This measuring device, however, was not adequate for measuring the maternal drive, because time of separation between mother and litter does not regularly intensify the need. Moreover, this procedure obviously does not permit a comparison of the strength of the maternal need with that of bodily hunger. To compare the strength of these different drives a measuring device had to be found which would permit the measurement of the strength of different drives under the same situation and with the same measuring stick. The obstruction box does fulfill these requirements, at least to some degree. It offers one situation in which a tendency related to the strength of the need (namely, what we have called the force in the direction to the goal $f_{P,G}$) is measured by the same measuring stick—namely, overcoming or not overcoming the grill.

There exists besides a possibility of viewing the obstruction box as a device for proving a certain empirical *law*, namely, a law relating the intensity of a need (tension) to the strength of a force: $f = F(t)$ corresponding to (26). Such a view would refer to the possibility of comparing after different periods of starvation the willingness of the animal to cross the grill to the goal. If one finds that after a longer time of starvation the animal would be willing to cross a more disagreeable grill, one could say that the formula (26) would have been proved, at least for these circumstances, and that this formula would have the character of an empirical law. We have mentioned that for every law at least two constructs have to be measured independently. Indeed, there are two logically independent constructs involved: namely, the tension (t) representing dynamically the need, and the force ($f_{P,G}$) representing the tendency to locomotion. Both constructs would have been independently measured, the intensity of the tension by the period of starvation, the strength of the force by the strength of the opposing force related to the grill.

A third view regarding the purpose of the obstruction box could hold that it intends to compare *two types of measurement* of the same construct. If one granted the proposition expressed in formula (26) as a hypothesis, or, as already proved otherwise, one could say that the obstruction box refers to two measurements of the intensity of a need (t): namely, 1.) by the period of starvation; and 2.) by the strength of the force (f) resulting from the need (t). The main purpose of the obstruction box then would be to compare the merits of these two ways of measuring t.

This example might show how much the meaning of a certain formula and a certain experimental procedure depends upon the historical setting.

Finally, we want to emphasize again that, with the progress of science, measurement and laws become more and more interwoven.

5. Interdependence of Two Observable Facts

One can relate by mathematical functions two directly observable facts like bodily height and circumference of the chest, or like the number of spontaneous approaches of one child to another and his refusal to relinquish a toy in the nursery-school situation.

One refers to this type of functional relation frequently as "purely statistical interrelations." However, the use of a statistical method is possible and customary as well for proving a law (b) and for measurement (c) and might be conceivable even as expression of conceptual interdependence (a). The important difference is neither the mathematical form of the equation nor the method used for the establishment, but the content of the formula, namely, its referring to two directly observable facts and not to constructs.

The interest back of the investigation of such functional interdependence is usually the interest in constructs or laws, that is, in interdependence of the type b or c. This is true even in those cases where the official doctrine of the investigator refuses to recognize any other goal than that of relating "facts with facts." Only very hard-boiled "empiricists" ever attempt to correlate facts indiscriminately without having at least some hope that the relation of these facts might have some meaning. Indeed, the value of a functional relation of type d depends upon whether or not it can be interpreted with sufficient probability as characteristic for a dependence of either type b or c.

E. CONTINUOUS AND DISCONTINUOUS FORCE FIELDS

One of the outstanding characteristics of the geometry of the life space is the fact that we have to deal, not with an infinitely structured space, but generally with macroscopic units. This characteristic of the psychological field was basic for our distinguishing of cells (1) as sub-parts of the life space and of steps (4) as units of locomotions. (Tolman 1932 refers to these units as "molar" behavior.)

Naturally these facts will show themselves also in the dynamics of the life space.

For instance, the eating situation of a child (C) who dislikes his food can sometimes be represented as a series of rather separate steps (Princ., p. 97). The otherwise united

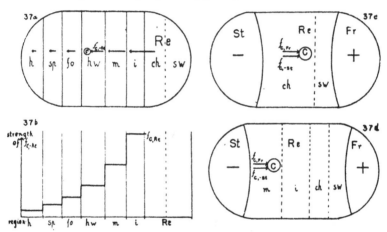

FINITELY STRUCTURED FORCE FIELD CONSISTING OF MACROSCOPIC REGIONS

Fig. 37a. Eating situation in case of disliked food. C, child; Re, real eating; h, putting hand on table; sp, taking spoon; fo, putting food on spoon; hw, bringing spoon half way to mouth; m, bringing spoon to mouth; i, taking food into mouth; ch, chewing; sw, swallowing; eating has a negative valence $(Va(Re) < 0)$; the force away from real eating $f_{C,-Re}$ increases stepwise with the decrease of distance between C and Re.

Fig. 37b. Curve representing schematically the strength of the force $f_{C,-Re}$ at different distances from Re.

Fig. 37c. Change of direction of forces after the child started real eating.

C, child; Re, real eating; St, struggle with adults; Fr, freedom; $f_{C,Fr}$, force in the direction to freedom; $f_{C,-St}$, force away from struggle.

Fig. 37d. In a later stage of "learning" to eat the disagreeable food, the situation might be restructured so that bringing spoon to mouth (m) is now seen as a sub part of the region of real eating (Re).

action of eating breaks up into putting the hand on the table (h); taking the spoon (sp); putting the food on the spoon (fo); bringing the spoon halfway to the mouth (hw); bring it to the mouth (m); taking the food into the mouth (i); chewing (ch); swallowing (sw). These steps correspond topologically to a series of regions (Figure 37a). The situation is dominated by the negative valence of the real eating (Re) (which contains the regions ch and sw). In other words, there exists a force $f_{C,-Re}$ away from the real eating. Observations on social pressure in such situations seem to prove that the force $f_{C,-Re}$ increases with the decreasing distance $e_{C,Re}$ (that is $|f_{C,-Re}| = F\left(\dfrac{1}{e_{C,Re}}\right)$). The structure of the force field is represented by arrows in Figure 37a.

The increase in the strength of the force seems to occur not gradually but rather stepwise: within the same cell no difference or at most only a very slight difference in the strength of the force $|f_{C,-Re}|$ can be observed; however, a marked difference exists of the strength of the force $f_{C,-Re}$ in neighboring cells. Figure 37b represents schematically the change of the strength of the force parallel to the topology of the situation.

When the child enters the region of real eating, the situation changes fundamentally. Ahead of him lies, then, the region of freedom (Fr) which has a positive valence (Figure 37c). Therefore, a force $f_{C,Fr}$ exists. To avoid eating, he would have to struggle (St) with the adult. This region of fight has a negative valence for him. Therefore, a force $f_{C,-St}$ exists. In other words, as soon as the child enters the region of real eating (Re) the forces existing in the situation will make him finish the real eating instead of resisting it as before.

It often happens when the child "learns" to eat a disagreeable food that the region of real eating (Re) increases so that it contains not only the region sw and ch but also the region i and m (Figure 37d). In this case the change in the constellation of forces (from that corresponding to 37a to that corresponding to 37c) will occur as soon as the child enters m.

This action shows that the extension of the cells plays an important role not only for the cognitive structure of the situation but also for the direction of the forces and the structure of the force field. In our case the greater unification of the regions m, i, ch, and sw, has the effect that directions and strengths of forces within these regions are about the same, whereas previously (Figure 37a) the regions m, i, and ch showed different directions and different strengths of forces.

We do not intend to say that in all cases the structure of the force field shows abrupt steps. Especially if the field has a semi-Euclidian character there might be a rather continuous decrease or increase of force observable, for instance, if the individual gradually approaches a goal in a homogeneous field. However, the stepwise increase seems to occur rather frequently.

It is a question of research to find out what the structure of the field is in a given situation.

V

EXAMPLES OF MEASUREMENT OF FORCES

The following examples should illustrate application of the concepts and principles which we have discussed thus far. They are merely illustrative examples. It is not the purpose of this study to give a systematic survey of the work done in the field of measurement of forces or to defend special theories. Rather, we are concerned here primarily with methodological problems.

As stated in the beginning, the concepts discussed should be applicable to problems of behavior in all branches of psychology. Unfortunately, experimental examples from human and social psychology are rather limited.

Our examples thus far referred only to the "plane of reality" in the life space of an individual (Princ., pp. 195 ff.). I wish to emphasize that the problem of forces in the various planes of irreality is not less essential. To my mind, behavior is not understandable without taking into account these different planes of the life space. However, we will continue to use only examples of the plane of reality.

I will limit my discussion here to the more simple problems of psychological forces, namely: (1) force, (2) force field, (3) overlapping force fields.

A. MEASUREMENT OF FORCES

Attempts already have been made to measure forces by quite a variety of methods. I intend to discuss merely some of the outstanding methods.

We have mentioned that any of these measurements can be viewed from rather different angles. Generally, they can be considered as devices for measuring different types of constructs or as devices for proving certain laws. The grouping of a given experiment under a certain heading is therefore more or less arbitrary.

1. Measuring a Force by an Opposing Force

The obstruction box can be viewed, as we have seen, as a measurement of one force by another which is opposite in direction.

There is an entire group of such methods of measurement which try to determine whether a force $f_{A,G}$ (which is to be measured) is greater or smaller than a second (standard) force $f_{A,H}$.

(Ex. 16) $$|f_{A,G}| \gtrless |f_{A,H}|$$

For this type of measurement the following requirements have to be fulfilled: 1.) Both forces have to be opposite in direction. That is, $d_{A,G} = d_{A,H}$. 2.) The point of application has to be the same region. For instance, both forces might act on the same individual P at the same time ($f_{A,G}^{P}$ and $f_{A,H}^{P}$).

In all these cases we have to deal with the problem of equilibrium. As a criterion for whether $|f_{A,G}| < |f_{A,H}|$ or whether $|f_{A,G}| > |f_{A,H}|$ one observes whether a locomotion occurs in the direction $d_{A,H}$ or in the direction $d_{A,G}$. As long as $|f_{A,G}| = |f_{A,H}|$ no locomotion should occur in the direction $d_{A,G}$ or $d_{A,H}$.

a. *Conflict between Two Driving Forces.*—Considering the possible constellation of valences which can lead to such a situation, one can distinguish the following three cases: 1.) A positive valence $Va(G) > 0$ and a negative valence $Va(H) < 0$ lying in the same direction from the individual P who should be located at the region A in such a way that $d_{A,G} = d_{A,H}$ (or that $d_{A,G} = d_{H,-H}$). In this case, there exist two forces $f_{A,G}$ and $f_{A,-H}$ (or $f_{H,-H}$) which are opposed in direction. This is a typical constellation of reward (Lewin 1935). The obstruction box is an example of this constellation. 2.) The individual might be located "between" two negative valences. An example is the situation of threat of punishment for not entering a disagreeable activity (Lewin 1935). In this case there are two negative valences:

$Va(G) < 0$ and $Va(H) < 0$. The two forces $f_{A,-G}$ and $f_{A,-H}$ are, in some respects, opposite to each other

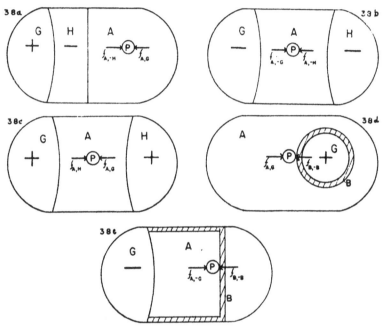

VARIOUS CONFLICT SITUATIONS (SCHEMATICALLY REPRESENTED)

I. Conflict between Two Driving Forces

Fig. 38a. A positive and a negative valence lying in the same direction. A, present position of the person P; $Va(G) > 0$; $Va(H) < 0$; $d_{A,G} = d_{A,H}$; $f_{A,G}$, force in the direction to G; $f_{A,-H}$, force in the direction away from H.

Fig. 38b. Two negative valences lying in opposite directions. $Va(G) < 0$; $Va(H) < 0$; $d_{A,G} = d_{A,H}$; $f_{A,-G}$, force away from G; $f_{A,-H}$, force away from H.

Fig. 38c. Two positive valences lying in opposite directions. $Va(G) > 0$; $Va(H) > 0$; $d_{A,G} = d_{A,H}$; $f_{A,H}$, force in the direction to H; $f_{A,G}$, force in the direction to G.

II. Conflict between a Driving and a Restraining Force

Fig. 38d. A Person Unable to Pass a Barrier to a Goal. P, person; G, goal $(Va(G) > 0)$; B, barrier; $f_{A,G}$, force in the direction to goal; $f_{B,-B}$, force hindering P from entering B.

Fig. 38e. Barrier Hindering Escape from a Negative Valence. $Va(G) < 0$; B, barrier; $f_{A,-G}$, force away from G; $f_{B,-B}$, force hindering P from entering B.

($d_{A,-G} = d_{A,-H}$ in some respect). 3.) The individual stands "between" two positive valences: $Va(G) > 0$ and $Va(H) > 0$. The two forces $f_{A,G}$ and $f_{A,H}$ are opposite in direction ($d_{A,B} = d_{A,C}$). This situation is generally called that of a choice between two attractions. (We will see later that one should distinguish rather carefully such a choice of goals from the choice of means.)

Figures 38 a, b, and c, represent schematically (not hodologically exactly) these three constellations. The behavior in these constellations can be understood only if one considers not only the two opposing forces at A, but the two force fields corresponding to the two valences. We prefer, therefore, to treat these problems later, when we discuss the effect of overlapping force fields.

b. Conflict between a Driving and a Restraining Force: Barriers and Paths.—One can create a set-up of reward, for instance, by letting an animal dig through a certain amount of sand before reaching his goal (Stone 1937). This constellation is similar to that of a positive and a negative valence in the same direction mentioned under 1.) However, the digging as such might not have a negative valence for the individual, as the electric grill had. It is questionable, at least, as to whether there are not obstacles of such a nature that passing through them is equivalent to something like friction but which do not possess a negative valence in themselves. In other words, if one indicates the region of digging by H one could not say that $Va(H) < 0$. Instead it would be $Va(H) = 0$. Nevertheless, passing through the obstacles might become more and more difficult the greater the obstacles are.

In this case we are accustomed to speak of the region of digging as a "barrier" B which shows resistance for a locomotion through it. The amount of resistance of such a barrier region might have any value between nearly zero and infinity. In the first case one is accustomed to speak of an easily passable "path." We will speak in both cases of a barrier region, in the second case of an impassable barrier (Princ., pp. 153-154). We will call forces which correspond to such barriers (or to friction) "restraining forces" and those which correspond to positive or negative valences "driving forces."

The resistance which a barrier offers hinders the locomotion into it. The forces corresponding to a barrier B might therefore be indicated by $f_{B,-B}$, at least at the boundary of the barrier. The direction of these forces is therefore similar to those corresponding to a negative valence. However, there exist also important differences. The strength (and also the direction) of the restraining forces, corresponding to a certain barrier does not depend only upon the character of this barrier. They depend always upon the direction and strength of the driving forces affecting the individual at that time. For instance, the strength of the force $f_{B,-B}$ which one has to correlate to an impassable barrier B depends upon the strength of the driving force $f_{A,G}$. Figures 39a and b shall represent the same impassable barrier B, but the positive valence $Va(G)$ shall be greater in case of Figure 39a than in Figure 39b, i.e., $|Va(G^a)| > |Va(G^b)|$. Therefore $|f_{A,G^a}| > |f_{A,G^b}|$.

If the impassable barrier B is sufficiently strong a locomotion in the direction to G will be prohibited in both cases as soon as the individual P reaches the boundary of B. In both cases, therefore, an equilibrium in regard to this locomotion will exist. In other words, in both cases, $d_{A,G} = d_{B,-B}$ and $|f_{A,G}| = |f_{B,-B}|$ according to (19a). From this together with $|f_{A,G^a}| > |f_{A,G^b}|$ it follows that $|f_{B^a,-B^a}| > |f_{B^b,-B^b}|$. That means: a greater restraining force is to be attributed to barrier B in the case 39a than in 39b in spite of the fact that the barrier has the same properties in both cases. In other words, *even if the character of B is not changed its restraining forces increase with the increase of the opposing driving forces.* In case the driving force is zero no restraining force can be attributed to B, even if the barrier is impassable.

Therefore, the properties of a barrier, for instance, the "strength" of a barrier, cannot be represented by a definite force, nor a definite force field. Rather the field of restraining forces, corresponding to a constant barrier, changes with the strength of the opposing driving forces. The *strength of a barrier* is characterized by the maximum driving force which can be applied to the barrier without breaking it.

In this respect, there exists a marked contrast with the grill of the obstruction box. The negative valence of the electric grill B and the force $f_{B,-B}$ which hinders the individual from entering B, depends directly upon the character of the grill. If B is kept constant the force $f_{B,-B}$ is (relatively) constant. At least, it does not decrease to zero or increase to infinity in the same way as the restraining force correlated to the impassable barrier. The grill B has a valence which can be represented by a definite force field (although, of course, the valence of B depends upon the state of the individual P and the character of the total situation).

The difference between driving and restraining forces is well known in physics (Planck 1928). The introduction of the concept of restraining forces is closely related to the ideas of equilibrium and of the correlation between resultant force and locomotion (19a). It would lead us too far afield to discuss this problem in detail here. It might be possible to avoid altogether the concept of restraining force in psychology if one did not refer to geographical regions one had to cross, but merely to different types of activities one had to fulfill, such as "crossing a certain area by foot." The activity of overcoming resistance often has a negative valence; sometimes it has a positive one. By referring to these activities of overcoming resistance rather than to the resistance itself it might be possible to substitute always a negative or positive valence of a region of activity for the restraining forces of a barrier. We might well leave this problem open.

It is an important characteristic of the force field which corresponds to a barrier that it does not extend, or at least does not extend to any important degree, outside the region of the barrier B. In other words, there are only forces $f_{B,-B}$ (Figures 39a and b), but not forces $f_{A,-B}$. The force field differs, at least in this respect, from those force fields corresponding to a negative valence which spread over an area considerably larger than the region of the valence (Figures 33a and 37a).

In case restraining forces are to be distinguished in psychology from driving forces one will have to enumerate two more conflict situations in which one can measure forces by an equilibrium: 4.) A barrier B lies "between" the individual P and a positive valence G (Figure 38d): $d_{A,G} = d_{B,-B}$. In this case a locomotion through B will occur only if $|f_{A,G}| > |f_{B,-B}|$. Such a situation is most common wherever the individual has to solve a problem or to

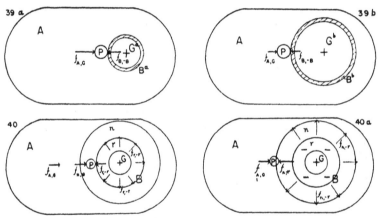

Figs. 39a and 39b. The Strength of a Restraining Force as a Function of a Driving Force. $Va(G) > 0$; P, person; B, impassable barrier; $f_{A,G}$, driving force in the direction to G is greater in 39a than in 39b; the restraining force $f_{B,-B}$ is greater in 39a than in 39b.

Figs. 40 and 40a. Measuring Forces by the Duration of the Attempt to Pass an Impassable Barrier. P, individual; G, the goal; B, the barrier consisting of the regions n (preparatory actions to overcome the barrier) and r (the actual passing of the barrier).

Fig. 40. Constellation shortly after the beginning of the attempt to pass the barrier. P is located in n; $f_{n,G}$, force in the direction to G; $f_{r,-r}$, restraining force hindering the entrance into r.

Fig. 40a. Constellation at the moment when the person relinquishes (temporarily or permanently) his attempt to pass through the barrier. P is leaving n in the direction to A; $Va(r) < 0$; $f_{A,G}$, force in the direction to G; $f_{n,-r}$, driving force away from r.

overcome an obstacle when he is to reach a goal. 5.) The individual P is prevented by a barrier B from going away from a negative valence G (Figure 38e): $d_{A,-G} = d_{B,-B}$. Again a locomotion through B presupposes that $|f_{A,-G}| > |f_{B,-B}|$. As an example of this situation, a child may wish to withdraw from the eating of undesired food but may be held back by the arm of the mother.

I will take up one example of measurement of forces in case of an impassable barrier, and a second example in case of a passable barrier.

c. Measuring of Forces in the Case of an Impassable Barrier.—To find out in what way the strength of the force depends upon the distance from the goal, Fajans (1933) has tried to compare the strength of the force at different distances. We will come back to the problem of distance later. Here we will discuss in detail Fajans' criterion for the strength of the force.

As subjects, Fajans used a group of infants and young children up to five and one-half years old. The infants, seated in a high chair (A), tried to reach a toy (G) actually out of reach. The older children tried to reach a piece of chocolate or a toy which was hung out of reach. Fajans used as symptoms for the strength of the force $f_{A,G}$ the total time (Ti) the individual spent in "action toward the goal" (as stretching the hand to the goal, asking the experimenter for help, looking for tools) during a three- or five-minute period. In other words, she used as a measuring stick the formula:

(Ex. 17) $f_{A,G} = F \ (Ti)$

where F means a constantly increasing function.

Fajans discussed the question whether the time (Ti) spent during a given interval in action toward the goal can be considered as a measuring stick. (I am quoting Fajans' considerations in a slightly changed form.) The topology of the situation corresponds roughly to Figure 39a or 39b if B indicates an impassable barrier and if the distance between the individual P and the goal G is larger in 39b than in 39a.

The statement (Ex. 17) involves that if $|f_{A,Ga}| > |f_{A,Gb}|$ then $Ti^a > Ti^b$.

There exists no logical necessity that a stronger force in the direction to the goal should involve a longer time before the person turns away from the barrier. Indeed, one could argue that the impassable barrier might be more disagreeable in case of a strong goal behind it and might tend to make the individual withdraw more quickly.

The actual behavior of the children in this case and in any similar case of an impassable barrier before a goal is nearly always the following: the individual tries for a time to overcome the barrier, then he withdraws, but returns after a time. New attempts to overcome the barrier are followed by new withdrawals. On the whole, the length of the withdrawal increases as the action toward the goal decreases (Fajans 1933) until the individual withdraws permanently. Relatively seldom is the first withdrawal permanent.

A more detailed representation of the situation is given in Figure 40. The activity corresponding to the physical distance between the child and the goal (which makes up the barrier B in our case) is that of overcoming this distance. One can distinguish within this activity at least two sub-regions: namely, preparatory actions (n) like looking to the goal, selecting tools (including unsuccessful attempts); and (r), the rest of the actions which would be necessary for actually overcoming the physical distance ($B = n + r$). The child P enters n in line with the force $f_{A,G}$ which has the direction $d_{A,n}$. There the driving force $f_{n,G}$ exists, which has the direction $d_{n,r}$. However, the subject finds himself unable to enter the region r: he is unable actually to bridge the physical distance to G. In other words, there exists a restraining force $f_{r,-r}$ which is equal in strength to the opposing driving force $f_{n,G}$ (it is $d_{n,G} = d_{r,-r}$ according to 15c). These forces constitute an equilibrium.

(Ex. 18) $$|f_{n,G}| = |f_{r,-r}|$$

As long as the region r is just an obstacle but has no negative valence in itself, or as long as the force field corresponding to a negative valence of r does not extend beyond the boundary of r, the individual should remain in n. Indeed, for a long time many children continue to reach for the goal in a serious or a gesture-like way.

An actual withdrawal from n presupposes that the situation changes to that represented in Figure 40a: there should exist in n a force $f_{n,-r}$ away from r which is greater than the force in n in the direction toward G:

(Ex. 19) $|f_{n,G}| < |f_{n,-r}|$

In this case the resultant of the forces in n will have the direction $d_{n,-r}$ which is in this situation equal to $d_{n,A}$:

(Ex. 19a) $f_{n,G} + f_{n,-r} = f^*_{n,A} > 0$; therefore
            $v_{n,A} > 0$ according to (19).

That means that the individual will locomote from n to A. In the usual language, the individual will cease to make actions toward the goal and will withdraw to other activities. It would have the same effect if not the region n, but the whole barrier region B (including n and r), would acquire a negative valence, or if the region G would become negative.

We can state now that the condition for this change, which terminates one period of action toward the goal, is a change in the character of the region r (or B). This region which previously has been an obstacle acquires a negative valence, of which the corresponding force field must be sufficiently strong and must spread at least into the region n.

According to Fajans, the barrier actually acquires such a negative valence, the strength of which increases the longer the child tries unsuccessfully to enter r. Such a change is typical for all situations where a subject tries in vain to reach a goal (Lewin 1935).

After the individual has withdrawn from n to A and has spent some time in A, the negative valence of the barrier may weaken until again:

(Ex. 20) $|f_{A,G}| > |f_{B,-B}|$

That is, a situation will arise similar to that existing in the beginning period (Figure 40). The individual will start anew an action toward the goal; i.e., he will enter the region n of B. Gradually a new experience of failure will develop leading again to temporary and eventually to permanent withdrawal.

Just as in the case of the obstruction box, the duration of the action toward or away from the goal G depends upon a "historical" process involving a change in the character of the situation. If one uses the total time (Ti) of "action toward the goal" as a measuring stick for the strength of $f_{A,G}$ in line with (Ex. 17), one presupposes that the negative valence of the barrier increases at such a rate that the state corresponding to (Ex. 19) and (Ex. 19a) is reached later the greater $|f_{A,G}|$ is. Of course, the greater $f_{A,G}$ is, the greater must become $f_{n,-r}$ before the individual withdraws. However, it is quite possible that the velocity of the increase of the negative valence of r is itself a function of $|f_{A,G}|$.

Fajans has shown that at least one factor in addition has to be considered which determines the length of Ti. A withdrawal can be caused not only by a sufficiently strong negative valence of r (or B) but also by a change in the *cognitive* structure of the situation. In case the individual understands fully that r is impassable, the step $w_{A,n}$ is no longer a step in the direction to the goal G. (It is not $w_{A,n} \subset w_{A,G}$; therefore $d_{A,n} \neq d_{A,G}$ according to (3).) In other words, the force $f_{A,G}$ has no longer the direction $d_{A,n}$. Therefore no locomotion $w_{A,n}$ (action toward the goal) will occur even in case the force to the goal $f_{A,G}$ is strong and the barrier has no negative valence.

Fajans concludes from her material that such a change of the cognitive structure of the situation is indeed the dominant factor for the withdrawal of the older children. The infants, on the other hand, withdraw mainly as a result of an increasing negative valence of the barrier.

Fajans arrives at this conclusion in the following way. It has been observed experimentally that the total action toward the goal (Ti) was greater in case of a small distance between individual and goal (Figure 39a) than in case of great distance (Figure 39b) :

(Ex. 21) $\qquad$ $T_i{}^a > T_i{}^b$

This was observed in both infants and older children. If, in line with (Ex. 17), this difference would be due to a different strength of the forces toward the goal ($|f_{A,G}{}^a| > |f_{A,G}{}^b|$), then also the opposing restraining force $f_{r,-r}$ should be greater in case of Figure 39a than in 39b ($|f_{r}{}^a{}_{,-r}{}^a| > |f_{r}{}^b{}_{,-r}{}^b|$) ; for, as long as the individual remains in n without being able to locomote through r, an equilibrium exists according to (19a), i.e., $|f_{n,{}^aG}{}^a| = |f_{r}{}^a{}_{,-r}{}^a|$ and $|f_{n}{}^b{}_{,G}{}^b| = |f_{r}{}^b{}_{,-r}{}^b|$.

The resultant of forces is in both cases zero. However, the strength of the two opposing forces and, therefore, the conflict should be greater in case 39a than in case 39b. A conflict leads, according to Lewin (1935) and Fajans, to an inner-personal tension (t). The intensity of this tension is a positive function of the strength of the opposing forces (in line with (26)):

(26a) $\qquad$ $t = F\ (f)$ aside from other factors.

Therefore if $|f_{A,G}{}^a| > |f_{A,G}{}^b|$ there should be $t^a > t^b$.

One can consider the amount of restlessness and of emotional behavior as a symptom for the intensity of inner-personal tension. Fajans found that the emotionality of the infants was decidedly greater in case 39a than in 39b. She concludes therefore that for the infants it is true that $t^a > t^b$ and therefore that $|f_{A,G}{}^a| > |f_{A,G}{}^b|$. The older children, on the other hand, did not show this difference in emotionality. This means that for them $t^a = t^b$ and therefore $|f_{A,G}{}^a| = |f_{A,G}{}^b|$.

In summary, on the average both the infants and the older children showed a greater amount of action toward the goal when its physical distance was small (39a) than when the distance was large (39b) ($T_i{}^a > T_i{}^b$). However, the quicker withdrawal in case of the larger distance had different causes for the two groups. For the infants, the forces to the goal are different in the two situations ($|f_{A,n}{}^a{}_{,G}{}^a| > |f_{A,n}{}^b{}_{,G}{}^b|$) and the time of the withdrawal is determined mainly by the increase in the negative valence of the barrier.

For the older children the forces to the goal are about equal ($|f_{A,n^a,G^a}| = |f_{A,n^b,G^b}|$) and the time of the withdrawal is mainly determined by the change of the cognitive structure of the field so that $d_{A,n} \neq d_{A,G}$.

That in case of the older children the increase of the physical distance does not correspond to a smaller force in the direction to the .goal, might be due 1.) to the greater size of the physical life space of the older children (differences of a few feet do not mean as much in their life space as in that of the infant) ; 2.) to the social character of the situation (the older children recognized that the main barrier to the goal was not the physical distance but the experimenter who did not permit the use of certain tools and who did not give in to their requests for assistance) ; 3.) to the greater intellectual maturity of the older children which made the problem of the cognitive structure more dominant for them.

Fajans' experiment seems to me a good example of a rather important problem in psychological measurements. *To keep a set-up physically constant does not secure psychological constancy.* On the contrary, practically always both the cognitive structure of the situation and its force field will change relatively rapidly. That the individual remains in n and is not able to proceed to r (in other words, the very fact that the situation remains physically constant) changes both the direction and the valences in the psychological situation. Measurement of forces in psychology will have to be aware of this basic fact which, as we have seen, is important also in case of the obstruction box. To my knowledge, only Fajans has attempted to take care of the dynamical questions involved in these "historical changes" by providing additional observations necessary for deciding among the different possibilities.

d. *Measuring Forces in the Case of a Passable Barrier.* As a barrier between a rat and a goal, Stone (1937) has used sand through which the animal must dig. The apparatus was constructed in such a way that new sand could be added to the barrier during the digging. Hamilton (1934) has let a rat pull a string to bring food within reach. The string could be arranged so that the animal might pull indefinitely without ever getting to the food. One could think of measuring the strength of the force $f_{A,G}$ to the goal G by the time (Ti) before the animal gives up.

The topology in these cases is relatively simple (Figure 41). The animal in the region A is separated by a region B, corresponding to digging or string pulling, from the goal G. As a result of previous experience, the direction $d_{A,G} = d_{A,B}$. Therefore, following the force $f_{A,G}$ the animal enters the region B. In contrast with the situation of the experiment of Fajans, the animal is not stopped after the first step ($w_{A,B}{}^1$) but can go on to B^2, B^3, ...

The time (Ti) the animal will spend in proceeding with the activity B depends obviously again on a "historical process." If we call n that subpart of the barrier region B where the individual is at present, and call r the rest of the barrier region between n and the goal G we can say: the animal enters B^1 if $|f_{A,G}| > |f_{B^1,-r}|$ and will go on as long as

(Ex. 22) $|f_{n,G}| > |f_{r,-r}|$

The animal will stop digging if the negative valences of the activities r in front of him and therefore $f_{r,-r}$ will increase sufficiently. Also, the animal will stop this activity if he understands that the region B does not lead to G, that is if the cognitive structure of the field changes so that

(Ex. 23a) $d_{n,G} \neq d_{n,r}.$

In cases where the activity is not unpleasant to the animal and where there is not much increase of the negative valence of this activity by satiation or by exhaustion, the time Ti should depend mainly upon the factors which determine the change in the cognitive structure of the field, that is, upon the intelligence of the animal and his persistency in remaining hopeful. I should expect that the change in the cognitive structure would occur less rapidly in cases where the individual seems to be able to proceed than in those cases where he has to stop at a definite point (as in the experiments of Fajans).

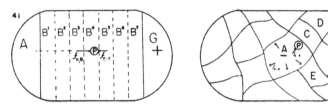

Fig. 41. Measuring Forces in Case of a Passable Barrier. G, goal; B^1, B^2, B^3 ..., parts of the barrier; $f_{n,G}$, force in the direction to the goal; $f_{r \cdot r}$, forces hindering the entrance into the rest of the barrier.

Fig. 42. Change of Activity in Case of Satiation. P, person, located in the activity region A; Va(A) $<$ 0; $f_{A,-A}$, forces at A in the direction away from A; C, D, E, regions of different activities.

e. Measuring Forces by Restraining Forces Which Permit Locomotion.—One can try to measure the driving force at every step by measuring the friction the individual is willing to overcome at that point. In this way one can eliminate at least some of the historical problems involved in the use of time periods as measuring sticks.

As a measuring stick for the psychological forces in the direction toward a goal, I have suggested the use of physical forces which one has to overcome. Such methods are limited of course to cases where the structure and direction of the physical surroundings correspond fairly adequately to the psychological situation and to the directions defined according to the hodological space.

Zener and Krechevsky have carried out such measurements under different conditions (unpublished).

2. Measuring Forces by Velocity of Locomotion

The basic coordinating definition of force (19) relates forces to a locomotion in the direction of their resultant. One might readily think of relating the strength of the resultant force to the speed of locomotion. That is, one might assume $v_{A,B} = F(|f^*_{A,B}|)$.

In physics the strength of a force is not related to velocity but to acceleration. Whether psychology, too, should coordinate the strength of the force to acceleration, to velocity, or to other characteristics of locomotion, is a rather complicated problem. We might first discuss measurements of psychological forces which try to use velocity of locomotion as a symptom of the strength of the resultant force.

We will have to remember that locomotion in psychology does not mean merely physical locomotion but might mean, as well, a social locomotion or the change from one activity to another.

We have mentioned, furthermore, that the speed of locomotion depends upon the properties of the motoric regions and the tools which are used as vehicles of locomotion. It might, therefore, be clear from the beginning that the actual speed of a locomotion $v_{A,B}$ will in a given case not be merely a function of the resultant force $f^{*}_{A,B}$ but might depend as well on other factors, for instance on whether the individual is walking or using a car, on whether the path offers great or little resistance, etc. We will designate as "h" the totality of these additional factors which might influence speed. We can then state as a possible assumption underlying the idea of measuring force by speed:

(33) $$v_{A,B} = F(|f^{*}_{A,B}|, h)$$

Different experimenters have attempted to correlate force with the speed of quite a variety of forms of behavior. We will discuss the following: the speed of a) restless movements, b) bodily locomotion to a goal, c) consumption, d) learning, e) decision.

a. *Force and Speed of Restless Movement.*—We have mentioned that a need may correspond not only to a goal G which has a positive valence ($Va(G) > 0$), but that it might also correspond to a negative valence of the present state A of the individual ($Va(A) < 0$); therefore, in case of a need not only a force $f_{A,G}$ might exist but also a force $f_{A,-A}$.

We do not assume that every need and every corresponding tension (t) goes hand in hand with a negative valence of the present state, although such an assumption might be correct. Certainly high tension corresponds to an unsatisfactory status of the person. At least for this case it holds that the negative valence $Va(A)$ increases if the tension (t) increases —somewhat parallel to the increase of the positive valences of the goal according to (31). In case the other factors are constant, one could say $Va(A) = F(t)$. That implies:

(34) $|f_{A,-A}| = F(t)$ in case other factors are constant

In other words, the force $f_{A,-A}$ to leave the present state will increase with increasing tension (need).

According to (15c) $d_{A,-A} = d_{A,X}$ for any $X \cdot A = 0$. The force $f_{A,-A}$ will lead, therefore, to a step $w_{A,C}$ to any region C which is different from A. When this locomotion is carried out, C will be the present state of the individual, and as a result of the tension (t) a force $f_{C,-C}$ will arise. This will lead to a step away from C, etc. (We have already discussed this problem.)

To my mind, the formula (34) represents one of the basic characteristics of the state of restlessness.

As to the measurement of restlessness, one might distinguish two situations, namely: 1) that of the absence, 2) that of the presence of a goal.

1) Restlessness without the presence of a positive valence. —In some respects the situation without the presence of a positive valence which is related to the need (tension) is more characteristic for the situation of restlessness. In this case the situation is dominated by the negative valence of A.

We have previously seen that the direction of the force $f_{A,-A}$ is multi-valued. It is a state which one can call "not-polarized" in comparison with a situation where a definite goal exists, because a step to any other region than the present one is in the direction of the force $f_{A,-A}$.

If one applies to restless movements the idea that the speed of locomotion is a function of the strength of the resultant force in its direction (33) and if one indicates the velocity of restless movement by $v(res)$, the formula (33) takes the form:

(Ex. 23) $v(res)_{A,-A} = F(|f_{A,-A}^{*}|)$

in case the other factors (h) are kept constant. We will mention several studies the results of which are in line with this assumption.

a) Velocity of Change of Activity in Satiation.—Karsten (1927) found that with increasing psychological satiation of an activity, the person tends to shift more and more rapidly from one activity to another. I might emphasize that this situation is not merely a restless situation. However, it is a clear case in which the character of the present occupation always becomes a negative valence and leads to a locomotion away from it. In this respect it is formally similar to the situation of restless movements.

Figure 42 represents a situation in which the individual P is located in A. If this activity A acquires a negative valence $(Va(A) < 0)$ and therefore $|f_{A,-A}| > 0$, the individual might shift, for instance, to the activity C. Soon C will acquire a negative valence and the individual will shift to some other region D, etc. Karsten found that, on the average, the satiation time becomes shorter and that therefore the velocity of locomotion from one activity to another increases if the general level of satiation gets higher.

Freund (1930) found that in the time of the menstruum the speed of psychological satiation is faster than during intermenstruum. That is in line with the fact that during that time the general emotional tension is greater and it is easier to touch the central regions of the person.

b) Velocity of Bodily Locomotion during Hunger.— Skinner (1932) has observed restless bodily movements in animals in different states of hunger. He found that both the area covered in a given time and the speed of the restless movements are functions of the starvation time. In other words, he found that the formula (Ex. 23) in connection with (34) is correct, namely,

(Ex. 23a)　　$v(res)_{A,-A} = F(|f_{A,-A}^{*}|) = F(t)$

His results can be viewed either as a measurement of force by speed according to (Ex. 23), or as a measurement of tension (t) by speed according to (Ex. 23a), or as an expression of a law which relates the tension (t) to the force $|f_{A,-A}|$ (34). In the last case the time of starvation has to be viewed as a measurement of (t) and the velocity as an independent measurement of the force $|f_{A,-A}|$ according to (Ex. 23).

Richter (1927) measured the number of drum revolutions by an animal. He, too, found that the formula (Ex. 23a) is correct because the speed of locomotion was greater if the time of starvation increased.

c) Amount of Random Movements during Hunger.—Irwin (1932) found that the amount of random movements of infants (measured with a stabilimeter) increases with increasing time after the last feeding. Therefore, the random movements are a function of the tension (need) in line with (Ex. 23a).

One should realize, of course, that in all probability the life space of the infant of a few days is not yet sufficiently structured to speak of definite regions of the life space and of locomotions, other than in a very vague and tentative way. On the other hand, the results of Irwin doubtless indicate a relation between the amount of random movements and the intensity of hunger (tension). One might prefer to think of these random movements more as a ''discharge of tension'' than as movements due to a general feeling of uncomfortableness (the latter interpretation would be more in line with a force $f_{A,-A}$).

In any case, the amount of random or of restless movements seems to be a rather good symptom of the amount of tension (other factors being equal) in line with (Ex. 23a) even if one does not relate the restless movements to a force $f_{A,-A}$.

2) Restlessness in the presence of a goal.—A typical case of restlessness in the presence of a goal is given if an individual P is unable to overcome a barrier B between himself and the goal G. In this case the force $f_{A,G}$ exists (Figure 39a) and tends to lead to a locomotion in the direction $d_{A,B} = d_{A,G}$. However, if the resistance of the barrier B is great enough to block locomotions, that is, if $|f_{B,-B}| = |f_{A,G}|$ no locomotion in the direction $d_{A,B}$ will occur according to (19).

The resultant f^* of these restraining and driving forces will be equal to zero ($f_{A,G} + f_{B,-B} = f^* = 0$) regardless of the strength of the driving force $f_{A,G}$. However, the state of the individual P under this condition is not the same as it would be if no opposing forces were acting on him. It is different if the equilibrium is due to weak or to strong opposing forces. For instance, we have seen, when discussing Fajans' experiments, that the tension of the individual will be greater in the case represented by Figure 39a than in 39b: $t^a > t^b$ if $|f_{A,G}^a| > |f_{A,G}^b|$. In other words:

(35) $t = F(f_{A,G})$ in a state of equilibrium.

If the tension (t) is high enough it will lead to restless movements, that is, to a force $f_{A,-A}$, the strength of which will be a function of the tension according to (34). The velocity of these restless movements should be a function of this force and, therefore, of the tension according to (**Ex. 23a**).

To my knowledge, there has been no specific measurement done of restless movements under this condition although the form of such restless movements behind a barrier has often been described (for instance by Koehler 1929, Tolman 1932). We may, however, add here a few remarks about the direction of these restless movements.

In the case without a goal, the restless movement might go in the direction to any other region because any of those directions will equal $d_{A,-A}$ (according to 15c). Therefore, it is not possible to make a general statement concerning the specific direction of the restless movements (aside from (34a)). This will depend upon the individual constellation.

However, in the case of presence of a goal, we have to deal with a "polarized field" of driving forces (central field) and a general statement about the form of the restless movements is possible: The locomotion $w_{A,X}$ resulting from the force $f_{A,-A}$ will be such that the resultant force ($f^*_{X,-X}$) opposite to the direction of this locomotion ($d_{A,X} = d_{X,-X}$) will be a minimum. In other words:

(34a)   The restless movement $w_{A,X}$ occurs so that
$$f^*_{X,-X} = \text{minimum}$$

The forces at every point X within the field are determined by the driving force $f_{A,G}$ related to the positive valence of G and by the restraining force $f_{B,-B}$ related to the barrier B. The restless movements will occur, therefore, in the lines of equilibrium of both force fields. Because, only in this case will the force $f_{A,-A}$ not encounter opposing forces.

I have discussed several examples elsewhere (1935). In the case of a circular barrier in a semi-Euclidian space with the goal inside and the individual outside the barrier, the restless movements should be circular. In case of a straight barrier, the restless movements should oscillate parallel with the barrier around the point which is nearest to the goal. This is true, of course, only if the life space has a semi-Euclidian character.

Theoretically, it seems possible to measure the strength of the force to restless movements $f_{A,-A}$ by creating such a situation where there exists a *point* of equilibrium but no *line* of equilibrium and where any locomotion away from A is opposed to a standard force. It would lead too far afield to discuss this problem in detail here.

b. Force and Speed of Consumption. 1) Areas of locomotion to be considered in case of a goal.—In case locomotion is possible from the region A where the person is at present to the goal region G, the following regions might be considered for measuring the speed of locomotion as a function of the force $f_{A,G}$.

The path $w_{A,G}$ might lead through: 1.) the "region of decision" D, including the making up of the mind to choose G as a goal and to start the action (Figure 43). 2.) the activity B corresponding to a change in physical position from A to that physical region where the goal G is available; we would call this the "region of translocation" using a term of Bingham (1928). 3.) the region G corresponding to "consumption."

Every one of these regions might have subregions. For

instance, the region of translocation B might contain a sub-region of preparation and actual translocation as in Figure 40.

One should notice that the graphical presentation in Figure 43 coordinates the regions to activities and not to geographical areas. A step from any region to any other means, therefore, a change in activities. *To stay within one region does not at all mean that nothing happens. Instead, it means that a certain activity continues to go on.*

One will have to realize that to stay in the same region generally implies a gradual change in the situation. That is true even for such an activity of "consumption" as lying quietly under a tree. We have mentioned that, after some time, the psychological character of the activity, especially its valence, will be changed because the person will become satiated or tired; or he may enjoy the activity increasingly. Also, in case of translocation (that is, if the person stays in the region B), the state of the person, and therefore the valence of this activity, will gradually change. Besides, the physical surroundings will be permanently changed by the activity B itself. The psychological surrounding is permanently changed also by the activity D and C, but this is not as obvious in the case of consumption and especially of decision as in the case of translocation.

We will discuss, first, the speed of locomotion in regard to consumption.

2) Topology of consumption.—With rats as subjects, Skinner (1937) investigated the following situation: Every tapping of a lever produces a small amount of food. Skinner found that the frequency with which a rat taps the lever within a time unit decreases as the animal approaches satiation.

The topology of the situation is given in Figure 44. The animal starts from the region A which represents its present state of activity. It might tap the lever L and reach the food G. The amount of food is small. Therefore, after consuming G the animal will find itself in a state which is approximately the same as that before tapping the lever. In other words, it will be again in a region A.

After several days of experience the cognitive structure of the situation will have somewhat changed (Figure 45). The animal knows that tapping the lever will produce food. Therefore, after consuming the food G^1 reached by the first tapping of the lever (L^1), the animal finds itself in A but can proceed immediately to the second tapping of the lever L^2, from there to G^2, A, L^3, G^3 and so on. (It might be appropriate to eliminate the regions A in the representation of at least a certain period of the experiment.)

The driving force in this situation is probably determined by the valence $Va(G)$ of the total amount of food the animal expects ($G = G^1 + G^2 + G^3 \ldots$). This amount is not limited. Therefore, the amount G ahead of the animal can be considered as practically the same during the whole experiment. Also, the distance ($e_{P,G}$) to the next food and to the rest of the food ahead can be considered as being constant. According to (21) is $f_{P,G} = F \left(\dfrac{Va(G)}{e_{P,G}} \right)$. In our case is $e_{P,G} = $ constant Therefore, the driving force $f_{P,G}$ can be considered to be a direct function of the valence of $G (f_{P,G} = F(Va(G))$ which decreases during satiation.

Indeed, Skinner found that the frequency of tapping the lever within a time unit decreases with the decrease in hunger (t). One can consider the frequency of tapping the lever in a time unit as the velocity v_{A,L^n,G^n} with which the animal passes through one group of regions A, L^n, G^n. Skinner's observation can then be expressed by the formula:

(Ex. 24) $v_{A,L^n,G^n} = F(t)$

The velocity v_{A,L^n,G^n} refers to the total time which the animal needed for: "tapping the lever once, consuming the food received, getting ready to tap the lever the next time." The time necessary for actually tapping the lever is probably rather short and relatively constant. Therefore, the difference of velocity is probably mainly a difference in consumption and getting ready for the next tapping of the lever.

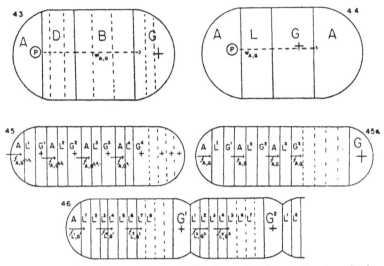

Fig. 43. Decision as a Region to Be Crossed in Locomotion to a Goal. P person; A, region of present activity; D, region of decision; B, change in physical (or social) position; G, goal region of consumption.

Fig. 44-46. Topology of Consumption (Experiment of Skinner).

Fig. 44. The animal P reaches the food G by tapping a lever L; after consumption of G he finds himself again in a situation A similar to the beginning situation.

Fig. 45. Structure of the life space after the individual is thoroughly acquainted with the situation. G^1, G^2, G^3 . . . ., food achieved by tapping the lever; L^1, L^2, L^3, . . . , various occasions of tapping the lever; A, a situation like the beginning situation (including being hungry); f_{A,G^1}, ^{2}, ^{3}, . . . , f_{A,G^2}, ^{3} . . and f_{A,G^3} . . , forces in the direction to the food G ahead of the position of P at a given time.

Fig. 45a. A slightly different representation of the same setting. Being satiated is regarded as the goal G, which dominates behavior; the single bites G^1, G^2, G^3 are regarded merely as a means to reach G; $f_{A,G}$, force in the direction to G.

Fig. 46. Situation where many tappings of the lever have to be made before a bite is reached. G^1, G^2, consumption of food; A, beginning situation; L^1, L^2, L^3 . . , various tappings of the lever; f_{L^1}, G^1, f_{L^4}, G^1, f_{L^2}, G^2, forces in direction of the goal at different positions of P.

The result (Ex. 24) of the experiment can be derived from the theory that the valence of the goal G, and therefore the force in its direction, is a function of the need of the individual $|f_{A,G}| = F(Va(G)) = F(t,G)$ according to (31), and that the speed of locomotion is a function of the resultant force in its direction ($\lceil v_{A,G} = F(|f^*_{A,G}|)$) according to (19) and (33). For, the restraining force $f_{L^n, -L^n}$ offered by the tapping of the lever probably can be considered to be relatively constant (and not very great) as soon as the animal is familiar with it. We have already mentioned that the driving force $f_{P,G} = F(Va(G))$. Therefore, the resultant $f_{P,G} + f_{L^n, -L^n} = f^*_{P,G} = F(Va(G))$.

If one applies these formulas in our case, one assumes that the velocity of consumption $v(cons)$ can be viewed as one type of velocity of locomotion. That means that formula (33) can acquire the form

(Ex. 25) $v(cons)_{P,G} = F(|f^*_{P,G}|) = F(t)$

in case the other factors are kept constant. Skinner's results are fully in line with these deductions.

The region of consumption is not always structured into such clearly distinguishable units as in the experiment of Skinner. Often G is a more homogeneous field or its subparts G^1, G^2 . . . are different in size and not clearly separated. Washburn (1924) has observed the speed of consumption by weighing the amount of food eaten during a time unit. She also found a gradual decrease in the speed of consumption with satiation. Her results are therefore in line with (Ex. 25).

It might be appropriate to mention one slightly different representation of the situation in Skinner's experiment. In Figure 45 the regions G^1, G^2 . . . ., in other words, the eating as such, are considered to have a positive valence. One might say, however, that the state of being satiated is the goal G of the animal. In this case the eating of the single bites is to be conceived as regions which do not themselves have a positive valence but are merely means, that is, regions one has to pass through to reach the goal G. This situation would correspond to Figure 45a.

In certain cases of "consumption" such a distinction is quite important. For instance, in case of dancing, the activity of consumption (dancing) is the goal (positive valence) itself.

Doubtless on many occasions, especially when the hunger is not too great, human beings eat mainly from pleasure of eating and not to escape the unpleasantness of the present state of hunger or to become satiated. Sometimes the getting satiated is definitely not the goal. A child might eat dessert particularly slowly for the purpose of staying as long as possible within the region of the pleasant consumption and of avoiding satiation as long as possible, because satiation would force him to leave the pleasant region of eating dessert.

Often, of course, especially in cases of great hunger, both the eating and the being satiated might have a positive valence. Frequently the eating has a positive valence and the present state (A) of being hungry has a negative valence. That means that besides the force $f_{A,G}$ a force $f_{A,-A}$ would have to be considered. This, however, would not affect the formula mentioned. The situation in Skinner's experiments is probably best represented by Figure 45 if one adds a negative valence to the present state A of the individual. This negative valence decreases with satiation.

c. *Force and Speed of Translocation.*—The problem of consumption might be a good illustration of the difficulties involved in the concept and measuring of speed in psychology. It is necessary to distinguish *two types of speed,* namely, the "speed of activity" and the "speed of locomotion from one region to another."

The "speed of consumption" cannot be viewed as identical with the speed of activity in physical terms. It would have, for instance, little meaning to relate the speed of consumption in dancing to the velocity of dancing. On the other hand, it should be noted that under certain conditions, as in the experiments of Skinner, situations might be set up so that the speed of activity and the speed of locomotion might be related to each other and might measure the velocity of consumption.

It is well to keep in mind these problems if one approaches the rather difficult question of the velocity of bodily locomotion. A number of authors relate the speed of locomotion to the force of the action to the goal. Especially Hull (1932) has used the criterion of speed for his goal-gradient theory.

If we apply the formula (31) and (33) to velocity of transportation v(trans) we could say that

(Ex. 26) $v(trans) = F(|f^*_{A,G}|) = F(t)$

in case other factors are kept constant.

1) Speed of tapping a lever.—A relatively clear situation is given in an experiment by Skinner (1936). The rat has to tap a lever to receive food. However, in contrast with the requirements in the previously mentioned experiment, it has to tap a great number of times before even a small amount of food will arise. Skinner found that the speed of tapping is relatively constant as long as the amount of food received does not essentially change the state of the hunger. If one views the speed of tapping as the velocity of locomotion from one pushing the lever (L^n) to the next one (L^{n+1}) and indicates this velocity by $v_{L^n, L^{n+1}}$ one can say that $v_{L^n, L^{n+1}} = $ constant, if $t = $ constant. He observed, furthermore, that the speed of tapping the lever decreased when the hunger decreased. In other words,

(Ex. 27) $v_{L^n, L^{n+1}} = F(t)$

Figure 46 represents the topology of the situation. The animal has to pass through quite a large number of regions $L^1, L^2, L^3 \ldots$ before he reaches the region G^1 corresponding to a small amount of food. The number of regions (L) is unknown to him, but he knows that G^1 exists somewhere at not too great a distance. Under these circumstances we will have to expect that

(Ex. 28) $|f_{L^1,G^1}| = |f_{L^2,G^1}| = |f_{L^3,G^1}|$

Namely, the situation of the animal in L^1 and L^2 will be about the same in relation both to its own state and to its environment: the hunger will not be changed; the animal will not be essentially tired, because pushing the lever is an easy task; the distance $e_{L^1,G^1} = e_{L^2,G^1} = e_{L^3,G^1}$, because the animal never knows how much must be done by him before he reaches G^1.

Of course, if the animal has to pass on and on without ever getting food, sometime a state will be reached where the cognitive structure of the situation is changed so that $d_{L^n,L^{n+1}} \neq d_{L^n,G^1}$. (Just as, for instance, in the experiment of Fajans.) However, if the number of taps of the lever is not too great, the force to the Goal G^1 or G^2 always will have the direction $d_{L^n,L^{n+1}}$.

Psychologically, the tapping of the levers can well be viewed as a locomotion to the goal, in spite of the fact that the animal physically does not locomote from one place to another. The results of Skinner can be taken as an example of velocity of translocation v(trans) and derived from (Ex. 26). The experiment can be viewed either 1.) as a measurement of the force $|f_{A,G}|$ by velocity of translocation v(trans), or 2.) as measurement of the need t by v(trans), or 3.) as the establishment of a law (26) relating force to tension $(|f_{A,G}| = F(t))$ where v(trans) is taken as measuring stick for the force, and the time of starvation as measuring stick for the tension.

With the same technique Heron and Skinner (1937) have measured the changes in hunger during starvation. They found a steady increase with an average peak at the fifth day, and a decrease in activity as the animal becomes too weak. This measurement is well in line with that of Warden (1931), who used the obstruction box as his measuring stick. This agreement between the two different types of measurement shows their value as means of determining the force $f_{A,G}$ and the tension t and can be considered an additional proof of (26).

We mentioned that the animal will stop tapping the lever if the tapping never leads to food because in this case the cognitive structure of the field will change. Skinner (1936), using the terminology of the conditioned-reflex theory, says: "the response" to the lever has to be "reinforced periodically." Otherwise, "extinction" will occur. Skinner emphasizes that "changing the drive does more than change the effect of the reinforcement." In our terminology, we could interpret this statement in the following way: A change of the state of the drive (t) changes the strength of the valence and therefore the strength of the force $f_{A,G}$ according to (26). The reinforcement might also change somewhat the valence, and therefore the drive ($f_{A,G}$), by making the goal more vivid and perhaps by creating a kind of fixation of the need on the specific goal. However, the main function of the "reinforcement" seems to be to prevent the change in the *cognitive structure* of the set-up. Without reinforcement, pressing the lever would not be an action towards the goal (G). That is, instead of $d_{A,L} = d_{A,G}$ we should have $d_{A,L} \neq d_{A,G}$. If this interpretation is right, the so-called curve of extinction would depend to a considerable extent upon the velocity with which this change in cognitive structure occurs. The great individual differences in the extinction rates (Skinner, 1936) are well in line with this interpretation.

2) Speed of walking and running.—One of the basic examples of transportation is, of course, walking or running. We have discussed the speed of such bodily locomotion as a function of restlessness (Ex. 23a). Hull (1932) has used the speed of locomotion as a measuring device for a force in the direction to a goal. His purpose is to show that this force, or, as he says, the "excitatory tendency," increases with a decreasing distance from the goal. The dependence of the strength of the force upon the distance from the goal is a problem of the structure of the force field which will be discussed later. We will limit the discussion here to the more general question of the relation between the speed of bodily locomotion and the strength of the force to a goal.

a) Speed of Locomotion in Psychology and Physics.— The relation between speed and force seems to me one of the most difficult of our problems. One is tempted, of course, to notice how physics handles this problem and to try to solve it in the same fashion. However, I become more and more convinced that such a treatment is not feasible.

In physics, force is related to acceleration rather than to velocity. An object will keep on moving at the same speed if no forces are acting upon it.

The coordinating of force to acceleration presupposes the law of inertia of physical bodies and the law of constancy of energy, or this coordination is at least closely related to both laws. Therefore, any assumption regarding the relation between speed and force in psychology should be conscious of its far-reaching consequences.

In psychology, as in physics, force is related to locomotion, according to the coordinating definition of force (19): a locomotion occurs in the direction of the resultant force if this resultant is greater than zero. This definition, however, leaves open the question whether acceleration or velocity of locomotion is coordinated to the strength of the force. To correlate acceleration to force would imply that in psychology as well as in physics inertia exists; that means that locomotion would go on with the same velocity after the forces which initiated the locomotion would cease to exist.

In my mind, such an assumption cannot be made in psychology. However, a proof of this negative statement is not as easy as it might seem. Many psychologists imply occasionally such an assumption or use it as a general theory. According to Goldstein (1931), the tendency to go on with an activity after it once started is characteristic of living beings. One can, of course, point to a great number of facts which seem to disprove such an assumption. For instance, the tapping of the lever in the experiment mentioned above should go on indefinitely even if food fails to appear. If inertia existed, a person who is running to a goal should proceed in the same direction after reaching the goal, then come back, and swing around the goal like a pendulum in physics. That is, of course, not the case. (I am not speaking here of the little excursions resulting from the physical momentum of the running body.) However, this does not suffice to disprove the theory of inertia, because in physics, too, the pendulum movements will occur only if friction is relatively small.

We have already stated (33) that in psychology the actual velocity depends not only upon the force ($f_{A,G}$) in the direction to the goal, but as well on other factors. One of them might be the friction which the movement encounters. (Doubtless the amount of friction one must overcome by walking on a paved road or through loose sand is quite different and is one of the factors determining the actual speed. In addition, there might be an inner friction of the motoric system involved in every locomotion.) To prove that the law of inertia does not hold in psychology, one should show that the absence of the pendulum movements around the goal and the cessation of tapping the lever are not due to this friction.

It seems to me within the reach of present-day psychology to decide these questions. However, I shall leave these questions open and limit the discussion to a survey of the factors which one must take into consideration in approaching this problem.

b) Factors Determining Speed Which Depend upon the Properties of the Present Region.—In case the law of inertia does not hold in psychology one could try to determine the actual speed by referring to two components, namely, one which makes for speed or higher speed and another which hinders higher speed. One factor limiting speed could be the restraining force due to friction at the present region of locomotion.

In our discussion of friction thus far we have dealt generally with situations where the individual has faced friction in a barrier-region B ahead of him. We have represented, therefore, the friction related to the region B as $f_{B,-B}$ similar to a negative valence of B (see discussion on page .?..). For discussing the effect of friction on speed it is well to separate more clearly the effect of friction from the totality of the driving forces. We may call $f_{A,G}$ the resultant of the driving forces of an individual in A and $rf_{A,-G}$ the restraining forces which hinder a locomotion in the direction $d_{A,G}$ at the region A. If the velocity $v_{A,G}$ of the locomotion in the direction $d_{A,G}$ in the region A would depend solely upon the resultant of the driving forces on the one hand and the friction at the present region, the formula would hold:

$$(\text{Ex. 29}) \qquad v_{A,G} = F\left(\frac{|f_{A,G}|}{|rf_{A,-G}|}\right).[1]$$

It is probably true in psychology as in physics that the friction one must overcome by crossing a certain region B is not a constant property of that region B but is greater for a greater speed of locomotion. In other words,

$$(\text{Ex. 30}) \qquad |rf_{A,-B}| = F\ (v_{A,B})$$

We might consider a certain velocity v^n as a "region of activity." A region of faster locomotion might then be represented as v^{n+1}. If the formula (Ex. 30) is correct we can consider friction as a force which hinders the transition from a lower to a higher velocity. The formula (Ex. 30) which expresses the dependence of the amount of friction on the velocity can then be written in the form:

$$(\text{Ex. 30a}) \qquad |f_{v^n,-v^{n+1}}| = F(v_{A,G}^n)$$

This formula (Ex 30a) in combination with (Ex. 26) would permit the determination of the actual speed $(v_{A,G}^n)$ in A, in case the driving force $f_{A,G}$ and the friction $rf_{A,-G}$ are the sole determining factors of the speed.

$$(\text{Ex. 31}) \quad v_{A,G}^n \text{ is such that } \left|f_{A,G}\right| = \left|f_{v_{A,G}^n,\ -v_{A,G}^{n+1}}\right|$$

For, if the velocity would increase from $v^n_{A,G}$ to $v^{n+1}_{A,G}$ the friction $|rf_{A,-G}|$ would increase according to (Ex. 30). Therefore, the force $\left|f_{v_{A,G}^{n+1},\ -v_{A,G}^{n+2}}\right|$ would increase according to Ex. 30a) so that the driving force $|df_{A,G}|$ would not suffice to keep up this velocity $\left(|f_{A,G}| < \left|f_{v_{A,G}^{n+1},\ -v_{A,G}^{n+2}}\right|\right.$

---

[1] This formula says merely that the speed increases with the driving and decreases with the restraining force without presupposing proportionality.

As a result, the velocity would decrease. In case the velocity would be smaller than $v_{A,G}^{n}$ namely, $v_{A,G}^{n-1}$. Then, the driving force $\left| f_{G,A} \right| > \left| f_{v_{A,G}^{n-1},\, v_{A,G}^{n}} \right|$ and the velocity would increase until the equation (Ex. 31) holds.

The equation (Ex. 31) thus determines the actual speed on the basis of an equilibrium between two forces ($f_{A,G}$ and $f_{v_{A,G}^{n},\, v_{A.G}^{n+1}}$) which is reached if a certain speed $v_{A,G}^{n}$ is maintained.

One could enumerate other factors which influence the velocity of locomotion in the same way as friction. For instance, fast running may be painful or disagreeable to a certain degree, and this negative valence might increase with the speed of running. Under this condition a force $f_{v^{n},\, v^{n+1}}$ would arise which again would be a function of the speed itself. Therefore, under this condition the actual velocity $v_{A,G}^{n}$ would be determined by an equation of the same form as (Ex. 31).

It is not correct to say that the negative valence of locomotion always increases with speed. Extremely slow walking is doubtless more disagreeable than a "normal" speed. The function in the formula (Ex. 30a) is, therefore, not a homogeneous function if we refer to the disagreeableness of speed rather than to friction. If one starts with the zero point of velocity one can probably say that with increasing speed the negative valence of locomotion decreases first to an optimum and then increases. However, if one knows this function (F) one could still use formula (Ex. 31) for determining the velocity "above or below normality."

An outstanding characteristic of the formula (Ex. 31) is the fact that the velocity at a given moment is determined on the one hand by the strength of the resultant driving force to the goal ($f_{A,G}$) (excluding those forces which are due to the activity of locomotion), and on the other by the force which could be said to be an expression of the total negative valence of a velocity higher than the present one. This force

($f_{\mathrm{v}n,-\mathrm{v}n+1}$) depends upon the state of the person, the type of locomotion, its velocity, and the character of the ground.

c) Characteristics of the Total Path Ahead Which Affect Speed.—Thus far we have considered as forces hindering higher velocity only those forces which are due to the locomotion at that region in which the individual is located at present. We should, however, consider a second possibility. The actual speed of locomotion is not influenced solely by the amount of friction and disagreeableness which the momentary speed as such has. Tolman (1932) emphasizes that the total amount of work the individual has to do before reaching the goal ("Means-End-Distance") influences action.

Indeed, for instance, a runner in a race decides his velocity by reference to the distance ahead of him. He runs more slowly and "economizes his energy" as long as the goal is far away.[2] We can designate the total amount of work to be done to cross a distance $e_{A,G}$ as $k_{A,G}$. (It should be noted that $k_{A,G}$ does not refer to a property of the locomotion at the region A—as $v_{A,G}$ and $rf_{A,G}$ do—but to a property of the locomotion as a whole (from A until G), as it appears in A.)

The total work $k_{A,G}$ (corresponding to the path $w_{A,G}$) is a function not only of the distance $e_{A,G}$ but also of something like an "average speed" ($av_{A,G}$) over the whole path $w_{A,G}$. (One will remember that $v_{A,G}$ does not refer to a speed during the whole path $w_{A,G}$ but to the speed in A in the direction $d_{A,G}$):

(Ex. 32) $$k_{A,G} = F(e_{A,G}, av_{A,G})$$

Of course, $k_{A,G}$ depends also upon other factors as, for instance, upon the type of the road.

The work $k_{A,G}$ might have a positive valence for the individual, especially if it is not too much. Often, however, it has a negative valence, particularly if it is merely a means to an end. The negative valence of the amount of work ahead,

[2] Robinson and Heron (1924) found that the speed in a tapping test was higher when a subject expected a short tapping period preceding rest than when he expected a long one. Yochelson (1930) found that more work was performed at the ergograph when longer rest periods were anticipated than when shorter ones.

in other words, the force $(f_{kA,G,-kA,G})$ depends according to (Ex. 32) upon the distance between the individual and the goal and upon the average velocity $av_{A,G}$ (besides other factors):

(Ex. 32a) $|f_{kA,G,-kA,G}| = F(e_{A,G}, av_{A,G})$

One can inquire in what way the negative valence of $k_{A,G}$ depends upon the average speed of locomotion $av_{A,G}$ by referring to a situation where all other factors, like distance, type of road and ability of individual, are kept constant.

Under this condition, the negative valence of $k_{A,G}$ does not homogeneously increase beginning with the average speed zero, but shows probably again an optimum. For, it is disagreeable not only to walk too fast, but also to walk too slowly for a certain time. However, above a certain speed probably $f_{k,-k}$ increases with $av_{A,G}$.

(Ex. 32b) $|f_{kA,G,-kA,G}| = F(av_{A,G})$
for $av_{A,G}$ greater than a certain amount.

If the velocity of locomotion would be limited solely by the factor $f_{kA,G,-kA,G}$ and if the individual would plan to use the same speed throughout $w_{A,G}$ which he uses at present $(v_{A,G} = av_{A,G})$ one could determine the actual velocity $(v^n_{A,G})$ at A with the help of (Ex. 32b). The actual velocity $v^n_{A,G}$ would be such that

(Ex. 32c) $\left| f_{A,G} \right| = \left| f_{k^n_{A,G}} - k^n_{A,G} \right|$ where $k^n_{A,G}$

refers to the total amount of work anticipated in crossing the distance $e_{A,G}$ with an average velocity $av^n_{A,G} = v^n_{A,G}$.

This formula again determines the actual velocity $v^n_{A,G}$ by an equilibrium between the driving force to the goal $f_{A,G}$

and a force which limits the speed, namely $f_{kn_{A,G}}, -kn_{A,G}$.
It is based on similar considerations, as those mentioned
after (Ex. 31). Also the form of the formula (Ex. 32c) is
similar to (Ex. 31). *There is, however, one important difference between determining the actual speed by the negative valence of higher speed at the present region ($f_{vn, -v^{n+1}}$)
and determining the speed by the negative valence of the
total amount of work ahead ($f_{kn, -kn}$).* Assuming, for instance, that the driving force ($f_{X,G}$) in the direction to G
would be constant for the whole path $w_{A,G}$ and that also the
type of road and the fatigue of the person would not change,
then (according to Ex. 31) the velocity ($v_{X,G}^n$) would be
constant at every point X of the path $w_{A,G}$ in case the force
$f_{vn_{A,G}}, -v^{n+1}_{A,G}$ would be the dominant factor. If, however,
the total amount of work ahead would be decisive
($f_{kn_{A,G}}, -kn_{,G}$) the speed of $v_{X,G}^n$ should increase with decreasing distance $e_{X,G}$ to the goal (according to 32a), even
if everything else, especially the force $f_{X,G}$ in direction to
the goal, would be constant.

We will come back to this problem when we discuss Hull's
results.

Probably the disagreeableness of a higher speed
($f_{vn, -v^{n+1}}$) at present and of the total amount of work ahead
($f_{kn, -kn}$) are both factors which determine the actual
velocity. In case the law of inertia does not hold in psychology or that in the given situation inertia does not play
an important role, the actual velocity $v_{A,G}^n$ in A would be
determined mainly by the formula:

(33a) $v_{A,G}^n$ is such that

$$\left|f_{A,G}\right| = \left|f_{vn_{A,G}}, -v^{n+1}_{A,G}\right| + \left|f_{kn_{A,G}}, -kn_{A,G}\right|$$

In this formula $f_{A,G}$ refers to the resultant of the driving
forces at A with the exception of the forces related to the

valence of the locomotion (including that due to friction) and of the work anticipated until reaching the goal.

The relative importance of the two factors ($f_v n, _{-v} n+1$ and $f_k n, _{-k} n$) within (33a) seems to vary under different conditions. For young individuals, the quality of the momentary activity ($f_v n, _{-v} n+1$) might be relatively more important. In adults, the total amount of work ahead and the will "to economize their own energy" tends to emphasize the factor $f_k n, _{-k} n^t$. There might be great individual differences as to the importance of both factors.

It might be mentioned that no factor of the form ($f_k n, _{-k} n$) enters the determination of velocity in physics. Velocity in physics does not depend upon whether the object is moving to a point near by or far away. This factor should, therefore, not be confused with the so-called "law of least action."

d) Determination of Speed if the Law of Inertia Holds.— The determination of the actual velocity becomes even more complicated if a law of inertia should hold in psychology. In this case a force will have to be coordinated to acceleration. The actual speed would depend upon the time during which the force affects the individual. In case of locomotion without friction even a small force should lead to an extreme velocity if the force affects the person long enough.

We do not wish to discuss here the many problems involved. It might, however, be appropriate to state that in my opinion it is very unlikely that such a law holds for psychology. Even if inertia existed, the formula (33a) would still be correct in case of sufficient friction.

e) Topological Representation of Speed.—We have treated the problem of speed of translocation, thus far, in a rather abstract "algebraic" fashion. It might be well to supplement this by discussing how the problem of speed of translocation ($v(trans)$) might be represented topologically.

We have already mentioned that in representing the life space of the person, one generally has to coordinate activities rather than geographical areas to its various regions. Bodily locomotion has to be viewed as one kind of region, namely, the barrier region (B) of translocation which might separate the momentary activity (A) of an individual and the goal region (G) he wishes to enter (Figure 47).

If one wishes to represent the different speeds possible, one can do that by a representation similar to that we used for the obstruction box (Figure 31a). One will first have to realize that the speed of a person is not a matter of continuous change from zero to infinity. If a person at the region A wants to locomote to the region G (Figure 47) by crossing the intervening region B, he must first make up his mind

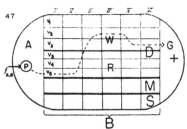

Fig. 47. Representation of Speed of Translocation. P, person; A, beginning region; G, goal; B, barrier region (between A and G) consisting of: S, going by train; M, going by automobile; D, going by foot. D consists of R, running, and W, walking; within R various speeds (v_3, v_4, v_5) of running might be distinguished; within W various speeds (v_3, v_2, v_1) of walking might be distinguished; I, II, III . . ,· various distances to G.

whether he is going by train (S) or by automobile (M) or by foot (D). That means the actual speed by a given force $f_{A,G}$ will depend upon the "instruments" used for translocation.

If the person is going by foot, he might locomote with different velocities. However, even then the different locomotions are not only a matter of speed. One should distinguish two qualitatively different types of locomotions, namely, walking W and running R ($D \supset W$; $D \supset R$). In each of these regions there is a very large number of possible velocities (v^1, v^2, v^3 . . .). The same physical velocity might occur in walking and running ($v^3 \subset W$; $v^3 \subset R$); psychologically, it will have in the two cases quite different characters. (For a small child it might be necessary to distinguish between crawling and walking and between different types of crawling.)

It may be advisable to represent in a given case the activity of translocation from A to G for a given velocity, for instance v^2, not as one region but as a series of regions, each representing the crossing of a certain subpart (I, II, . . .) of the path from A to G.

It is not always possible to shift in the middle of the road from one type of transportation to another, for instance, from running (R) in subpart III, to using a train (S), because the train may stop at I but not at III. However, it is generally possible to shift from one velocity, for instance v^4, of running to a faster velocity v^5 or to walking.

The problem of speed should, in my mind, be handled as the problem of such a shift in kind of translocation. From the point of view of the hodological space, the different speeds appear at the time of the start in A as different paths $(w_{A,v^1,G}; \ w_{A,v^2,G}; \ w_{A,v^3,G}; \ w_{A,M,G})$ from A to G. What kind of speed (v^n) is used is a problem which could be handled similarly to the problem of choice between different paths to the same goal. The choice, and therefore the special instrument, of transportation, and the special speed, will depend upon the positive or negative valence which the various regions of transportation between A and G have. This positive or negative valence will depend upon the character of the activity $(v^n_{A,G})$ and the total amount of the activity $(k^n_{A,G})$ necessary. This positive or negative valence might well change during locomotion. A person might decide to run because he is in a hurry and does not have an automobile available. He starts with his top speed (v^5). However, after some time, for instance at the sector III he might find this velocity too disagreeable and drop down to a medium speed of walking (v^2). Close to the goal G he might start to walk faster, that is, he might shift from v^2 to v^3 without running.

According to this consideration, the choice of a certain velocity is determined by the same two factors (the valence of $v_{A,G}^n$ and the valence of $k_{A,G}^n$) as those which are found on the one side of the formula (33a) which we previously considered as important for determining the actual velocity of translocation. If one views the actual velocity as a result of a kind of choice situation, it can be considered a choice between "the desired result which a higher velocity would have for reaching the goal faster," and "the undesired result of this higher velocity due to the greater momentary and permanent effort necessary." The actual velocity $v_{A,G}^n$ would then be determined in the following way:

(33b)[3] $v_{A,G}^n$ is such that

$$|f_{v^n,v^{n+1}}| + |f_{k^n,-k^n}| = |f_{v^n,-v^{n+1}}| + |f_{k^{n+1},-k^{n+1}}|$$

In other words, the positive valence of a higher speed is confronted with the negative valence of the greater effort. The positive valence of the higher speed (v^{n+1}) is itself a function of the importance of the goal and of reaching it fast; it is, therefore, a function of the force $f_{A,G}$.

(33c) $$|f_{v^n,v^{n+1}}| = F(|f_{A,G}|)$$

As a whole, therefore, we are led to the same factors as determinants of the actual speed as we considered previously (in (33a)). The formula (33b) should be considered as rather tentative. One would have to discuss in detail whether (33a) and (33b) are fully equivalent or not.

   d. *Force and Speed of Learning.*—The coordinating definition of force (19) relates the force to either a locomotion

[a] Instead of separating the positive valence of the higher speed $pVa(v^{n+1})$ due to the quicker result from the negative valence of this speed $nVa(v^{n+1})$ due to the greater momentary effort, one can consider the total valence $Va(v^{n+1})$ of this speed and can coordinate the force $f_{v',v^{n+1}}$ to this total valence. The formula 33b then takes the form:

(33b1) $v_{A,G}^n$ is such that $|f_{v',v}^{n+1}| = |f_{k}^{n+1,-k^{n+1}}|$.

or a change in the structure of the field. One might ask, therefore, whether it is possible to relate the speed of restructuring (v(stru)) to the strength of the force. In other words, one can ask whether

(Ex. 33) $v(stru) = F(f^*_{A,G}) = F(t)$ [holds only within narrow limits]

There are two types of restructuring we could mention here, namely, decision and learning.

Decision is, in my mind, essentially a restructuring of the field (Koffka 1934, Lewin 1935). Before the decision is reached an overlapping situation (Princ.) exists for the person. The forces resulting from the two overlapping situations are opposed to each other. The decision means that one of the overlapping situations becomes predominant. We might say that the relative potency of this situation increases and that of the other decreases. In case the decision is definite, the relative potency of one of the two situations becomes nearly zero.

The velocity of the decision depends upon the type and strength of the overlapping force fields. We might, therefore, discuss this question later.

The velocity of learning has often been related to the strength of the force in the direction to the goal (Elliot 1928, Blodgett 1929, Dashiell 1937). For instance, Tolman and Honzik (1930) have shown that the velocity of learning to run a maze is a function of the intensity of the drive and the type of incentive (valence). However, it has been emphasized correctly (Lashley 1929, Tolman 1932, Leeper 1935, Maier and Schneida 1935) that one should distinguish clearly between the effect of a force on performance and the effect on learning. On the whole, the results of experiments with human beings and animals indicate that the formula (Ex. 33) is correct in so far as a minimum of force $(f_{A,G})$ toward a goal is necessary for learning. Roughly speaking, the speed of learning will increase with the interest in achievement. However, two facts should be emphasized. If the force in the direction toward the goal $(f_{A,G})$ is too great, a decrease in learning probably will result, because learning requires a sufficient survey of the total situation. Experiments by Koehler and others indicate that too high an emotional tension rather hinders the solution of a problem. Therefore, (Ex. 33) should prove to be correct only within rather narrow limits. The results of Yerkes and Dodson (1908) are well in line with this statement (compare also P. T. Young, 1936, pp. 282 and 309).

Furthermore, the velocity with which a field changes its cognitive structure depends largely upon the *specific* structure of the situation and upon the specific ways or ''methods of learning.'' A systematic change of ''hypotheses'' (Krechevsky 1932) regarding the road to the goal should lead on the average to faster learning than a random 'change of hypotheses. Obviously, the intelligence and the stubbornness of the individual play a great role. Experiments on frustration (Barker, Dembo and Lewin, in preparation) seem to indicate that constructiveness and intelligence decrease if the tension increases too much.

All this makes it rather probable that the velocity of restructuring (v(stru)) will not be as good a yardstick for the measurement of forces as the velocity of restless movement (v(res)), of consumption (v(con)), and of translocation (v(trans)).

3. Summary

The examples of measurement of forces we have discussed thus far are by no means a complete survey of what has been done or could be done. We will, however, limit our discussion to these cases.

As a symptom for the measurement of forces, one can use the overcoming of opposing forces in some type of choice situations or by taking as a criterion the velocity of locomotion in its various forms, as restless movements, speed of consumption, speed of translocation, or of learning. One can, furthermore, use the criterion of tension as an indirect measurement of forces. All these measurements can be said to measure one force by another force. Only the type and direction of forces (friction, negative valence of means, negative valence of ends) and the constellation of measurement are different in the different cases.

B. MEASUREMENT OF VALENCES

We have mentioned previously that one will have to distinguish clearly between a force and a valence. A positive valence corresponds to what is known as a goal. It is correlated to a field of forces. Mathematically, a valence is a scalar and can be said to possess strength, but not direction. We have already discussed (31) the point that the valence $Va(G)$ which an object or activity G possesses at a given time is a function of the need in question (tension t) and of the nature of G: $Va(G) = F(t,G)$.

1. Comparison of the Valence of Different Incentives

There exists a whole field of experiments both with human beings and with animals which compare the valence of different incentives for a given amount of hunger. That is, they ask whether for a given (t) the valence of the incentive G^1 is greater, equal, or smaller than the valence of the incentive G^2.

(Ex. 34) $$Va(G^1) \gtreqless Va(G^2).$$

Experiments are generally conducted in the form of a normal choice experiment. That is, the distance $e_{R,G}$ and other factors are kept equal and the strength of the valence $Va(G)$ is measured by the relative strength of the corresponding force $(f_{A,G})$. In case the decision of the individual shows that $|f_{A,G^1}| > |f_{A,G^2}|$ one concludes that $Va(G^1) > Va(G^2)$.

This conclusion is well in line with our previous discussion: Under equal conditions, especially if the psychological distance $(e_{A,G})$ is kept constant, the comparative measurement of one force within each force field is sufficient to compare the strength of different valences.

2. The Realm of Regions with Positive Valence

From the formula (31) which states that an increase of tension (t) increases the strength of the corresponding valence ($Va(G)$) one could make the following conclusion: For a group of objects or activities (G^1, G^2, G^3. . . .) the valence might be below or equal to zero ($Va(G^1) \leqq 0$ $Va(G^2) \leqq 0$; . . . .) in case the need ($t(G)$) related to the goal G is small. An increase of ($t(G)$) should increase the valence of some of these objects and activities so that $Va(G^1) > 0$; $Va(G^2) > 0$; . . . . If we indicate by R $Va(G)$ the totality of objects or activities the valence of which is greater than zero ($Va(G) > 0$) we can say that:

$$(36) \qquad RVa(G) = F(t(G))$$

In other words, the realm of objects or activities which have the character of a positive valence for a given need should increase with the increase of the need. The experiments on "appetite" (Katz 1935 and others) are in line with this conclusion. For instance, an increase in hunger makes the individual willing to eat types of food which he rejects if the hunger decreases.

3. Substitute Valence and Substitute Value

This fact has an important bearing on the problem of substitution. One can define the "substitute value" SV which an activity G^2 has for the activity G^1 (i.e., $SV(G^2$ for $G^1)$) by the property of the "consumption" of G^2 (indicated as cons (G^2)) to satisfy the need correlated to G^1, in other words, to decrease the tension $t(G^1)$.

$$(36a) \quad SV(G^2 \text{ for } G^1) > 0, \text{ if } t(G^1) = F\left(\frac{1}{\text{cons } (G^2)}\right)$$

Lissner (1933) and Mahler (1933) have measured this substitute value and have determined its dependence upon various factors such as similarity, degree of difficulty and degree of reality of the substitute activity.

There seem to be, however, cases where an individual may start an activity G^2 (or approach an object G^2) obviously as a substitute for the activity G^1 even if G^2 later on proves to have no substitute value for G^1. (This has been shown by Dembo (1931) and Sliosberg (1935)). In other words, the substitute valence $SVa(G^2)$ might be high, even if the substitute value $SV(G^2)$ is low.

This statement seems to be true not only in the case of substitution, but seems to hold generally in regard to all needs. The "satisfaction value" of an activity G^1 is not necessarily parallel to its valence. In other words, it would not be appropriate to measure the strength of the valence by its ability to satisfy the need when consumed, because valences which show force fields of the same strength may be quite different in their "satisfaction value." It would be interesting both for the problem of need and the problem of substitution to study the relation of the satisfaction value and valence more in detail.

C. DETERMINING THE STRUCTURE OF THE FORCE FIELD

Many factors determine the area which is covered by a force field corresponding to a valence. The force field corresponding to a dangerous-looking animal in the life space of a child is spread over a different area than that corresponding to an immovable hot stove. We have mentioned already that the structure of a central field corresponding to a positive valence is often different from that corresponding to a negative valence. Also, the character of the region surrounding the valence is important for the spread and the structure of the force field.

We will limit our discussion to the question of how the intensity of the force $f_{A,G}$ corresponding to a valence (G) changes with the distance $(e_{A,G})$ and how this change can be measured. In other words, we ask within formula (32), how can the importance of the distance $(e_{P,G})$ be determined? What is the function (F) in the formula

(Ex. 35) $$f_{A,G} = F\left(\frac{1}{e_{A,G}}\right)$$

if the other factors determining f are kept constant?

The distance $e_{A,G}$ between the individual P located in A, and the valence G, is determined by the regions that the path $w_{A,G}$ has to cross (14). This locomotion does not need to be bodily locomotion but might be a social one. We will, however, not enter here into a discussion of the measurement of social distances (Lewin 1936) and will limit the discussion to cases where the psychological distance is measured either by physical or temporal distance.

1. The Strength of Force and the Physical Distance to the Goal

a. *Measurement by Speed.*—A theorem derived by Hull from his goal-gradient hypothesis, taken together with certain accessory conditions (1932), states that the excitatory tendency, or as we say, the force $f_{A,G}$ in direction to the goal G, is a function of the physical distance between the animal and the goal. This proposition is, therefore, identical with formula (Ex. 35) if one interprets the distance $e_{A,G}$ as physical distance.*

* Hull does not state his goal-gradient theory originally in the form of a field theory. That is, he does not link the greater velocity to the smaller distance as such. His theory rather concerns the origin (historical cause) of certain behavior: he states ''that the goal reaction gets conditioned the most strongly to the stimuli preceding it, and the other reactions of the behavior sequence get conditioned to their stimuli progressively weaker as they are more remote (in time or space) from the goal reaction'' (1932, p. 26). In other words, the excitatory tendencies are said to have been more ''reinforced'' the closer the individual is to the goal. Of course, Hull's statement includes certain field theoretical propositions. For, one can describe the effect of the process of reinforcement in no other way than by statements which are equivalent to field-theoretical propositions about the distribution of forces at two moments (one concerning the situation before reinforcement and one concerning the situation after reinforcement) plus a statement concerning the cause of the change of this situation.

The discussion of the goal-gradient theory here refers only to the field-theoretical statement included in it. The field-theoretical proposition as such on the other hand is independent of statements regarding historical causes and could hold even if the historical statement included in Hull's theory is, as I suspect, not entirely correct.

Hull's experiments have shown a variety of interesting and complicated results. He found that the speed of running in a simple maze increases with decreasing distance:

(Ex. 36) $\qquad v_{A,G} < v_{B,G}$ if $e_{A,G} > e_{B,G}$

In other words, he observed that the speed of bodily locomotion is an inverse function of physical distance:

(Ex. 36a)[4] $\qquad v_{A,G} = F\left(\dfrac{1}{e_{A,G}}\right)$

Hull found that this inverse relation between speed and distance does not hold for every distance. For instance, the animals slow down if they come rather close to the goal. I will not enter here a discussion of this and other interesting findings of Hull (although it seems to me possible to explain them if one takes into account the topology of the situation more in detail). We merely ask here whether, within the limits in which the observation is actually expressed by formula (Ex. 36), one can conclude from the observed difference in speed that there is a difference in force (excitatory tendency). In other words, can one derive from the observation (Ex. 36) the statement about the force expressed in (Ex. 35)?

From our previous discussion it will be clear that such a conclusion presupposes a definite assumption about the relation between velocity of locomotion and strength of force. We have discussed some of the possible assumptions in detail already. A conclusion from observations about speed, that a force (excitatory tendency) is a function of distance from a goal, is permissible only if the speed of locomotion is determined by the formula (Ex. 31) and not by the formula (Ex. 33a). In other words, the conclusion holds only if the forces which keep the animal from running faster than it actually does are a function only of the momentary velocity ($v^n_{A,G}$) and not of the total amount of work ahead ($k^n_{A,G}$). If something like inertia should exist also in psychology, the direct conclusion from velocity to force would not be permissible either.

[4] The formula 36a should express merely that we have to deal with a constantly decreasing function without making more far-reaching statements.

The experiments of Hull seem to me to show particularly clearly what is necessary to derive from observations statements about such constructs as the strength of the excitatory tendency or of a force. The observation on differences of speed in different distances from the goal does not permit any definite conclusion regarding the relation between the strength of the force and the distance. Such a conclusion presupposes not only a coordinating definition of force but also some definite assumption regarding the factors and laws determining speed in psychology, including statements about such problems as resultant of forces, friction, and inertia. This example shows how closely measurement, concepts, and laws are interwoven, as Brown (1934) has emphasized.

b. *Measurement by Amount of Action towards Goals.*— Fajans (1933) has investigated the relation between the distance ($e_{A,G}$) to the goal and the strength of the force $f_{A,G}$ with children, using the total amount of action toward the goal within a given period as a criterion. This type of measurement is in some respects conceptually simpler than that by speed. We have mentioned, however, that this observation alone does not permit a conclusion about the strength of the force. To make a conclusion possible, Fajans has employed a second independent measurement, namely, the comparison of the intensity of emotional tension (t) which the children showed when the goal was located at different distances. On the basis of a certain theoretical assumption regarding the relation between force and tension (which is equivalent to formula (35)), the two observations permit a statement regarding the relation between distance and force. As mentioned before, Fajans comes to the conclusion that, under the conditions studied, the formula (Ex. 35) holds only for infants, but that the force $|f_{A,G}|$ did not decrease with increasing physical distance in the older children.

c. *Measurement by Choice between Two Paths.*—There might exist a third way to determine the relation between the strength of the force and physical distance. We refer to the many experiments (Gengerelli 1930, Tolman 1932) regarding the choice of short and long paths to the same goal. Hull is correct in stating that if the force is an inverse function of the distance, one could conclude that the individual should use the shorter of two paths to the goal. (Such a conclusion is, by the way, permissible only if the physical laws of the resultant of forces do not hold, but if the principles of the hodological space are applied.)

However, one cannot argue the other way around: If the animal chooses the shorter path $w_{A,B,G}$ (Figure 48) instead of the longer path $w_{A,C,G}$ one can conclude only that the *resultant* of forces $f^*_{A,B,G}$ is greater than the resultant of forces $f^*_{A,C,G}$.

(Ex. 37) $$f^*_{A,B,G} > f^*_{A,C,G}$$

This resultant depends not only upon the forces $|f_{A,B,G}|$ and $|f_{A,C,G}|$ corresponding to the valence of G, but also upon the forces correlated to the regions B and C. Even if the physical properties of the two paths would be equal, the total amount of work ahead (k) is greater for the longer path ($w_{A,C,G}$) than for the shorter one ($w_{A,B,G}$). One should expect, therefore, that $|f_{C,-C}| > |f_{B,-B}|$. In other words, the forces, which are opposed to using the path $w_{A,C,G}$ are greater than the forces opposed to using $w_{A,B,G}$. Therefore, (Ex. 37) would hold for the resultant of forces and would lead to the choice of the shorter path even if it would be that $f_{A,B,G} = f_{A,C,G}$.

The experiments on long and short paths, therefore, do not permit a definite conclusion about the relation between the strength of the force and the distance from the valence.

d. Distance and Force in a Power Field.—I might mention here a group of studies related to what one might call the strength of a social power field, although a social power field can not be viewed as identical with a normal force field of the type we have discussed so far.

Wiehe (1935) found that the effect of the power field of a stranger upon a child depends not only upon the character of the child, the stranger and the situation, but also upon

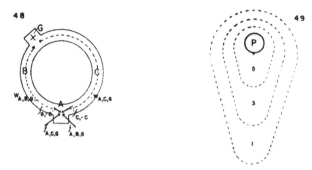

Fig. 48. Choice Between Two Paths to the Same Goal. A, starting region (position of the individual) ; G, goal ; B and C, two adits to G; $w_{A,B,G}$ and $w_{A,C,G}$, two paths to the goal; $f_{A,B,G}$ and $f_{A,C,G}$, driving forces to G along different paths; $f_{B,-B}$ and $f_{C,-C}$, restraining forces against entering B and C, respectively; the choice of a shorter path might not be due to a difference in driving forces (it might be $|f_{A,C,G}| = |f_{A,B,G}|$) but to a difference in the strength of restraining forces (it might be $|f_{C,-C}| > |f_{B,-B}|$).

Fig. 49. Power Field. P, the person; 5, 3, 1, representing different degrees of strength of power field; often this strength increases with a decrease in distance to P; the scope of the power field is a function of the activity of P, such as, looking, talking to, etc.

the physical distance between the child and the stranger. He distinguishes five degrees of strength of a power field by means of certain behavioral criteria. The strength of the power field of the stranger generally decreases with the time of adaptation. However, it can be increased again by decreasing the distance from the child.

One can represent the strength of the force field and that of a power field by connecting the points of equal strength (just as in a potential field). Wiehe has found that the shape of the power field in an otherwise homogeneous surrounding corresponds roughly to Figure 49. Its strength decreases much faster with the distance in back of the person than in front of him. A turn of the stranger so that he looks at the child will greatly increase the pressure on the child (see Lewin 1935).

Observations of Dembo, Frank, Waring and Lewin (in preparation) on the effects of social pressure on the eating behavior of nursery school children at dinner time, also show how pressure is increased by decreasing the physical distance. They also confirm the fact that looking at the child, especially into his eyes, or talking to the child, might increase the pressure greatly. J. Frank has found a quantitative proof of the same dependence with students.

2. The Strength of Force, and the Temporal and Other Types of Distances

Sams and Tolman (1925) found that animals prefer temporally shorter routes to food. Topologically, we have to deal here again with a choice between two paths (Fig. 48). Therefore, in this case also, we can make a statement only with regard to the resultant forces ($f^*_{A,B,G}$ and $f^*_{A,C,G}$) in the direction of each of the paths. But we cannot derive from the actual behavior conclusions regarding the strength of the separate forces ($f_{A,B,G}$ and $f_{A,C,G}$) without making assumptions about the nature of the opposing forces.

The situation is technically somewhat more conclusive if we have to deal with negative valences. We have mentioned that the force away from eating a disagreeable food generally is increased by coming closer to the actual eating (Figure 37a). The distance from eating is, of course, not merely a time distance.

One might take the experiments of Zeigarnik (1927) and of Ovsiankina (1928) as indirect measurements of the strength of the force to the goal. They compared the tensions (t) of quasi-needs resulting from simple tasks when these activities were interrupted at different distances from the completion of the work. Using frequency of resumption or memory as a measuring stick, they found that within certain limits the tendency to resumption was greater if the distance from finishing the work was smaller.

3. Forces, the Strength of Which Increases with Distance, and the Law of Parsimony

Tolman, discussing the several types of "Means-End Distances" (1932), emphasized that a path requiring more effort sometimes is preferred to paths requiring less effort. Rats, for instance, tend to crawl up inclined planes.

The reasons for such action might be manifold. If one viewed this behavior as a "geotropism," one probably considers the activity of climbing up as a positive valence in itself, and not as a means. We would then have a simple case of two overlapping force fields (which we discussed previously, Figure 35).

It is possible, however, that a certain amount of resistance of means brings the individual to a higher tension level (t) in line with (35) and in this way indirectly increases the force $f_{A,G}$ toward the goal in line with (26). The experiments of Ach (1910) show this "stimulating" effect of a certain amount of difficulty. A similar effect was shown by experiments on distraction (Bills 1934).

We might, finally, mention here problems related to the level of aspiration. Experiments of Hoppe (1931), J. Franck (1935, 1936), and Dembo (1931) show that a strong tendency exists to choose, after success, more difficult rather than easier tasks. Children of three years of age often refuse help and prefer to do things alone. That is, they choose the more difficult rather than the easier path.

It is possible, however, that here again we must deal, not with a means-end relation, but with the positive valence of the more difficult means which follows from the higher social status connected with the using of such means.

The examples might suffice to show that one should be rather careful in applying the so-called "law of parsimony." This law will not have definite meaning in psychology until it is defined more precisely in terms of forces, distances, or whatever it refers to. Besides, one will have to be careful to apply it only to choices of means not to choices of ends.

4. Forces and Tension in a Region of Positive Valence

We will conclude our discussion of the structure of force fields by pointing briefly to a rather complicated problem. How should one represent the forces acting on a person who is located in a region which has a positive valence, for instance, on a person who is in a happy state?

This question already came up in the problem of consumption. Consumption, such as eating, often changes the state of the person rather rapidly in the direction toward satiation. It can, therefore, be viewed as a type of locomotion through subregions of consumptions, the character of which is progressively different: the beginning subregions of the series have a distinctly positive valence, but eating soon becomes neutral and the later sub-parts of the series have a negative valence (state of over-satiation). It may be that every consumption has to some degree this character. However, there are cases where at least for some time a happy state without much change might be enjoyed, such as lying quietly under a tree.

Let us discuss first the situation when a person is located in a region G which has a negative valence (where he feels unhappy or uncomfortable). In this case the dominant forces can be characterized as $f_{G,-G}$ (Figure 50). The direction of this force is $d_{G,-G} = d_{G,X}$ where X is any region outside of G (15). In other words, the force $f_{G,-G}$ is equivalent to a force $f_{G,X}$ toward a region outside of G. There seem to be no problems involved which we have not discussed already. In case a barrier B hinders the individual from leaving the region G he will be in a conflict situation. The strength of the force $|f_{B,-B}|$ and, therefore, the tension (t) resulting from such a conflict situation will be a function of the strength of the negative valence of G according to (35).

In case the region G in which the individual is located at present has a positive valence, the problem seems to be less simple. As long as the individual P is outside G, for instance, in the region C (Figure 50a), there exists a force $f_{C,G}$ the strength of which depends on the strength of the

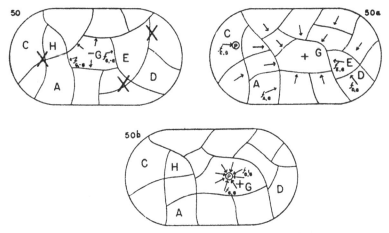

FORCES TOWARD AND AWAY FROM THE REGION IN WHICH A
PERSON IS LOCATED

Fig. 50. Forces Away from the Present Region. G, region in which
the individual is located; $f_{G,-G}$, forces in G away from G.

Fig. 50a and 50b. A force ($f_{G,G}$) toward the present region G is
equivalent to a force field corresponding to Fig. 50a, i.e., equivalent to
forces ($f_{C,G}$, $f_{A,G}$, $f_{E,G}$, $f_{D,G}$) outside the region G toward G. A force
$f_{C,G}$ does not correspond to a pressure acting from all sides against
the person P as represented in Figure 50b.

valence G and which increases generally with the decreasing distance to G, according to (21a). One might, therefore,
conclude that the force $f_{X,G}$ from any region X outside
of G reaches its maximum in the region $G(|f_{G,G}| = |f_{X,G}^{max}|)$.

After P reaches G, he will not leave G again because he
would have to locomote against the forces of the positive
central field which all point in the direction $d_{X,G}$. One might
be tempted, therefore, to conclude that the individual will be
in G in a state where he is affected by a number of forces
$f_{X,G}$ acting from all sides on P (Figure 50b). In other
words, we would be led to the same picture which one can
use to represent a person in a conflict situation standing under
pressure from all sides. The strength of these forces $f_{X,G}$
are supposed (for the given valence Va(G)) to be a maximum

in G itself. Therefore, the tension (t) resulting from this conflict should be rather high, according to (35).

This is obviously not the case. The person, being in a region in which he enjoys himself, is not in such a pressure or conflict situation. (We will not enter here into a discussion of the type of tension which is sometimes observable in a state of very great happiness.)

It might appear more adequate to say that the person in a region with positive valence is not affected by any forces: there are no forces existing which make him move from this region to another one.

This statement also, however, would not be fully adequate because if one attempts to take the individual out of the present region he will resist. It has, therefore, a good meaning to speak of the positive valence of the present region (Va(G) >0) and to coordinate to this valence forces which are opposite to leaving the region. The strength of these forces should vary with the strength of Va(G).

We come then to a rather peculiar conclusion. The force field which is correlated to a region of positive valence in which the person is located can be represented only outside this region. It is a force field like that represented in Figure 50b. There exist forces $f_{X,G}$ in the regions X outside the region G (up to the boundary of G). They all are directed toward G. However, they cannot be said to exist inside the central region G of this central force field if one thinks about forces as directed entities.

Formalistically, the forces acting on an individual who is located in a region of positive valence are to be represented as $f_{G,G}$ according to (20) and (17). It seems to me to speak for the consistency of the axioms of hodological space and for the adequacy of this geometry for representing the dynamics of the life space that this symbol represents all the properties of the situation discussed: The force $f_{G,G}$ has the direction $d_{G,G}$. One will remember that this direction had to be defined in a rather roundabout way. A direction is a relation between *two* regions. $d_{G,G}$ refers only to one region and as such would not be directed. Thus, the direction $d_{G,G}$ could be defined only as a direction opposed to leaving G ($d_{G,G} = d_{G,-G}$) according to (17).

If one applies these considerations of directions to the concept of the force $f_{G,G}$ one can make the following statement: the force $f_{G,G}$ *means in itself not a tendency to a directed action but merely a tendency which is opposed to leaving the present region G, that is, opposed to $f_{G,-G}$*. This is exactly the description of the situation of a person enjoying himself in G. The positive valence of the present region G does not include a tendency to a directed locomotion. However, it includes the resistance against a force in the direction of leaving G in case such a force should come up.

D. OVERLAPPING FORCE FIELDS

Nearly always the life space contains more than one positive or negative valence. Besides, there always exist some barriers or paths with friction. The life space, therefore, contains always a number of overlapping force fields.

Behavior depends upon the resultant of forces. Thus, the dominant problem is that of determining the resultant of the forces of the overlapping fields at a given point. A special problem in this connection is the determination of the points or regions of equilibrium within the field.

The number of constellations of force fields corresponding to various positive and negative valences is obviously infinite. I will confine myself here to the treatment of one or two simple cases.

1. Choice between Two Positive Valences

a. Two Positive Valences Lying in the Same Direction from the Person.—When we discussed the measurement of forces we gave a survey of the constellations of force fields which involve conflict (page 122). One of these conflict situations exists if the person stands "between" two positive valences.

The existence of two positive valences ($Va(G^1) > 0$ and $Va(G^2) > 0$) does not necessarily involve a conflict for the individual P. If both valences lie in the same direction ($d_{P,G^1} = d_{P,G^2}$), the forces might strengthen instead of weaken each other (Figure 51); the resultant $f^*_{P,N}$ of the forces $f_{P,G^1} + f_{P,G^2}$ will have the direction toward G^1 and G^2 ($d_{P,N} = d_{P,G^1} = d_{P,G^2}$), and the strength of the resultant, generally, will be greater than that of either of the components.

(Ex. 38 $|f^*_{P,N}| > |f_{P,G^1}|$; $|f^*_{P,N}| > |f_{P,G^2}|$,
$$\text{if } Va(G^1) > 0 \text{ and } Va(G^2) > 0 \text{ and}$$
$$\text{if } d_{P,G^1} = d_{P,G^2}$$

The situation represented in Figure 35 is such a case as long as the person is located in A.

(Ex. 38) might not hold always, but experiments with animals (Grindley, 1929) indicate that it holds at least within certain limits if the individual thinks he can get both goals rather than merely one of them.

Sometimes the person faces a situation where it seems that he has to choose one of two goals, in the beginning. However, the person might be able to change the structure of the field so as to avoid the choice.

A student wishes to prepare for his examination but he also would like to be with a friend. He is confronted with a situation similar to that represented in Figure 38a, where G represents the activity of studying and H the being with the friend. It occurs to the student that it might be possible to combine both goals by interesting the friend in the topic of the studies. He succeeds in doing this. This means that he changes the situation first cognitively (as a wish), then actually, so that G and H become overlapping regions or unseparated parts of one region GH which corresponds to "studying for the examination in the presence of his friend" (Figure 51a) and which has the positive valence of both G and H.

This case is typical of many in which a choice is avoided by restructuring the field. It is at the same time an example of the fact that a force might lead either to locomotion or to restructuring of the field (according to (19)).

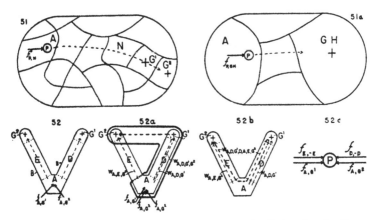

Fig. 51. Two Positive Valences (G^1, and G^2) Lying in the Same Direction.

Va(G^1) > 0; Va(G^2) > 0; direction $d_{P,G^1} = d_{P,G^2} = d_{P,N}$; $f^*_{P,N}$, the resultant force.

Fig. 51a. A Situation of Conflicting Positive Valences (G and H in Figure 38c) are chanted so that both valences are combined (to GH) now lying in the same direction. $f_{P,GH}$, force in the direction to the combined valences.

Fig. 52. Driving Force in Case of Choice Between Two Incompatible Positive Valences Va(G^1) = Va(G^2) > 0; A, region where the individual is located; B, impassable barrier; f_{A,G^1} and f_{A,G^2}, opposing forces (direction $d_{A,G^1} = d_{A,G^2}$).

Fig. 52a. Choice in a Situation of Two Valences Where It Is Uncertain Whether Only One or Both Valences Might Be Reached. This constellation can be represented by two overlapping situations: in the one the direction to G^1 is opposite to the direction to G^2 ($d_{A,G^1} = d_{A,G^2}$) in view of the paths w_{A,D,G^1} and w_{A,E,G^2}; in the other, these directions are the same ($d_{A,G^1} = d_{A,G^2}$) in view of the path w_{A,D,G^1,G^2}. f_{A,G^1}, force toward G^1; f_{A,G^2}, force toward G^2.

Fig. 52b. A situation similar to that represented in Fig. 52a. G^2 is accessible either by the direct path w_{A,E,G^2} or by the path w_{A,D,G^1}, D,A,E,G^2 which leads first to G^1, then back to A, and then to G^2.

Fig. 52c. Driving and Restraining Forces in Case of Two Conflicting Positive Valences. P, person located at A (Fig. 52); f_{A,G^1} and f_{A,G^2} driving forces to G^1 and G^2; $f_{D,-D}$, a force against entering the adit D to G^1; $f_{E,-E}$, force against entering the adit E to G^2. $d_{D,-D} = d_{A,G^1}$; $d_{E,-E} = d_{A,G^2}$.

Such restructuring implies often merely a cognitive change in structure. For instance, one might "rationalize" the giving up of one of two positive valences by thinking that the way to the other positive valence might lead later also to the first one (see Figure 51). In our case the change in the structure of the situation involves that the student makes his friend actually move into the region G.

b. Survey of Choice Situations.

1) Choice between two equally distant but incompatible valences.—To simplify problems of direction, we might refer to the situation in a simple maze. The individual P is located in A (Figure 52). Regions G^1 and G^2 are positive valences and the intermediate regions D and E are such that $e_{A,G^1} = e_{A,G^2}$. The regions A, D, G^1, E, G^2, might together be surrounded by an impassable barrier B. In this case, we can say that $d_{A,G^1} = d_{A,G^2}$ according to (13) because $w_{G^1G^2} \supset w_{A,G^2}$. The forces f_{A,G^1} and f_{A,G^2} are, therefore, opposite in direction.

The individual is in a conflict situation and the choice can be used directly as a measurement of the relative strength of the valences $Va(G^1)$ and $Va(G^2)$. The constellation will approach an equilibrium the more nearly $|f_{A,G^1}| = |f_{A,G^2}|$.

This constellation is, of course, independent of the physical angle of both paths. Hodologically, the psychological directions d_{A,G^1} and d_{A,G^2} will be opposed to each other even if the angle between them is less than 180°.

The same constellation can exist in a free field without a surrounding barrier. It is characteristic of any choice between two positive valences (at the time of the decision), in case one can choose only one.

2) Choice between two equally distant valences which are not known to be incompatible.—Figure 52 does not fully represent the situation discussed above, because it permits a path, not only from A to G^1, but also from G^1 to G^2, after the individual has reached G^1. That is, it permits getting both goals G^1 and G^2. To make the representation adequate, one would have to say that the regions D and E (or the boundaries between D and G^1 and between

E and G^2) are passable only in one direction, namely, in the direction $d_{A,G}{}^1$ and $d_{A,G}{}^2$. (Physically, that would correspond to one-way doors at D and E or to any other device which prevents the individual from reaching G^2 after he has been in G^1.)

There are, of course, situations where the individual might reach the second valence, too, or might have at least a chance to do so. (Sometimes the attainment of both goals is possible only if one goes first to G^1, but not if one goes first to G^2.) The topology of this situation is given in Figure 52a. It can be viewed as the overlapping of two situations. The one situation corresponds to that in Figure 52, and there the direction $d_{A,G}{}^1 = d_{A,G}{}^2$. Besides, however, these exists a path $w_{A,D,G}{}^1{}_{,G}{}^2$ from A to G^2 by way of G^1, even if this path $w_{A.D,G}{}^1{}_{,A,E,G}{}^2$ has first to lead back to A (Figure 52b).

So far as the force fields are concerned, we have to deal here (Figure 52a) with two pairs of overlapping force fields. The forces $f_{A,G}{}^1$ and $f_{A,G}{}^2$ which correspond to the one pair are opposed to each other ($d_{A,G}{}^1 = d_{A,G}{}^2$), just as in the case discussed under 1). The forces $f_{A,G}{}^1$ and $f_{A,G}{}^2$ corresponding to the other pair are acting in the same direction ($d_{A,G}{}^1 = d_{A,G}{}^2$), as in the situation discussed under a (Figure 51).

The process of decision will be influenced under this condition by the relative potency of both overlapping situations. The set-up will have less the character of a conflict situation the greater the relative potency of that situation where $d_{A,G}{}^1 = d_{A,G}{}^2$, that is, where B can be reached by way of A. I would expect that the time of decision, on the whole, will be shorter in this case than in the case discussed under 1).

3) *Two equal valences at different distances. One valence accessible by two different paths.*—This is a situation widely used in animal psychology to investigate the effect of different properties of paths, for instance, of the length of the path.

In this case one refers to a group of forces which existed

also in the cases represented in Figures 52, 52a, and 52b, although we did not mention them—namely, to the forces $f_{D,-D}$ and $f_{E,-E}$. These forces correspond to the resistance, or to the negative valences, of the paths to the goals. In the situation represented in Figure 52, one must deal, in the region A at least, with four forces, each of them part of a separate force field, namely, the forces f_{A,G^1}, f_{A,G^2}, $f_{D,-D}$, and $f_{E,-E}$ (Figure 52c). In the situation discussed under 1), the forces $f_{E,-E}$ and $f_{D,-D}$ are kept equal in strength ($|f_{D,-D}| = |f_{E,-E}|$). The decision, therefore, depends only on the relative strength of $|f_{A,G^1}|$ and $|f_{A,G^2}|$—in other words, on the relative strengths of the valences $Va(G^1)$ and $Va(G^2)$. However, the time of the decision might well be influenced by the strength of $f_{D,-D}$ and $f_{E,-E}$ as well.

For comparing the effects of different kinds of paths on behavior, one tries to keep $|f_{A,G^1}| = |f_{A,G^2}|$. These forces depend partly on the strength of the valences $Va(G^1)$ and $Va(G^2)$, partly on other factors such as distance. To make sure that one deals with the same intensity of the valence, one can use instead of two valences only one and let both paths lead to the same valence (G), corresponding to a constellation represented in Figure 48.

One is accustomed to view such a consideration as a case of choice. However, psychologically such a situation is quite different from that of two different valences even if the strength should be equal.

We might exemplify that by comparing a study of Hull (1933) with that of Leeper (1935). Hull tried to condition animals so that they would choose in a maze, schematically represented in Figure 53, the path $w_{A,D,C}$ to C if they were hungry, and the path $w_{A,E,C}$ to C if they were thirsty. In the first case they found food (G^1), in the second case water (G^2), in C. In the training periods the animals were prevented from entering C by a door (R^2) if they were thirsty, and by another door (R^1) if they were hungry. Hull found that an exorbitantly high number of repetitions was necessary to train the animals, and that even then the performance was rather imperfect.

Leeper repeated the experiment using, besides other arrangements, a set-up which might roughly be represented by

Figure 54. The region C was divided into two parts H and K, one with food (G^1 in H) accessible through D, the other with water (G^2 in K) accessible through E. Physically this situation in Figure 54 is so similar to that in 53 that one should expect little or no difference for the forces governing the decision of the animal in A. However, Leeper found that the animals now learned very rapidly to make the right choice.

These results seem less paradoxical if one translates them into human situations. Let us suppose a person must cross a river to a library to get books. He can use either one of two bridges, the length of both paths being equal. The experiment of Hull would be equivalent to the following proposal: the person might get either mathematical books or psychological books from the library. Sometimes he will find the left and sometimes the right bridge blocked. Objectively, the right bridge always will be blocked if the person wants to get mathematical books from the library, the left bridge always if he wants to get psychological books. I assume that it would take a human being a very long time to find out this rule, because he always wants to go to the same place. It is to be expected that one of the last "hypotheses" (Krechevsky 1932) which the individual will happen to think of will be that the blocking of the specific bridge has something to do with *what* he expects to do in the library.

Leeper's experiment corresponds to the situation where two libraries exist, one for mathematical books which can be reached only by the right bridge, and one for psychological books which can be reached only by the left bridge. Of course, the person will soon learn to use the correct bridge to get the book he wants.

As a matter of fact, the situations represented in Figures 53 and 54 are, in spite of their physical similarity, very different from the point of view of hodological geometry. Topologically, there is no difference between the situation represented in Figure 54 and Figure 52. However, both are quite different from the situation represented in Figure 53.

In Leeper's experiment (Figure 54) the force to the food f_{A,G^1} and the force to the water f_{A,G^2} have the directions $d_{A,H}$ and $d_{A,K}$, respectively. These directions are clearly different and can even be said to be opposed to each other for the same reasons as in Figure 52.

(Ex. 39) $d_{A,H} = d_{A,K}$; therefore $d_{A,G^1} = d_{A,G^2}$ and

(Ex. 39a) $d_{A,D} = d_{A,E}$, according to (3).

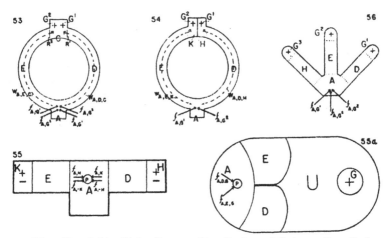

Figs. 53 and 54. Choice Between Two Paths and Between Two Goals (in physically nearly identical settings)

Fig. 53. Situation in an Experiment of Hull. The goals, G^1, and G^2, are located in C; in the direction $d_{A,D,C}$ there exist two forces $f_{A,G}^1$, and $f_{A,G}^2$ (according to the path $w_{A,D,C}$ to G^1 and G^2); in the direction $d_{A,D,C}$ there exist again the two forces $f_{A,G}^1$ and $f_{A,G}^2$ (according to the path $w_{A,E,C}$ to G^1 and G^2).

Fig. 54. Situation in an Experiment of Leeper.

The goal G^1 is located in K; goal G^2 is located in H; in the direction $d_{A,D,H}$ there exists only the force $f_{A,G}^1$ (according to the path $w_{A,D,H}$ to G^1); in the direction $d_{A,E,K}$ there exists only the force $f_{A,G}^2$ according to the path $w_{A,E,K}$ to G^2).

Fig. 55. Constellation of forces if it is not known in which of two positions a valence is located. P, person located at A; H and K, the possible locations of the goal; H, has a positive valence (Va(H) $>$ 0) corresponding to the possibility that the goal is located there, and a negative valence (Va(H) $<$ 0) corresponding to the possibility that the goal is not located there; the same holds for K; $f_{A,H}$, force toward H; $f_{A,K}$, force toward K; $f_{A,-H}$, force away from H; $f_{A,-K}$, force away from K.

Fig. 55a. Slightly different representation of the same situation emphasizing the "intellectual" character of this type of conflict. P, person located at A; G, goal; U, cognitively undetermined region separating G from A; $f_{A,D,G}$ and $f_{A,E,G}$, forces toward G in the direction $d_{A,D}$ and $d_{A,E}$ respectively.

Fig. 56. Choice Between Three Mutually Exclusive Positive Valences. Va(G^1) $=$ Va(G^2) $=$ Va(G^3) $>$ 0; $f_{A,G}^1$, force toward G^1; $f_{A,G}^2$, force to G^2; $f_{A,G}^3$, force to G^3; these forces are mutually in opposition: $d_{A,G}^1 = d_{A,G}^2$; $d_{A,G}^2 = d_{A,G}^3$, $d_{A,G}^1 = d_{A,G}^3$; in regard to determination of resultant of these forces see text.

In Hull's experiment both water and food appear in the same region C. Therefore, the forces to the food $f_{A,G}^1$ and to the water $f_{A,G}^2$ have the same direction, namely $d_{A,C}$.

(Ex. 40) $$d_{A,G}^1 = d_{A,C} = d_{A,G}^2.$$

Of course, as far as consumption is concerned, in both cases the forces are directed to two different ends (water and food). However, as far as translocation is concerned, the sub-goal of reaching a certain geographical area is different for both paths in the experiment of Leeper, but identical in the experiment of Hull.

For determining the directions of the forces $f_{A,G}^1$ and $f_{A,G}^2$ at the point A in the experiment of Hull, there remains the question of determining the relation between the directions $d_{A,D}$ and $d_{A,E}$. In Leeper's experiment both are clearly opposed (Ex. 39a). In Hull's experiment we have to deal with a rather complicated relation between the directions of two paths from the same starting region to the same end-region. By discussing the geometry of this situation (p. 35) we have seen that those directions have to be considered as "partly equal." That would mean in our case:

(Ex. 40a) $$d_{A,D} (=) d_{A,E}$$

which involves both a certain amount of equality and difference of these directions. We expected (p. 35) that the *difference* of both directions should become more important the greater is the potency of the means, relatively to that of the ends. Indeed, I would assume that one of the reasons for the difficulty of learning in Hull's experiments is that the regions E and D are relatively slightly emphasized means to a common end.

At any rate, the directions $d_{A,D}$ and $d_{A,E}$ are not clearly opposed to each other, as in Leeper's experiments. In addition, the force $f_{A,G}^1$, in Hull's experiment, points in two directions, namely, in the direction $d_{A,D}$ and in the direction $d_{A,E}$. Also, the force $f_{A,G}^2$ points in these two directions. In Leeper's experiment each of these forces points only in one of these directions.[5]

[5] Leeper (pp. 31 and 32) explained the different results of his and Hull's experiments by pointing to the fact that in his experiments "when a rat chose incorrectly, its run led it into the end-box containing the material which the rat did not desire at that time and the rat thus had an opportunity to learn what materials were in what places.... When

The experiments with animals on two paths to one goal seem to be well in line with our interpretations. If two paths of equal length are leading to the food, the animal tends to alternate between these two paths (Tolman 1932; according to Krechevsky (1937) finally one path becomes habitual). If both paths are different in length or in other qualities, the preference should be established according to the forces represented schematically in Figure 52c. According to Kuo (1930), the order of preference of paths under similar circumstances is 1.) short path w^s; 2.) long path w^l; 3.) path including a period of confinement for reaching the goal w^c; 4.) path crossing electric grill w^g. That would mean that in these experiments

(Ex 40b) $\quad |f_{w^s,-w^s}| < |f_{w^l,-w^l}| < |f_{w^c,-w^c}| < |f_{w^g,-w^g}|$

That $f_{w^g,-w^g}$ shows the greatest strength is well in line with our discussions. We have here a clear case where a path itself has a negative valence to which driving forces correspond, whereas a short path probably involves only certain restraining forces. Confinement might involve both restraining forces and a certain amount of negative valence.

   4) One valence located in one of two equally distant positions.—Many choice experiments in animal psychology use a set-up which amounts more or less to a simple T-maze with one valence. The animal has a choice between going to the right or to the left, but does not know whether the valence is located at the end H of one arm or at the end K of the other one (Figure 55). At first glance one might think that, psychologically, the situation should be presented by Figure 52. For, could one not say that, psychologically, for the in-

---

a rat made an error in Hull's maze, its path led it to a door which firmly obstructed its entrance into the end-box. . . . Now, if the effect of an incorrect run is not to be described as a 'stamping out of the connections leading to that response', nor as the 'development of a negative conditioned response to that side of the maze', but is to be described rather as a matter of the rat's learning the nature of the situation to which each response leads, the results seem to be understandable.''

   This might add to the basic hodological difference in making the result of the two experiments so unlike.

dividual in A a force $f_{A,H}$ and a force $f_{A,K}$ exist both directed to the valence G, located either in H or in K?

One could even say that in this experiment one is sure that $|f_{A,H}| = |f_{A,K}|$ because it is the same valence Va(G) at each side of the maze and the distance and other factors are equal.

Such a representation, however, would not be adequate, It would be incorrect to say that the valence G is located both in H and in K, because the individual is not sure of its location. This uncertainty about the location of G is one of the major factors which dominates the decision of the individual in A. If one uses a representation similar to Figure 52, one would have to say that (Figure 55) there exists in A in relation to the region H two forces: a force $f_{A,H}$ toward H resulting from the possibility that G is located in H, and, in addition, a force $f_{A,-H}$ away from H, corresponding to the possibility that G is not located in H. Likewise, there exist two forces in A in relation to K: a force $f_{A,K}$ toward K corresponding to the possibility that G is located in K, and, in addition, a force $f_{A,-K}$ corresponding to the possibility that this is not the case.

The situation is, therefore, rather different from that of the choice between two more or less equal valences, each having a definite location (our case 1) or 2)). There the relative strength of two valences was decisive for the choice. This time we must deal rather with a decision within an *unclear* situation. It is an "intellectual" decision rather than a choice between two different attractive valences or two different agreeable paths.

The situation may be best represented by Figure 55a. The individual is located in A. There exists somewhere a valence G, the character of which is known to the individual. However, the path between A and G is not known sufficiently. In other words, the region A and G are separated by what we have called (see Figure 18) a cognitively unstructured region U. The regions D and E are part of U, because it is questionable for the individual which of the paths is con-

nected with G. In other words, the individual does not know
whether $d_{A,D} = d_{A,G}$ or $d_{A,D} \neq d_{A,G}$ and whether
$d_{A,E} = d_{A,G}$ or $d_{A,E} \neq d_{A,G}$.

On the whole, the situation is rather similar to that of
learning a new maze (Figure 18). The main difference is
that the geography of the place itself is well known to the
animal, and that in this respect the field does not have the
character of U. However, it is not known where G is located.
The field is, therefore, undetermined (U) in respect to the
connectedness with G (see page 62).

A second difference between this situation and that of
learning a maze is the knowledge of the individual that,
in the former, he cannot go back, for instance, from D to A
when he once has entered D and found that this is the wrong
path. In the usual situation of maze learning, the individual
can correct the mistake of entering a blind alley. The decisions in the learning situation, therefore, have a less definite
character. I would expect, then, a shorter decision time, ceteris
paribus, in the learning situation.

The act of decision itself involves here, as in the learning
situation, a change of the cognitive structure of the field: for
the time being it might become, for instance, $d_{A,D} = d_{A,G}$
and in this case the force $f_{A,G}$ would lead to a locomotion
to D.

5) *Ends against means.*—One might count as a separate
group of choice situations those where a conflict exists between choosing a certain end and avoiding a certain means.
For instance, a path with a negative valence might lie between the individual and a positive valence (as in case of
the obstruction box). In those cases the means always has
a valence in itself. These cases might therefore be treated
as were the cases discussed under 1) and 3).

2. *Choice between Three or More Positive Valences.*—In
many experimental set-ups the individual has to choose between three or more possibilities. We will discuss here only
the case where a choice has to be made between three different
positive valences G^1, G^2, and G^3 (Figure 56). Only one of

them should be obtainable. The other constellations of a choice between three possibilities could be handled accordingly by taking into account our discussion of the various cases of choice between two valences.

For the individual located in A there exist the forces f_{A,G^1}, f_{A,G^2} and f_{A,G^3}. The direction $d_{A,G^1} = d_{A,G^2}$ for the same reason as in Figure 52. Further, $d_{A,G^2} = d_{A,G^3}$, and $d_{A,G^1} = d_{A,G^3}$. In other words, the direction toward every one of the goals is opposite to that of either of the other goals.

In Euclidian space the three equations could not hold true together, because from any two of these equations would follow that at least two of the directions are equal to each other. In hodological space, however, where equality of direction is not always transitive (7a), no two of these directions are equal and the three equations do not contradict each other.

In determining the resultant of the forces $f_{A,G^1} +$ $f_{A,G^2} + f_{A,G^3}$ *it would not be correct to proceed as in physics* and to determine at first the resultant $f^*_{A,N}$ of two of these forces (for instance $f_{A,G^1} + f_{A,G^2}$) and to determine then the resultant of $f^*_{A,N}$ and the third force f_{A,G^3}. For, the resultant $f^*_{A,N}$ of the two first forces will be nearly equal zero ($f_{A,G^1} + f_{A,G^2} = f^*_{A,N} = 0$) in case the three positive valences are nearly equal in strength ($|Va(G^1)| = |Va(G^2)| = |Va(G^3)|$), because it is nearly $|f_{A,G^1}| = |f_{A,G^2}|$ and $d_{A,G^1} = d_{A,G^2}$. Therefore, the resultant of the resultant force $f^*_{A,N}$ and the third force f_{A,G^3} would be nearly equal to this third force ($f^*_{A,N} + f_{A,G^3} = f_{A,G^3}$). In other words, the resultant of $f_{A,G^1} +$ $f_{A,G^2} + f_{A,G^3}$ would have to be considered either equal f_{A,G^1} or f_{A,G^2} or f_{A,G^3} according to which two of the forces have been calculated first. This obviously is an impossible proposal. Therefore, the resultant of these three forces in a situation of choice cannot be calculated in this way.

The procedure becomes meaningful, however, if one takes

into account any two of the forces in question, and determines what the result is *after* the decision (that is, after the choice between the two valences has been made), before one proceeds to take into account the third force. For instance, the individual might consider at first G^1 and G^2 and might choose G^1. This decision changes (as we have seen) the life space so that the potency of the region containing G^2 becomes nearly zero. Therefore, from now on, only the forces corresponding to the preferred valence G^1 have to be considered. The choice between the remaining valences G^1 and G^3 takes place in about the same way as if only two valences had been present from the beginning. This is true, however, only in case that the choice between G^1 and G^2 had the character of a final decision.

The order in which the valences are actually considered by the individual has doubtless some influence on his choice. However, if the valences are sufficiently different in strength the procedure of calculating the result will be adequate independent of order in case the individual is confronted with the three valences simultaneously.

3. Conflict Situations with Stable and with Labile Equilibria

Thus far we have discussed the problems of overlapping force fields from the point of view of finding out under what conditions one of the opposing forces is dominant. In other words, we have asked under what conditions the resultant force $|f^*_{A,X}| \neq 0$ and what is the direction $d_{A,X}$ of $f^*_{A,X}$.

In case the opposing forces are equal in strength their resultant $|f^*_{A,X}| = 0$. In this case an equilibrium exists. Then according to (19) no directed locomotion occurs ($v_{A,X} = 0$). There are, however, important differences between various cases of such equilibria, or, as we might say, "conflict situations."

We have already mentioned that the tension (t) existing in a conflict situation is a function of the strength of the opposing forces (35). Besides, there exist important differences in the type of equilibrium. It seems to be possible to distinguish in psychology, as in physics, stable, labile, and indifferent equilibria. A stable equilibrium is defined by the fact that a small change of the object away from the position of equilibrium should involve a change in the constellation of forces such that the object should return to the position of equilibrium. In a labile equilibrium, however, a small shift of position should bring the object into a constellation of forces such that it will not return to the position of equilibrium but move in some other direction. In case of an indifferent equilibrium a small change of position leaves the object in a state of equilibrium.

The type of equilibrium is psychologically important for what one might call the lability of the situation and for the velocity of decision. It is a question closely related to problems of time and of probability of change. To discuss these questions, it is necessary to represent the constellation of forces resulting from the overlapping force fields not merely at one point but in the points of a whole area.

We will limit the discussion to relatively simple cases of two valences, and will compare at first the conflict situation regarding two positive and two negative valences.

   a. *The Space of Free Movement Is Limited.*—We compare both situations, at first under circumstances where the space of free movement of the individual is limited in such a way that he can move from his location in A only either toward G^1 or toward G^2. Other movements might be prohibited by barriers B. Let us assume that otherwise the field is relatively homogeneous and that

(Ex. 41) $Va(G^1) = Va(G^2)$

Figure 57 represents schematically the situation where both valences are positive $Va(G^1) > 0$ and $Va(G^2) > 0$. Figure 58 represents the case where both valences are negative $(Va(G^1) < 0$ and $Va(G^2) < 0)$, under otherwise equal circumstances. (Physically, the regions represented in Figures 57 and 58 might have any kind of shape.)

Let us first compare the forces existing at A in both cases. If the valences are positive (Figure 57) and the distances from

A equal $(e_{A,G^1} = e_{A,G^2})$ there should exist the forces f_{A,G^1} and f_{A,G^2} in A. The strengths of these forces should be equal, their directions opposite.

(Ex. 41a) $|f_{A,G^1}| = |f_{A,G^2}|$; $d_{A,G^1} = d_{A,G^2}$

We have to deal here, therefore, with an equilibrium.

In case of negative valences (Figure 58) there should exist in A the forces $f_{A,-G^1}$ and $f_{A,-G^2}$. Their strengths should be equal, their directions opposite.[8]

(Ex. 41b) $|f_{A,-G^1}| = |f_{A,-G^2}|$; $d_{A,-G^1} = d_{A,-G^2}$

In both cases, we have to deal with a state of equilibrium $(f_{A,G^1} + f_{A,G^2} = 0$ and $f_{A,-G^1} + f_{A,-G^2} = 0)$ or, psychologically speaking, with a conflict situation. There are, however, important differences which come into the open if one considers the whole force fields resulting from G^1 and G^2 rather than the forces only in A.

We can ask whether we have to deal here with a labile or a stable equilibrium. We can decide the problem of stabile or labile equilibrium in our cases if we assume that the strength of the force decreases with increasing distance both for the positive and for the negative valences (32).

In case of positive valences (Figure 57) the individual might, for instance, move from A in the direction toward G^1 to the point 1. There the forces f_{1,G^1} and f_{1,G^2} would exist. The locomotion to 1 increases the distance from G^2 and decreases the distance from G^1, i.e., $e_{1,G^1} < e_{1,G^2}$, therefore, $|f_{1,G^1}| > |f_{1,G^2}|$. The directions of both forces are again opposite to each other, but since f_{1,G^1} is the stronger, the resultant of $f_{1,G^1} + f_{1,G^2} = f^*_{1,G^1} > 0$. In other words, when the individual moves somewhat in the direction to G^1, the resultant of forces at the new place will lead to a further locomotion in this direction. Similarly, a slight locomotion in the direction to G^2 would lead to further locomotion in

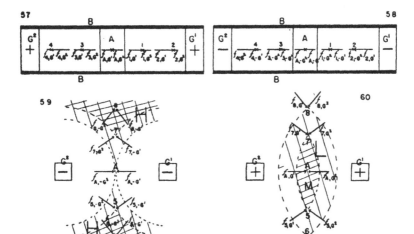

I. CONFLICT SITUATIONS IN A RESTRICTED SPACE OF FREE MOVEMENT.

Fig. 57. Conflict between Two Positive Valences. Labile Equilibrium. B, impassable barrier; $Va(G^1) = Va(G^2) > 0$; f_{A,G^1}, f_{1,G^1}, f_{2,G^1}, f_{3,G^1} and f_{4,G^1}, forces toward G^1 at the points A, 1, 2, 3 and 4, respectively; f_{A,G^2}, f_{1,G^2}, f_{2,G^2}, f_{3,G^2}, and f_{4,G^2}, forces toward G^2 at the point A, 1, 2, 3, and 4, respectively.

Fig. 58. Conflict between Two Negative Valences. Stabile Equilibrium. B, impassable barrier; $Va(G^1) = Va(G^2) < 0$; $f_{A,-G^1}$, $f_{1,-G^1}$, $f_{2,-G^1}$, $f_{3,-G^1}$, and $f_{4,-G^1}$, forces away from G^1 at the point A, 1, 2, 3, and 4, respectively; $f_{A,-G^2}$, $f_{1,-G^2}$, $f_{2,-G^2}$, $f_{3,-G^2}$, and $f_{4,-G^2}$, forces away from G^2 at the points A, 1, 2, 3, and 4 respectively.

II. CONFLICT SITUATIONS IN AN UNRESTRICTED SPACE OF FREE MOVEMENT.

Fig 59. A Conflict between Two Negative Valences. $Va(G^1) = Va(G^2) < 0$; $f_{A,-G^1}$, $f_{5,-G^1}$, $f_{6,-G^1}$, $f_{7,-G^1}$ and $f_{A,-G^1}$, forces away from G^1 at the point A, 5, 6, 7, and 8, respectively; $f_{A,-G^2}$, $f_{5,-G^2}$, $f_{6,-G^2}$, $f_{7,-G^2}$ and $f_{8,-G^2}$, forces away from G^2 at the points A, 5, 6, 7, and 8, respectively; H, the totality of points in the direction to which exists a resultant of the conflicting forces $f_{A,-G^1}$ and $f_{A,-G^2}$; K, the totality of points in the direction of which exists a resultant of the forces $f_{6,-G^1}$ and $f_{6,-G^2}$; $K \subset H$.

Fig. 60. Conflict between Two Positive Valences. $Va(G^1) = Va(G^2) > 0$; f_{A,G^1}, f_{5,G^1}, f_{7,G^1}, and f_{8,G^1}, forces toward G^1 at the points A, 5, 6, 7, and 8, respectively; f_{A,G^2}, f_{5,G^2}, f_{6,G^2}, f_{7,G^2}, and f_{8,G^2} forces toward G^2 at the points A, 5, 6, 7, and 8 respectively; A, point of unavoidable decision; M, the totality of points in the direction to which a resultant exists of the forces f_{5,G^1}, and f_{5,G^2} (or of the forces f_{7,G^1} and f_{7,G^2}); L, the totality of points in the direction of which a resultant exists of the forces f_{6,G^1}, and f_{6,G^2} (or of the forces f_{8,G^1}, and f_{8,G^2}); $M \subset L$.

the same direction. Therefore, we have to deal in case of *two positive valences with a labile equilibrium.*

The situation is different if G^1 and G^2 are negative valences (Figure 58). A locomotion from A to the point 1 would bring the individual under the forces $f_{1,-G^1}$ and $f_{1,-G^2}$. Again the distance $e_{1,G^1} < e_{1,G^2}$. Therefore, $|f_{1,-G}| > |f_{1,-G^2}|$. This time, however, the resultant of $f_{1,-G^1} + f_{1,-G^2} = f^*_{1,-G} > 0$. In other words, there would be a resultant force in the direction *away* from G^1, and that would lead, under the given circumstances, to a locomotion back to A. Therefore, we have to deal in the case of *two negative valences with a stable equilibrium.*

Our considerations concerning the type of equilibrium refer, of course, only to the period before the decision is reached. The decision changes the structure of the field considerably.

b. The Duration of Decision.—One can derive from these considerations a conclusion about the time of decision, if one assumes that the decision involves something like "virtual locomotion." We would conclude that, ceteris paribus, the *time of decision between two positive valences is shorter than the time of decision between two negative valences.* For, in the latter case, any movement toward one of the negative valences will lead to an increase of the force away from this valence. In the case of two negative valences the situation is such that a start in any one direction should be met by increasing opposing forces, and, therefore, the individual should turn back to A. That means actually the individual should stay in A longer before choosing G^1 or G^2.

This consideration might suffice for cases where the whole problem is not very important for the individual. However, other factors might enter, especially in important situations when much time is used for making up one's mind. One of the additional factors which one will have to take into account in discussing the decision-time is the valence of the momentary state of affairs. In some cases a decision might be postponed again and again, because the undecided state of affairs might have a higher positive valence for the individual than either of the situations after the decision. In other cases, the tension related to an undecided state might increase so much that the negative valence of this state will be greater than any decision, even if the individual has to choose something disagreeable.

In case of a conflict between two positive valences G^1 and G^2, generally the valence of the present undecided state (A) is probably less positive than the valence of the state in either G^1 or G^2, i.e., $Va(A) < Va(G^1)$ and $Va(A) < Va(G^2)$. The individual will have, therefore, a tendency to leave the present undecided state and make a quick decision in either one of the directions. In the case of the conflict between two negative valences G^1 and G^2 the present undecided situation A might have a higher positive valence than either of the valences G^1 and G^2, i.e., $Va(A) > Va(G^1)$; $Va(A) > Va(G^2)$. In other words, there exists in this case a force $f_{A,A}$ which keeps the person in A and makes for a slow decision. In the case of positive valences (if $Va(A) < Va(G^1)$ and $Va(A) < Va(G^2)$), there existed a force $f_{A,-A}$ which makes for a quick decision.

c. The Space of Free Movement Is Not Restricted. Determination of the Resultant Force.—Our statement concerning stability and lability of equilibrium in case of conflict between two negative and two positive valences pre-supposes the restrictedness of the space of free movement by the barrier B. The situation is quite different without such restrictions. Figure 59 represents a situation where the individual is again located in A between two negative valences G^1 and G^2 $(Va(G^1) = Va(G^2))$ at equal distances from A $(e_{A,G^1} = e_{A,G^2})$. The field should be homogeneous and should have a semi-Euclidian character. The forces acting in A would be again $f_{A,-G^1}$ and $f_{A,-G^2}$ $(|f_{A,-G^1}| = |f_{A,-G^2}|)$.

We have seen that in case of the barrier B which permits only locomotion toward G^1 or toward G^2, one could state that both forces are opposite in direction $(d_{A,-G^1} = d_{A,-G^2})$.

In case of unrestricted locomotions one can say that $d_{A,G^1} = d_{A,G^2}$, according to (13), if the paths w_{G^1,G^2} and w_{G^2,G^1} cross A (this would be the case in a semi-Euclidian space). However, one cannot conclude that $d_{A,-G^1} = d_{A,-G^2}$, because the direction $(d_{A,-G^1})$ away from G^1 is a multi-valued direction (15). It is the direction $d_{A,X}$ to every point X which is farther away from G^1 than A $(e_{G^1,X} > e_{G^1,A})$. Therefore, both the directions $d_{A,-G^1}$ and $d_{A,-G^2}$ correspond to a group of positive directions.

One can show even that both directions are not opposite to each other in so far as a direction d exists which is equal to both the direction away from G^1 *and* to the direction away from G^2 (i.e., $d_{A,X} = d_{A,-G^1}$ and $d_{A,X} = d_{A,-G^2}$). Every one of the points 5, 6, 7, or 8, for instance, has the property that $e_{G^1,5} > e_{G^1,A}$ and that at the same time $e_{G^2,5} > e_{G^2,A}$. Therefore $d_{A,5} = d_{A,-G^1}$ and $d_{A,5} = d_{A,-G^2}$. In other words, *the forces $f_{A,-G^1}$ and $f_{A,-G^2}$ have a common resultant* in the direction $d_{A,5}$ or to any point X which is farther away from G^1 and at the same time farther away from G^2 than A is:

(Ex. 41c) $f_{A,-G^1} + f_{A,-G^2} = f^*_{A,X} > 0$, if
$e_{G^1,X} > e_{G^1,A}$ and $e_{G^2,X} > e_{G^2,A}$

The area H (Figure 59) indicates the totality of such points X.

These considerations make it clear that one can speak of an equilibrium in case of a position between two negative valences only in regard to a locomotion *toward* either of those valences. We have seen that in this respect, the equilibrium is to be considered even as relatively stable. However, considering a field of unrestricted movements, the forces away from the negative valences have definite resultants toward places (X) of increased distance from both valences. Therefore, one can hardly speak about equilibrium at all, and certainly not about a stable equilibrium.

The observations about threat of punishment (Lewin 1935) and the studies on social pressure show that the individual actually will move from A in the direction $d_{A,X}$ toward such places X. Even where a barrier B limits the space of free movement, this resultant $f^*_{A,X}$ exists, and might lead to an attack against the barrier B.

The situation of an individual between two *positive* valences G^1 and G^2 in an unrestricted space of movement is rather different. The forces f_{A,G^1} and f_{A,G^2} (Figure 60) can be said to be opposed in direction in case of a homogeneous semi-Euclidian space ($d_{A,G^1} = d_{A,G^2}$, according to (12)), even if no barrier B limits the space of free movement. This time the forces f_{A,G^1} and f_{A,G^2} have no common resultant different from zero. In other words, there is no point X so that $d_{A,X} = d_{A,G^1}$ and $d_{A,X} = d_{A,G^2}$. In regard, for instance, to point 5, one cannot state that $d_{A,5} = d_{A,G^1}$ and $d_{A,5} = d_{A,G^2}$. Therefore:

(Ex. 41d) $$f_{A,G^1} + f_{A,G^2} = 0.$$ *

That means that the situation containing two positive valences is not much different in case the space of free movement is restricted by the barrier B or when it is not restricted. Especially, there exists no component of the forces f_{A,G^1} and f_{A,G^2} in the direction toward the barrier B, quite in contrast with the situation containing two negative valences. (We have seen that the situation represented by (Ex. 41d) is a labile equilibrium in regard to locomotions in the directions d_{A,G^1} or d_{A,G^2}.)

We have discussed up to now the effect of these overlapping central fields of forces located "between" the centers G^1 and G^2 of these fields, or to speak in hodological terms, at points of the distinguished path from G^1 to G^2. We shall ask now: what is the resultant of the forces of these two central fields at other points, for instance, at the point 6?

The resultant of the forces existing at the point 6 can be relatively easily determined in case of two negative valences (Figure 59).

(Ex. 41e) $f_{6,-G^1} + f_{6,-G^2} = f^*_{6,X} > 0$, if
$e_{G^1,X} > e_{G^1,6}$ and $e_{G^2,X} > e_{G^2,6}$.

In other words, the individual will move on to places still farther away, both from G^1 and G^2, as long as $|f_{6,-G^1}| > 0$ and $|f_{6,-G^2}| > 0$. On the whole, the resultant in point 6 can be determined in the same way as in point A. The area K (Figure 59) indicates the totality of points X, for which (Ex. 41e) holds. This area K is a part of the area H (i.e., $H \supset K$).

The situation is less simple in case of two positive valences (Figure 60). The forces at that point 6 are f_{6,G^1} and f_{6,G^2}. Our previous discussion of the geometry and dynamics of forces does not provide a sufficient basis for the determination of the resultant of $f_{6,G^1} + f_{6,G^2}$. Psychologically, the situation at 6 can be characterized as the situation of the individual who (a) has to make a choice between two positive valences (we still assume that he shall not be able to reach both valences), but (b) has not yet reached the point where he cannot proceed further without making a decision. At the point 6 it is possible for the individual to come closer both to G^1 and to G^2, for instance, by locomoting toward A.

In other words, there are points Y so that $e_{Y,G^1} < e_{6,G^1}$ and at the same time $e_{Y,G^2} < e_{6,G^2}$. At the point A, however, no such points Y exist. Instead, every decrease of the distance between A and G^1 increases the distance between A and G^2 and vice versa. We will call such a point A *"point of unavoidable decision."*

(37)   A is a "point of unavoidable decision" if from $e_{Y,G^1} < e_{A,G^1}$ follows that $e_{Y,G^2} > e_{A,G^2}$.

It is probably fair to make the following general assumption concerning the resultants of forces (not restricted to semi-Euclidian spaces):

(38)   Principle concerning resultants of forces:
$f_{N,G^1} + f_{N,G^2} = f^*_{N,Y}$ so that $e_{Y,G^1} < e_{N,G^2}$ and $e_{Y,G^2} < e_{N,G^2}$ in case such a region Y exists;

furthermore,

(38a) $|f^*_{N,Y}| > 0$ if $|f_{N,G^1}| > 0$ and $|f_{N,G^2}| > 0$.

Formula (38) deals with the direction, formula (38a) with the strength of the resultant force. In regard to forces *toward* two regions, these formulas serve the same purpose as the principle of the parallelogram of forces in physics. It should, however, be noticed that Y determines not only one point but an area of points, namely, the whole region (L) in Figure 60.

It is interesting to observe how this area narrows down in Figure 60, the closer the individual comes to the point of un-avoidable decision (A) (at the point 5 the area corresponds to M, at the point A it is zero). Also, in the case of two negative valences the resultant of the forces $f_{N,-G^1} + f_{N,-G^2} = f^*_{N,X}$ determined not only one point X but a field H (Figure 59), the shape of which changes with the departure from A.

The formulas (38) and (38a) deal with rather specific constellations of forces. However, it might be possible to make a more general statement about the resultants of forces along the same line.

The statements concerning the resultant of forces in case of two positive valences or two negative valences have been formulated so that they are immediately applicable also in such situations which have not the character of a semi-Euclidian homogeneous field. It does not seem necessary, therefore, to discuss these applications in detail.

d. The Point of Decision.—To avoid misunderstanding, it might be well to discuss briefly the location of the point of decision within two overlapping force fields, although this problem is a rather complicated one and demands a more detailed treatment. Here I wish to point merely to the fact that the actual decision does not necessarily occur at the "point of unavoidable decision" but might as readily occur previously.

The decision, as we have seen, is essentially a restructuring of the field so that one of two or more overlapping situations becomes dominant. The act of decision is a psychological process. Therefore, it can be represented as any other psychological activity by a region (D) of the life space. "Making the decision" would then have to be represented as a locomotion through this region D.

In a conflict situation between two positive valences, the individual P has to carry out mainly the following activities: starting at his present state in A, he must cross the region of decision (D) and the region of translocation (Tr) to reach the goal activities (either G^1 or G^2, Figure 61). If the goals G^1 and G^2 are not located at the same geographical point, then the translocation to G^1 and G^2 will cross at least partly different regions. In case A is already a point of unavoidable decision, the person will have to cross first the region of decision D (at least in the form of a temporary decision) before he can enter the region of translocation TrG^1 in direction to G^1, or TrG^2 in direction to G^2 (Figure 61a). However, if A is not a point of unavoidable decision but corresponds, for instance, to the point 6 in Figure 60, the time order of the activities decision and translocation is somewhat free.

The person might make the decision right away and only then start the translocation. In this case, the restructuring of the field which accompanies the decision takes place when the person still remains geographically at 6. As a result of the restructuring, the force f_{6,G^1} will approach zero (in case the individual decided to choose G^2) and the individual will locomote from 6 in direction of the force f_{6,G^2} directly to G^2.

However, the person might not cross the region of decision D when located at the point (region) 6. Instead, he might enter first a region of translocation (TrG^1G^2; Figure 61b) which decreases his distance to both goals until he reaches the point of unavoidable decision. In this case the translocation will be carried out partly before and partly after the decision.

Finally, the decision can be done at any point between the starting point and the point of unavoidable decision. Often transportation and decision can occur at the same time and

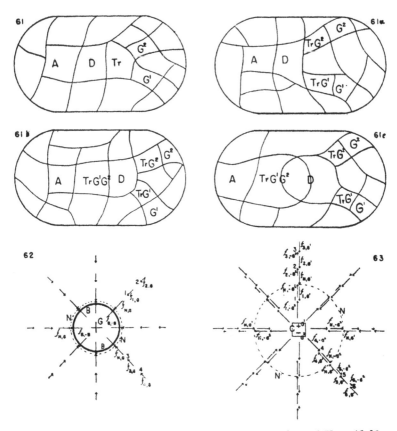

Figs. 61 to 61c. Decision and Translocation. Points of Unavoidable Decision.

Fig. 61. An individual located at A has to pass to the region of decision D, and the region of translocation Tr to reach the goal regions G^1 or G^2.

Fig. 61a. The Point of Unavoidable Decision. If the region A is so located that the translocations TrG^1 and TrG^2 from there to G^1 or to G^2 are different, the person has to first pass through the region of decision D before entering the regions of translocation.

Fig. 61b. If A is not a point of unavoidable decision, the person might first enter the region TrG^1G^2 of translocation toward both goals G^1 and G^2; TrG^1 and TrG^2, those parts of the translocation to G^1 and G^2 for which different paths must be used; D, region of decision.

might be represented then as partly overlapping regions of activities (Figure 61c).

At which point the decision actually will occur depends to a high degree upon the positive or negative valence which the act of decision itself has under the given circumstances. We have mentioned already the importance of this factor for the duration of the process of decision. It is important also for the place of decision whether the individual prefers to postpone disagreeable decisions or to "get it over" as soon as possible.

4. Force Fields Containing an Indifferent Equilibrium

The choice between two positive or between two negative valences contains only one point (region) in which an equilibrium exists, namely, the point A in Figures 59 and 60. There are other cases of force fields where a line (zone) of equilibrium might exist.

Figure 62 represents a case where a positive valence G is surrounded by an impassable barrier B (Lewin 1935). The field shall have, otherwise, the character of a homogeneous semi-Euclidian field. If B corresponds to a circle with G

Fig. 61c. Case where decision is partly made during translocation. TrG^1G^2, region of translocation toward G^1 and G^2; D, the region of decision partly overlapping TrG^1G^2; TrG^1 and TrG^2, translocations to G^1 and G^2 where different paths must be used.

Figs. 62 and 63. Force fields containing a line of indifferent equilibrium.

Fig. 62. Indifferent Equilibrium in Case of Conflict Between a Driving and a Restraining Force. G, goal $(Va(G) > 0)$; B, impassable barrier; person is located outside the barrier; $f_{N,G}$, $f_{1,G}$, $f_{2,G}$, $f_{3,G}$, $f_{4,G}$, forces to G at the points N, 1, 2, 3, 4, respectively; $f_{B,-B}$, restraining force against entering B; N, line of indifferent equilibrium; restless movements occur on N.

Fig. 63. Indifferent Equilibrium in Case of Conflict between Two Driving Forces. C, location of a positive and a negative valence G^1 and G^2; $Va(G^1) > 0$; $Va(G^2) < 0$; f_{N,G^1}, f_{1,G^1}, f_{2,G^1}, f_{3,G^1}, f_{4,G^1}, f_{5,G^1}, f_{6,G^1}, forces toward G^1 at the points N, 1, 2, 3, 4, 5, 6 respectively; $f_{N,-G^2}$, $f_{1,-G^2}$, $f_{2,-G^2}$, $f_{3,-G^2}$, $f_{4,-G^2}$, $f_{5,-G^2}$, $f_{6,-G^2}$, forces away from G^2 at the points N, 1, 2, 3, 4, 5, 6 respectively; N, line of equilibrium; restless movements occur on N.

as the center, a line of equilibrium exists at any point N directly outside the barrier. For, $|f_{N,G}| = |f_{B,-B}|$ and $d_{N,G} = d_{B,-B}$.

A similar situation exists (Figure 63) (a) if a positive valence G^1 and a negative valence G^2 are located at the same place C, (b) if in addition at the points near C the forces corresponding to the positive valence G^1 are weaker than the forces corresponding to the negative valence G^2, and (c) if the forces corresponding to the positive valence decrease less rapidly with increasing distance than do the forces corresponding to the negative valence. In other words, it is a situation where

(Ex. 42) $Va(G^1) > 0$; $Va(G^2) < 0$; $G^1 \subset C$
and $G^2 \subset C$; $|f_{X,G^1}| < f_{X,-G^2}|$, if
$e_{X,C}$ is sufficiently small; $|f_{X,G^1}| >$
$|f_{X,-G^2}|$ if $e_{X,C}$ is sufficiently great.

Such a situation is often realized (Lewin 1935) if an individual wishes to approach a region which implies some danger (negative valence).

Under these conditions there exists a zone of points N where $|f_{N,G^1}| = |f_{N,-G^2}|$. The forces at these points are equal in strength and opposite in direction. In other words, there exists a zone of equilibrium. A locomotion along this zone does not change this state of equilibrium. This equilibrium can be said, therefore, to be at least partly indifferent.

I have mentioned elsewhere (1935) that such lines of equilibrium are important determinants for the form of restless movements.

E. FORCE AND POTENCY OF A SITUATION

1. The Concept of Potency of a Situation

We have referred on several occasions to the concept of potency of a situation. The problem of potency or relative weight of a situation arises if the life space at a given·time consists of two or more overlapping situations (Princ., p. 217). A child eating his dinner might at the same time enjoy some conversation. In case he does not like his dinner he often tries to create a conversation to "distract" the adult from the eating situation. Being "inattentive" is a typical overlapping situation: the relative potency of one of the overlapping situations, i.e., that of work, is not as great for the child as the teacher wishes it to be. The situation of decision can frequently be treated as that of an overlapping situation. The relative potency is important for group membership in case of belonging to several overlapping groups (see Lewin 1935, Brown 1936).

The characteristics of an overlapping situation might then be described as follows:

Generally, the totality of a situation (S) has a certain unity of content (such as dinner situation, work, being at a movie, etc.). Such a situation might contain many subregions, a certain set of positive or negative valences, barriers and paths, and might be related to certain needs of the person. In case of an overlapping situation (L) the life space contains more than one of such units of situations (S^1, S^2, . . .).

Formalistically one can define an overlapping situation in the following way:

(39)   Definition: If $L = S^1 + S^2$ and $S^1 \cdot S^2 \neq 0$,
         S^1 and S^2 are said to be two overlapping
         situations[1])

We will deal here only with the case where the person P is located in the common part of S^1 and S^2 and where only two overlapping situations exist. The extension to more overlapping situations can easily be made.

We know from everyday observation and experiments that the two overlapping situations do not need to be of equal weight. The one situation might be the main situation and the second of lesser importance. There are all degrees of relative weight of the situation S^1, from zero (e.g., only the situation S^2 exists for the person) through a medium

[1] + and · in this formula refer to the topological sum and the intersection.

degree of potency until full dominance (which means that only the situation S^1 exists for the person).

We will characterize the relative potency $Po(S^1)$ by its fraction-of weight within the life space. That is, we will regard the potency of the total life space $Po(L)$ equal to one. The relation between the potencies of two overlapping situations will then be given by the formula:

$$(40) \qquad Po(S^1) + Po(S^2) = 1.$$

For instance, if both situations would have the same relative potency we would say in using a ten-point scale that: $Po(S^1) = 0.5$ and $Po(S^2) = 0.5$. $Po(S^1) = 0.1$ would mean then a rather low potency of S^1 and would imply that $Po(S^2) = 0.9$.

2. Potency of a Situation and Strength of Forces

There seems to exist a close relation between the effect which the forces existing in a situation have upon a person and the potency of this situation.

As an example, I might refer to the previously discussed dinner situation (p. 117) where a child P (Figure 64) does not like to eat (E) his food ($Va (E) < 0$). One of the typical ways in which the adult (Ad) tries to make the child eat is by distracting the child. That is, he tries to involve the child in a second situation, (S^2), for instance, of conversation, so much that he "forgets" his resistance. The forces in the eating situation (S^1) can be represented as follows: the adult tries to induce a force $f_{P,E}$ acting on the child in the direction of eating. Corresponding to the child's own need there exists a force $f_{P,-E}$ due to the negative valence of E and generally in addition a force against the pressure of the adult. The second force has the character of a restraining force. It is an attempt by the child to stand pat in his momentary situation A (for instance, of having his spinach on his spoon but not opening his mouth to allow the spoon to enter). The resistance can therefore be represented here as a restraining force $rf_{A,A}$ the direction of which is opposed to that of $f_{P,E}$ ($d_{A,A} = d_{P,E}$). As the force $f_{P,-E}$ due to the negative valence of eating has the same direction we can represent the total forces opposing the pressure of the adult by $f_{A,A}$ (Figure 64) the strength of which depends only upon the negative valence of the eating and upon the "will to resist."

(Ex. 43) $|f_{A,A}| = F(|f_{P,-E}| + |rf_{A,A}|)$

Distracting the child by a conversation means making the potency of that situation (S^2) relatively high ($Po(S^2) = 0.8$). In this way the potency of the eating situation S^1 is decreased ($Po(S^1) = 0.2$). As a result of it, the valences and forces related to this situation S^1 are obviously weakened to such a degree that the child does not resist the action of the adult.

To express this as a general statement, we could say that the actual strength of a force is a function of the potency of the situation to which it belongs.

(41) $|f| = F(Po(S))$ other factors being equal.

In our case the negative valence of E and the resistance of the child will diminish with the decrease of potency of the S^1 situation so that instead of the force $|f_{A,A}|$ we will have to deal with the much smaller force $|f_{A,A}| \cdot Po(S^1)$ $= |f_{A,A}| \cdot 0.2$.[1]

Of course, the decrease of potency of S^1 also decreases the potency of the adult's pressure in the eating situation. In other words, also the strength of the force $f_{P,E}$ will be smaller, namely $|f_{P,E}| \cdot Po(S^1) = |f_{P,E}| \cdot 0.2$. Therefore, nothing may seem to have been gained by decreasing the potency of S^1, from the point of view of the adult. Indeed, the trick of this type of feeding is to weaken the potency so that the resistance of the child becomes very weak and also the pressure of the adult becomes very weak but then to keep $f_{P,E}$ just a little ahead of his resistance at this low level:

(Ex. 44) $|f_{P,E}| \cdot Po(S^1) > |f_{A,A}| \cdot Po(S^2)$

[1] The sign "·" in this and the following formulas means "times" (not "common part").

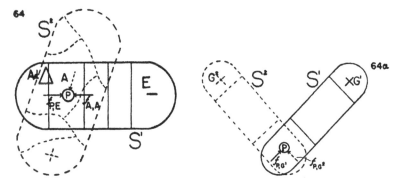

Fig. 64. Overlapping of Situations of Eating S^1 and Conversation S^2. P, child being in both situations; Ad, adult being in both situations; A, situation in which a child is at present (having spinach on spoon); E, actual eating; $f_{P,E}$, force toward E induced by adult; $f_{A,A}$, force to stay pat in A corresponding to the child's own need.

Fig. 64a. Decision Between Two Positive Valences Represented as Overlapping Situation. $Va(G^1) > 0$; $Va(G^2) > 0$; S^1, situation corresponding to a decision for G^1; S^2, situation corresponding to a decision for G^2; P, person located in S^1 and S^2; f_{P,G^1}, force toward G^1 corresponding to situation S^1, f_{P,G^2}; force toward G^2 corresponding to situation S^2.

It is in line with this representation that the tension (t) in this situation is very small. This follows from the relation between tension and the strength of the opposing forces in a conflict situation (35). Indeed, the adult has to be careful that the absolute level of his pressure ($f_{P,E}$) is kept on a rather low level. Otherwise the very effect of pressure will increase the potency of the situation S^1 and render the whole method void.

There is a second method used by adults to make the child eat which uses an increase rather than a decrease of potency of the eating situation. Every overlapping situation which might have existed is carefully ruled out by the adult and the potency of the eating situation brought up to the full strength ($Po(S^1) = 1$). In this situation, then, the force $f_{P,-E}$ resulting from the negative valence of E and also the resistance against the adult's pressure $rf_{A,A}$ will have maximum value. If the adult wishes to make the child eat, he will have, therefore, to exert a pressure greater than these forces ($|f_{P,E}| > |f_{A,A}|$). That means he will have to go to a rather high absolute level of pressure. Indeed, a high tension (t) is typical for this situation as compared with the situation mentioned above.

We have treated these examples without entering the problem of power fields and the more complicated problems related to them. High potency of the eating situation sometimes makes the child see the hopelessness of resistance and might then lead to abandonment of resistance.

The child frequently tries to use, against the adult, means similar to those which the adult uses against him.

Another example of an overlapping situation is that of a decision. In case a person P must decide between two goals G^1 and G^2 of nearly equal valence ($Va(G^1) = Va(G^2)$) one can say that P finds himself in two situations (S^1 and S^2) of about equal relative potency (Figure 64a): $Po(S^1) = Po(S^2) = 0.5$. Generally, an oscillation between the relative potencies of the two situations occurs until one becomes somewhat permanently dominant. In case one situation (S^1) becomes fully dominant we will have a full decision and only the force related to it will rule. In this case, namely, it will be:

(Ex. 45)　　$\begin{aligned} |f_{P,G^1}| \cdot Po(S^1) &= |f_{P,G^1}| \text{ and} \\ |f_{P,G^2}| \cdot Po(S^2) &= 0 \end{aligned}$

The representation of the decision situation by means of overlapping situations (Figure 64a) gives certain possibilities, not included in a previous representation (Figure 52). It permits us to take more fully into account the factors involved in a decision: rather frequently the decision is influenced not only by factors which concern directly the positive or negative valences involved in both possibilities, but also by an arbitrary increase of the relative potency of one of the situations at the moment of decision.

It is, by the way, easily understood why frequently

after the decision is made, the goal not chosen seems to be the more attractive one: the tension $t(G^1)$ related to the chosen goal G^1 decreases somewhat through the choice (see Wright, 1938), particularly in a case where no difficulties in reaching that goal are foreseen. At that time, therefore,

$$\text{(Ex. 46)} \qquad t(G^1) < t(G^2) \text{ and according}$$
$$\text{to (32) } f_{P,G}^2 > f_{P,G}^1$$

An adequate treatment of the problem of decision and potency must include the question of time perspective.

I am mentioning but one additional example related to change in "habits."

D. K. Adams and T. L. McCulloch (1934) report an experiment where two groups of rats have been trained in two simple T mazes, one with a short, and the other with a long common alley (Figures 65a and 65b). After the rats have been overtrained with the food being at C, the position of the food is changed to D. Physically, there seems to be not much difference between both constellations. However, psychologically, one should expect a difference which is rather important for the relearning. In the short maze the run from the start to the food is probably carried out in one undifferentiated unit of action, or, as we can say, by one unsegmented path (4a). If the path to the goal, however, is sufficiently long (Figure 65b), one would expect the path to be a segmented one with the running of the long section (B) as the first path.

During relearning the two situations would therefore be essentially different. In case of the short maze the animal will have to learn to use the unsegmented path $w_{A,D}$ (Figure 65c) instead of $w_{A,C}$ (Figure 65d). In other words, it has to learn to do an entirely different activity which contains no common steps with the previous one. In case of relearning of the long maze, however, the new path would be $w_{A,B,D}$ (Figure 65e), instead of the old one $w_{A,B,C}$: that is, the new and the old path contain a common step ($w_{A,B} \subset w_{A,B,C}$ and $w_{A,B} \subset w_{A,B,D}$). In other words, in this case the individual is likely to be in an overlapping situation during his run through B, namely, in a situation S^2 corresponding

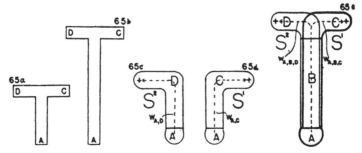

Change in "habits" and the unit of action (experiments of D. K. Adams and T. L. McCulloch).

Figs. 65a and 65b. A T-Maze with a Short, and One with a Long Alley (physical setting). A, starting point of the rat; C, location of food during learning; D, location of food after shift.

Figs. 65c, d, and e. The Psychological Situation.

Fig. 65c. Situation (S^2), a few repetitions after the shift of food to D. A, starting region; D, relatively undifferentiated region containing the food and including the approach-alley; $w_{A,D}$, unsegmented path from A to D.

Fig. 65d. Situation (S^1) before the shift. C, relatively undifferentiated region containing the food and including the approach-alley; $w_{A,C}$, unsegmented path from A to C.

Fig. 65e. Overlapping situation, a few repetitions after the shift in the position of the food is made. S^1, situation corresponding to the food in C; S^2, situation corresponding to the food in D; B, approach-alley contained as a relatively separated region both in situation S^1 and S^2; $w_{A,B,C}$, segmented paths from A through B to C; $w_{A,B,D}$, segmented paths from A through B to D.

to the new position of the goal, and in the situation S^1 corresponding to the old position of the goal (Figure 65e).

We have previously mentioned that such cases of "partly equal directions" (5a) can be treated with the help of the concept of potency of the situation. In case of the short maze the individual is, after a few experiences with the new constellation, already in the new situation S^2 (Figure 65c) which does not contain a common path with S^1 (Figure 65d). In other words, the potency of the situation S^1 is zero and that of the situation S^2 is 1 and the corresponding force $f_{A,D}$ alone governs the situation ($f_{A,D} \cdot Po(S^2) = f_{A,D} \cdot 1$

$= f_{A,D}$). In case of the long maze, however, we have to deal with an overlapping situation: the potency of the old situation S^1 during the individual running through B is not zero but greater than zero. The resultant force is, therefore, characterized by the formula $f_{A,C} \cdot Po(S^1) + f_{A,D} \cdot Po(S^2)$. If the potency $Po(S^1)$ during the run through B were still 0.7 this formula would amount to $f_{A,C} \cdot 0.7 + f_{A,D} \cdot 0.3$. In view of $f_{A,C} = f_{A,D}$ (because it is the same goal which the individual expects to reach in C or in D) one could conclude that $f_{A,C} \cdot 0.7 > f_{A,D} \cdot 0.3$, and, therefore, the resultant force $f^*_{A,C}$ would have the direction to C. In other words, the individual will run to C, that is to say, he will err. A weakening of the potency of S^1 is required before errors will be eliminated. This process will be considerably slower than in the case of the short maze because the common part B of the overlapping situation (Figure 65e) is apt to give the situation S^1 a relatively great potency for quite a while.

The results of Adams and McCulloch bear out these conclusions rather strongly in that they found about twice as many repetitions necessary for relearning in case of the long as in case of the short maze.

SUMMARY

We have attempted to describe the position of the concept force in psychology and to discuss major methods of measuring psychological forces. One of our objectives is to bring into the open and to apply scientific standards to those concepts which actually underlie certain recognized research methods and to eliminate those unnecessary accessories which create much discussion but little progress.

One of the outstanding properties of force is its directedness. Direction in psychology cannot be defined as physical direction and cannot be determined by Euclidian geometry. A geometry applicable in psychology is that of hodological space. The geometrical properties of this space are described, and examples of its application in determining directions and distances in the life space are offered.

The conceptual properties of the construct force are given and its coordinating definition to observable processes. The conceptual and dynamic relation between psychological forces, valences, and tension are discussed and certain basic theories concerning the relation between need, environment, and the "mechanics" of locomotion.

Various methods of measuring forces and valences are surveyed, especially those related to opposing forces and to velocity of locomotion, including velocity of restlessness, consumption, translocation, and learning. The problem of the structure of the force field and of overlapping force fields is discussed, including several choice and conflict situations with stable and labile equilibria. We have limited our discussion mainly to relatively simple problems of driving and restraining forces.

One of the main objectives of both the geometrical and the dynamical concepts is to develop a frame of reference useful as much in social as in quasi-physical situations. An adequate treatment of social problems, especially social conflicts, however, makes certain distinctions necessary, particularly that between "own" and "foreign" forces, which we have merely mentioned.

SYMBOLS USED

A. GENERAL

Be	Behavior
L	Life Space
S	Situation
P	Person
E	Environment
U	Cognitively Undetermined Region
(10)	Formula expressing general relationships between certain factors (of the type of a law or a logical connection).
(Ex. 10)	Formula referring to the interdependence of certain factors in regard to a special example.

B. FOR MATHEMATICAL CONCEPTS

I. Topological

$+$	Topological Sum of Regions
	Intersection of Regions (common part)
$\supset$	Includes
$\subset$	Being Included In

II. Metrical

$=$	Equal
$(=)$	Partly Equal
$\neq$	Unequal
$>$	Greater Than
$<$	Smaller Than

III. Functional Dependence

$F(a)$ A Constantly Increasing Function of a

$F(\frac{1}{a})$ A Constantly Decreasing Function of a (it is not assumed that arithmetic proportionality exists)

IV. Hodological

a) Path

$w_{A,B}$ Path from A to B (generally: distinguished path from A to B)

$w_{A,B,C}$ Path from A through B to C

b) Direction

$d_{A,B}$ Direction at A from A to B

$d_{A,-B}$ Direction at A away from B

$\overset{d}{}_{A,B}$ Direction at A opposite to $d_{A,B}$

$d_{A,A}$ Direction at A toward A

$d_{A,-A}$ Direction at A away from A

c) Distance

$e_{A,B}$ Distance between A and B measured along the path $w_{A,B}$

C. FOR DYNAMICAL CONCEPTS

I. Force

$f_{A,B}$ Force in the Direction $d_{A,B}$

$|f_{A,B}|$ Strength of force $f_{A,B}$ disregarding its direction

$f_{A,-B}$ Force in the direction $d_{A,-B}$

$|f_{A,-B}|$ Strength of force $f_{A,-B}$ disregarding its direction

$f_{A,B,C}$ Force in the direction $d_{A,B,C}$

$f_{A,B}^{P}$ Force $f_{A,B}$ with P as point of application (if the point of application is clear from the context, generally the symbol $f_{A,B}$ is used)

$f_{P,B}$ Used for $f_{X,B}^{P}$ in case the position of P was not determined

$f_{A,X}$ Force in the direction $d_{A,X}$ where X stands for a variable region

$f_{Y,B}$ Force in the direction $d_{Y,B}$ where Y stands for a variable region

$\Sigma f_{A,X}$ Totality of forces existing at the region A

$f_{A,B}^{*}$ Resultant of Forces in the Direction $d_{A,B}$

$rf_{A,-B}$ Restraining Force at A hampering locomotion in the direction $d_{A,B}$

$df_{A,B}$ Driving Force in the direction $d_{A,B}$

→   Diagrammatically forces are represented by arrows. The strength of the force is represented by the length of the arrow; its point of application by the point of the arrow. (In physics the tail of the arrow represents the point of application. We prefer the other representation to indicate that we deal with psychological rather than with physical forces.)

II. Valence

$Va(G)$ A Valence a Region G has for a Person at a Given Time

$RVa(G)$ The Totality of Regions which have a Valence for a Person in Relation to the Need $t(G)$

SVa Substitute Valence

III. Tension

$t(G)$	Tension in Relation to the Need G (or to the system G)
$t(M)$	Motoric Tension (particularly tonus)
$t(I)$	Tension of Inner Personal Regions
SV	Substitute Value

IV. Potency

$Po(S)$	Relative Potency of a Situation S

V. Velocity

$v_{A,B}$	Velocity at A in the Direction $d_{A,B}$
$v(\text{trans})_{A,B}$	Velocity of Translocation in the direction $d_{A,B}$
$v(\text{res})_{A,-A}$	Velocity of Restless Movements at A
$v(\text{cons})_{P,G}$	Velocity of Consumption of G by P
$v(\text{stru})$	Velocity of Change of Cognitive Structure of the Situation (for instance, in case of learning)

GLOSSARY

CHAPTER ONE

The Geometry of the Life Space. Direction and
Distance in Psychology

A. A Geometry Applicable to the Life Space
  I. Hodological Space
                Summary: Table I (p. 55)
  II. Semi-Euclidean Space
      p. 36

B. Basic Geometrical Constructs

1. Cell	(1) Definition: If A is a cell, no regions a, b, ... , n ($a \neq b \neq \ldots . \neq n$) should be distinguished such that $a + b + \ldots . + n = A$.
2. Step	(4) Definition: $w_{M,N}$ is a "step" within $w_{A,B}$ if $w_{A,B} \supset w_{M,N}$ and if $w_{M,N}$ has common parts with no other cells than M and N.
	(4a) Definition: A path is called "segmented" if it contains more than one step.
3. Unity of Path	(5) The degree of unity of a path w is greater the more $Po(w_{A,B}) > Po(w_{M,M+1})$ where $w_{A,B}$ indicates the path as a whole and $w_{M,M+1}$ that step of the path which a person is undertaking at present.

C. Direction

 I. Direction Toward

  a) Distinguished Path

   (1a) A distinguished path in the life space is (probably) characterized by: $Va(M) = \max$ where $Va(M)$ indicates the valence of the different paths from A to B as a means.

  b) Direction Defined

   (2) Definition: The direction at A toward B $(d_{A,B})$ is a relation between the regions A and B which is determined by the beginning step $(w_{A,Q})$ of the distinguished path $(w_{A,B})$ from the region A to B (with $w_{A,Q} \subset w_{A,B}$).

 II. Equality of Direction

  a) If only one distinguished path exists between two regions

   1. Equality of Direction at the Same Point

    (3) $d_{A,B} = d_{A,C}$ if there exists a $w_{A,H}$ such that $w_{A,H} \subset w_{A,B}$ and $w_{A,H} \subset w_{A,C}$.

    (3a) $d_{A,B} = d_{A,C}$ if $w_{A,C} \subset w_{A,B}$ or $w_{A,C} \supset w_{A,B}$

   2. Partly Equal Directions

    (5a) $d_{A,B} \;(=)\; d_{A,C}$

   3. Equality of Directions at Different Points

    (6) $d_{A,B} = d_{H,D}$ if $w_{A,B} \supset w_{H,D}$

    (6a) $d_{A,B} = d_{D,B}$ if $w_{A,B} \supset w_{D,B}$

   4. Equality of Direction as a Symmetrical Relation

    (8) $d_{A,B} = d_{C,D}$ if $d_{C,D} = d_{A,B}$

   5. Equality of Direction not Transitive

    (7) If $d_{A,B} = d_{A,C}$ and $d_{A,C} = d_{A,E}$ then $d_{A,B} = d_{A,E}$ in case there exists a $w_{A,Q}$ such that $w_{A,Q} \subset w_{A,B}$, $w_{A,Q} \subset w_{A,C}$ and $w_{A,Q} \subset w_{A,E}$.

(7a) If $d_{A,B} = d_{C,E}$ and $d_{C,E} = d_{G,K}$ then $d_{A,B} = d_{G,K}$ in case there exists a $w_{M,N}$ so that $w_{M,N} \supset w_{A,B}$, $w_{M,N} \supset w_{C,E}$ and $w_{M,N} \supset w_{G,K}$.

6. Equality of Direction at the End Point of a Path

(9) $d_{B,X} = d_{A,B}$ if $w_{A,X} = w_{A,B} + w_{B,X}$

b) If more than one distinguished path exists between two regions

1. Difference of Direction

(10) $d_{A,E,B} \neq d_{A,H,B}$ if no path $w_{A,X}$ exists such that $w_{A,X} \subset w_{A,E,B}$ and $w_{A,X} \subset w_{A,H,B}$.

2. Equality of Direction

(10a) $d_{A,E,B} = d_{A,H,B}$ if there is a $w_{A,X}$ such that $w_{A,X} \subset w_{A,E,B}$ and $w_{A,X} \subset w_{A,H,B}$.

III. Opposite Directions

1. At Different Points

(11) Definition: $d_{A,B} = d_{B,A}$

(11a) $d_{B,A} = d_{A,B}$ if $d_{A,B} = d_{B,A}$

(12) $d_{A,B} = d_{D,C}$ if a $w_{M,N}$ and $w_{N,M}$ exists such that $w_{M,N} \supset w_{A,B}$ and $w_{N,M} \supset w_{D,C}$

2. At the Same Point

(13) $d_{A,X} = d_{A,B}$ if $w_{X,B} \supset w_{A,B}$ or if $w_{B,X} \supset w_{B,A}$

(13a) It can be $d_{A,G} = d_{A,B}$ and $d_{A,E} = d_{A,B}$ in spite of $d_{A,G} \neq d_{A,E}$.

IV. Direction Toward the Present Region

(17) $d_{A,A} = d_{A,-A}$

V. Direction Away From

(15) Definition: $d_{A,-B} = d_{A,X}$ if $e_{B,X} > e_{B,A}$.

1. Relation between "away from" and "opposite" direction

$$(15a)\ d_{A,-B} = d_{A,B} \text{ or } d_{A,-B} \neq d_{A,B}$$

2. Direction away from the present region

(15b) Definition: $d_{A,-A} = d_{A,X}$ if $A \cdot X = 0.$

(15c) $d_{A,-A} = d_{X,A}$ for any $X \cdot A = 0.$

D. Distance

1. Distance between Two Regions

(14) $e_{A,B} > e_{H,D}$ if $w_{A,B} \supset w_{H,D}$ and $w_{A,B} \cdot w_{H,D} \neq w_{A,B}$

(14a) $e_{A,B} > e_{H,D}$ shall not imply $w_{A,B} \supset w_{H,D}$

2. Distance Zero

(16) $e_{A,A} = 0$

E. The Hodological Space Applied

I. The Cognitively Unstructured

1. Direction to Goal

(Ex. 4) $d_{C,G} = d_{C,U}$

(Ex. 4a) $d_{C,L} = d_{C,G}$ as long as $L \subset U.$

2. Orientation and Search

(Ex. 5) $d_{A,G} = d_{S,U}$

(Ex. 5a) $d_{A,G} = d_{S,-S}$

3. Orientation and Restless Movements

(Ex. 6) $d_{A,-A}$

II. Round-about Route

(Ex. 8) $d_{A,G} = d_{A,B}$

(Ex. 8a) $d_{A,R} = d_{A,-G}$

(Ex. 9) $d_{A,R} = d_{A,G}$

III. Use of Tools

(Ex. 10) $d_{A,G} = d_{A,T}$

IV. The Maze
    1. The Familiar Maze

        (Ex. 1) $d_{A,G} = d_{A,B}$
        (Ex. 2) $d_{A,G} = d_{C,D} = d_{E,T}$ etc.
        (Ex. 3) $d_{C,G} \neq d_{C,L}$ according to (3) because $w_{C,G}$ does not include $w_{C,L}$.

    2. The Unfamiliar Maze

        (Ex. 4) $d_{C,G} = d_{C,U}$
        (Ex. 4a) $d_{C,L} = d_{C,G}$ as long as L $\subset$ U.

    3. Maze with One-Way Doors
        p. 61

V. The Insane Asylum

        (Ex. 7) $d_{H,G} = d_{H,N}$; $d_{H,G} = d_{H,T}$; and $d_{H,G} = d_{H,D}$.
        (Ex. 7a) $d_{ph,G} \neq d_{ph,ct}$
        (Ex. 7b) $d_{ph,G} = d_{ph,ct}$

CHAPTER TWO

The Dynamics of the Life Space

A. *Behavior and Life Space*
    The basic formula of a field theory
        (25) $Be = F(L) = F(P,E)$.

B. *Force*

    1. The Resultant of Forces
        (18) Definition: $\Sigma f_{A,X} \equiv f_{A,B} + f_{A,C} + \ldots + f_{A,N}$.

    2. Force and Locomotion
        (19) Definition: If $\Sigma f_{A,X} = f^{*}_{A,B}$ and $|f^{*}_{A,B}| > 0$, then $v_{A,B} > 0$.
        (19a) If $v_{A,B} > 0$ then a resultant $f^{*}_{A,B} = \Sigma f_{A,X}$ exists such that $|f^{*}_{A,B}| > 0$.

3. Restraining Force

(Ex. 29) $v_{A,G} = F\left(\dfrac{|f_{A,G}|}{|rf_{A,-G}|}\right)$

(Ex. 30) $|rf_{A,-B}| = F\ (v_{A,B})$

4. Principle Concerning the Resultant of Forces

(38) $f_{N,G}{}^1 + f_{N,G}{}^2 = f^*{}_{N,Y}$ so that $e_{Y,G}{}^1 < e_{N,G}{}^2$ and $e_{Y,G}{}^2 < e_{N,G}{}^2$ in case such a region Y exists.

(38a) $|f^*{}_{N,Y}| > 0$ if $|f_{N,G}{}^1| > 0$ and $|f_{N,G}{}^2| > 0$.

C. Valence

1. Positive Valence

(20) Definition of positive valence: If $Va(G) > 0$, then $|f_{P,G}| > 0$.

2. Negative Valence

(20a) Definition of negative valence: If $Va(G) < 0$ then $|f_{P,-G}| > 0$.

3. Valence and Force Field

(20b) A positive valence corresponds to a force field where all forces are directed toward the same region. (This region is said to have a positive valence).

(20c) A negative valence corresponds to a force field where all forces have the direction away from the same region. (This region is said to have a negative valence).

(20d) A positive valence $(Va(G) > 0)$ corresponds to a positive central field $(f_{X,Y} = f_{X,G})$.

(20e) A negative valence $(Va(G) < 0)$ corresponds to a negative central field $(f_{X,Y} = f_{X,-G})$.

4. Valence, Force, and Distance

(21) $|f_{P,G}| = F(\dfrac{Va(G)}{e_{P,G}})$

D. Tension

  1. Definition

    (27) If $t(S) \neq t(S^1)$ and $b_S \cdot b_S{}^1 \neq 0$, a tendency exists to change t so that $t(S) = t(S^1)$.

  2. Coordinating Definition of Tension

    (29) Hypothesis: Wherever a psychological need exists, a system in a state of tension exists within the individual.

  3. Spreading of Tension

    (28) If $t(S) > t(S^1)$ and $b_S \cdot b_S{}^1 \neq 0$ there exist forces $f_{b_S, S^1 > 0}$

  4. Muscular and Inner Personal Tension

    (30) $t(M) = F(t(I), N)$

E. Force Field

  1. Valence, Force and Distance

$$(21)\ f_{P,G} = F\left(\frac{Va(G)}{e_{P,G}}\right)$$

  2. The Force Field

    (22) Definition: A force field correlates to every region of a field the strength and direction of the force which would act on the individual if the individual were in that region.

  3. Central Field

    (23) Definition: A positive central field is a field in which for every region X a force towards the same region G exists $(f_{X,Y} = f_{X,G})$.

    (24) Definition: A negative central field is a field in which for every region X a force away from the same region G exists $(f_{X,Y} = f_{X,-G})$.

  4. Force and Distance from a Valence

$$(Ex.\ 35)\quad f_{A,G} = F\left(\frac{1}{e_{A,G}}\right)\quad \text{other}$$

factors being equal.

5. Velocity and Distance

(Ex. 36) $v_{A,G} < v_{B,G}$ if $e_{A,G} > e_{B,G}$.

(Ex. 36a) $v_{A,G} = F\left(\dfrac{1}{e_{A,G}}\right)$

6. Choice between Two Paths

(Ex. 37) $f^*_{A,B,G} > f^*_{A,C,G}$

7. Distance and Force in Power Field

p. 168

8. Forces and Tension within the Region of Positive Valence

p. 172

F. *Some Dynamical Relations between Force, Valence, Tension, Potency of the Situation and Locomotion*

1. Valence as a Function of Tension and the Nature of the Goal

(31) $Va(G) = F(t,G)$

2. Force as a Function of Tension, Distance to the Goal, and Nature of Goal

(32) $f_{P,G} = F\left(\dfrac{t}{e_{P,G}}, G\right)$

3. Force Away from a Present Region of Negative Valence as a Function of Tension

(34) $f^{P}_{A,-A} = F(t)$ aside from other factors.

4. Tension as a Function of Force

(26a) $t = F(f)$ aside from other factors.

5. Tension as a Function of Force in a State of Equilibrium

(35) $t = F(f_{A,G})$ in a state of equilibrium.

6. Velocity as a Function of Force

(33) $v_{A,B} = F(|f^*_{A,B}|, h)$

7. Path of Restless Movement

(34a) The restless movement $w_{A,X}$ occurs so that $f^*_{X,-X} = $ minimum.

8. Restraining Force and Velocity of Locomotion

(Ex. 29) $v_{A,G} = F \left(\dfrac{|f_{A,G}|}{|rf_{A,-G}|} \right)$

(Ex. 30) $|rf_{A,-B}| = F(v_{A,B})$

(Ex. 31) $v_{A,G}^{n}$ is such that $f_{A,G} = f_{vA,G}^{n}, - v_{A,G}^{n+1}$.

9. Force, Velocity of Locomotion and Amount of Work Anticipated

(33a) $v_{A,G}^{n}$ is such that $|f_{A,G}| = |f_{v_{A,G}^{n}}$

$- v_{A,G}^{n+1}| + |f_{kA,G}^{n}, - k_{A,G}^{n}|$.

(33b) $v_{A,G}^{n}$ is such that

$|f_{v^{n}, v^{n+1}}| + |f_{k^{n}, -k^{n}}| =$
$|f_{v^{n}, -v^{n+1}}| + |f_{k^{n+1}, -k^{n+1}}|$

(33b^{1}) $v^{n}{}_{A,G}$ is such that

$|f_{v^{n}, v^{n+1}}| = |f_{k^{n+1}, -k^{n+1}}|$

(33c) $|f_{v^{n}, v^{n+1}}| = F \ (|f_{A,G}|)$ aside from other factors.

G. *Measurement of Force*

a) By Another Force

(Ex. 16) $|f_{A,G}| \lessgtr |f_{A,H}|$

b) By the Total Action Time Toward the Goal in Case of an Impassable Barrier

(Ex. 17) $f_{A,G} = F(T_{i})$

(Ex. 18) $|f_{n,G}| = |f_{r,-r}|$

(Ex. 19) $|f_{n,G}| < |f_{n,-r}|$

(Ex. 19a) $f_{n,G} + f_{n,-r} = f_{n,A} > 0$: therefore $v_{n,A} > 0$ according to (19).

(Ex. 20) $|f_{A,G}| > |f_{B,-B}|$

c) By the Total Action Time Toward the Goal in Case of a Passable Barrier

(Ex. 22) $|f_{n,G}| > |f_{r,-r}|$

(Ex. 23a) $d_{n,G} \neq d_{n,r}$

d) By Restraining Forces
                    p. 134
e) By Velocity of Locomotion
                    (33) $v_{A,B} = F(|f^*{}_{A,B}|, h)$
1. By Speed of Restless Movements
                    (34) $|f_{A,-A}| = F(t)$ in case other factors are constant.
   (a) Without a Goal Being Present
                    (Ex. 23) $v(\text{res})_{A,-A} = F(|f^*{}_{A,-A}|)$.
   (b) If a Goal is Present
                    (Ex. 23a) $v(\text{res})_{A,-A} = F(|f^*{}_{A,-A}|)$
                    $= F(t)$ in case other factors are constant.
2. By Speed of Consumption
                    (Ex. 25) $v(\text{cons})_{P,G} = F(|f^{*}{}_{P,G}|)$
                    $= F(t)$ in case other factors are constant.
3. By Speed of Translocation
                    (Ex. 26) $v(\text{trans}) = F(|f^*{}_{A,G}|) = F(t)$ in case other factors are constant.
   (a) If Only Restraining Forces Hamper Translocation
                    (Ex. 29) $v_{A,G} = F\left(\dfrac{f_{A,G}}{rf_{A,-G}}\right)$
                    (Ex. 30) $|rf_{A,-B}| = F(v_{A,B})$
                    (Ex. 30a) $|f_{v^n, -v^{n+1}}| = F(v^n{}_{A,G})$
                    (Ex. 31) $v^n{}_{A,G}$ is such that $|f_{A,G}|$
                    $= |f_{v^n{}_{A,G'}} - v^{n+1}|$.
                                                        A,G
   (b) If a Negative Valence of Total Work Ahead Influences Translocation
                    (Ex. 32) $k_{A,G} = F(e_{A,G}, av_{A,G})$
                    (Ex. 32a) $|fk_{A,G'} - k_{A,G}| = F(e_{A,G} \cdot av_{A,G})$.
                    (Ex. 32b) $|fk_{A,G'} - k_{A,G}| = F(av_{A,G})$ for $av_{A,G}$ greater than a certain amount.

(Ex. 32c) $|f_{A,G}| = |f_k{}^n{}_{A,G'} - k^n{}_{A,G}|$ where $k^n{}_{A,G}$ refers to the total amount of work anticipated in crossing the distance $e_{A,G}$ with an average velocity $av^n{}_{A,G} = v^n{}_{A,G}$.

(33a) $v^n{}_{A,G}$ is such that $|f_{A,G}| =$

$$\left|f_v{}^n{}_{A,G} \cdot {}_{-v}{}^{n+1}{}_{A,G}\right| + \left|f_k{}^n{}_{A,G} \cdot {}_{-k}{}^n{}_{A,G}\right|$$

(33b) $\overset{n}{v}_{A,G}$ is such that

$$\left|f_v{}^n{}_{,v}{}^{n+1}\right| + \left|f_k{}^n{}_{,-k}{}^n\right| =$$

$$\left|f_v{}^n{}_{,-v}{}^{n+1}\right| + \left|f_k{}^{n+1}{}_{,-k}{}^{n+1}\right|$$

(33b¹) $\overset{n}{v}_{A,G}$ is such that

$$\left|f_v{}^n{}_{,v}{}^{n+1}\right| = \left|f_k{}^{n+1}{}_{,-k}{}^{n+1}\right|$$

f) By Velocity of Restructuring

   (e.g. by Speed of Learning)

   (Ex. 33) $v(stru) = F(f^*{}_{A,G}) = F(t)$ within narrow limits.

g) Specific Examples

   1. Obstruction Box

   (Ex. 11) $|f_{A,C}| > |f_{B,-B}|$

   (Ex. 12) $d_{A,C} = d_{B,-B}$

   (Ex. 13) $d_{A,C} = d_{B,-B}$ according to (15c).

   (Ex. 14) $v_{A,C} > 0$ if $|f_{A,C}| > |f_{B,-B}|$.

   Frequency of Crossing the Grill

   (Ex. 15) $|f^2{}_{A,C}| > |f^1{}_{A,C}|$ if $pe^2 < pe^1$ in case $|f_{B,-B}| =$ constant.

   (Ex. 15a) $|f_{A,C}| = F\left(\dfrac{1}{pe}\right)$

2. Tapping the Lever (Skinner's experiments)

(Ex. 24) $v_{A^\cdot, L^n, G^n} = F(t)$

(Ex. 27) $v_{L^n, L^{n+1}} = F(t)$

(Ex. 28) $|{}^f L^1, G^1| = \cdot |{}^f L^2, G^1| = |{}^f L^3, G^1|$.

3. Training for Different Paths in Case of Different Needs (Comparison of experiments of Hull and Leeper)

(Ex. 39) $d_{A,H} = d_{A,K}$;   therefore $d_{A,G^1} = d_{A,G^2}$.

(Ex. 39a) $d_{A,D} = d_{A,E}$

(Ex. 40) $d_{A,G^1} = d_{A,C} = d_{A,G^2}$

(Ex. 40a) $d_{A,D} (=) d_{A,E}$

H. Measurement of Valence

a) Valence as a Function of Tension and Nature of Goal

(31) $Va(G) = F(t, G)$

b) Comparison of Strength of Two Valences

(Ex. 34) $Va(G^1) \gtreqless Va(G^2)$

c) The Realm of Regions with Positive Valence as a Function of Tension

(36) $RVa(G) = F(t(G))$

d) Substitute Value

(36a) $SV(G^2 \text{ for } G^1) > 0$, if $t(G^1) =$

$$F\left(\frac{1}{\text{cons }(G^2)}\right)$$

I. Overlapping Force Fields

a) Two Valences Lying in the Same Direction

(Ex. 38) $|f^*{}_{P,N}| > |f_{P,G^1}|$; $|f^*{}_{P,N}| > |f_{P,G^2}|$, if $Va(G^1) > 0$ and $Va(G^2) > 0$ and if $d_{P,G^1} = d_{P,G^2}$.

b) Choice between Valences and Choice between Paths
to the Same Valence

(Ex. 39) $d_{A,H} = d_{A,K}$; therefore
$d_{A,G^1} = d_{A,G^2}$.

(Ex. 39a) $d_{A,D} = d_{A,E}$

(Ex. 40) $d_{A,G^1} = d_{A,C} = d_{A,G^2}$.

(Ex. 40a) $d_{A,D} (=) d_{A,E}$

(Ex. 40b) $|f_{wS,-wS}| < |f_{w1,-w1}| <$
$|f_{wc,-wc}| < |f_{wg,-wg}|$

c) Choice as an Overlapping Situation

(Ex. 45) $|f_{P,G^1}| \cdot Po(S^1) = |f_{P,G^1}|$
and $|f_{P,G^2}| \cdot Po(S^2) = 0$.

(Ex. 46) $t(G^1) < t(G^2)$ and $f_{P,G^2} >$
f_{P,G^1}.

d) Conflict Situations

1. If the Space of Free Movement Is Restricted

(Ex. 41) $Va(G^1) = Va(G^2)$

(a) Concerning Two Positive Valences

(Ex. 41a) $|f_{A,G^1}| = |f_{A,G^2}|$; d_{A,G^1}
$= d_{A,G^2}$.

(b) Concerning Two Negative Valences

(Ex. 41b) $|f_{A,-G^1}| = |f_{A,-G^2}|$; $d_{A,-G^1}$
$= d_{A,-G^2}$.

2. If the Space of Free Movement Is Unrestricted

(a) Concerning Two Positive Valences

(Ex. 41d) $f_{A,G^1} + f_{A,G^2} = 0$

(b) Concerning Two Negative Valences

(Ex. 41c) $f_{A,-G^1} + f_{A,-G^2} = f^*_{A,X}$
> 0, if $e_{G^1,X} > e_{G^1,A}$ and
$e_{G^2,X} > e_{G^2,A}$.

(Ex. 41e) $f_{6,-G^1} + f_{6,-G^2} = f^*_{6,X} >$
0 if $e_{G^1,X} > e_{G^1,6}$ and
$e_{G^2,X} > e_{G^2,6}$.

(Ex. 42) $Va(G^1) > 0$; $Va(G^2) < 0$; $G^1 \subset C$ and $G^2 \subset C$; $|f_{X,G^1}|$ $< |f_{X,-G^2}|$, if $e_{X,C}$ is sufficiently small; $|f_{X,G^1}| >$ $|f_{X,-G^2}|$ if $e_{X,C}$ is sufficiently great.

3. The Point of Unavoidable Decision

(37) A is a "point of unavoidable decision" if from $e_{Y,G^1} < e_{A,G^1}$ follows that $e_{Y,G^2} > e_{A,G^2}$.

e) Principle Concerning Resultant of Forces

(38) $f_{N,G^1} + f_{N,G^2} = f^*_{N,Y}$ so that $e_{Y,G^1} < e_{N,G^2}$ and $e_{Y,G^2} < e_{N,G^2}$ in case such a region Y exists.

(38a) $|f^*_{N,Y}| > 0$ if $|f_{N,G^1}| > 0$ and $|f_{N,G^2}| > 0$.

J. Potency of a Situation

a) Definition of Overlapping Situations

(39) If $L = S^1 + S^2$ and $S^1 \cdot S^2 \neq 0$, S^1 and S^2 are said to be two overlapping situations.

b) Potency of Two Situations

(40) $Po(S^1) + Po(S^2) = 1$.

c) Force and Potency of a Situation

(41) $|f| = F(Po(S))$ other factors being equal.

d) Examples

1. Distraction as a means of overcoming resistance

(Ex. 43) $|f_{A,A}| = F(|f_{P,-E}| + |rf_{A,A}|$.

(Ex. 44) $|f_{P,E}| \cdot Po(S^1) > |f_{A,A}|$ $Po(S^2)$.

2. Decision

(Ex. 45) $|f_{P,G^1}| \cdot Po(S^1) = |f_{P,G^1}|$ and $|f_{P,G^2}| \cdot Po(S^2) = 0$.

(Ex. 46) $t(G^1) < t(G^2)$ and $f_{P,G^2} > f_{P,G^1}$.

BIBLIOGRAPHY

1. Ach, N. *Über den Willensakt und das Temperament*. Leipzig: Quelle und Meyer, 1910.

2. Adams, D. K., and McCulloch, T. L. On the structure of acts, *J. Gen. Psychol.*, 1926, **10**, 450-455.

3. Allport, G. W. *Studies in expressive movement*. New York: The Macmillan Co., 1933.

4. Barker, R., Dembo, T., and Lewin, K. *Experiments on frustration and regression*. Univ. Iowa Stud. in Child Welfare (in press).

5. Bills, A. G. *General experimental psychology*. New York: Longmans, Green and Co., 1934.

6. Bingham, H. C. Chimpanzee translocation by means of boxes, *Comp. Psychol. Monog.*, 1928, **5**, 92.

7. Birenbaum, Gita. Das Vergessen einer Vornahme. Isolierte seelische Systeme und dynamische Gesamtbereiche, *Psychol. Forsch.*, 1930, **13**, 218-284.

8. Blodgett, H. C. The effect of the introduction of reward upon the maze performance of rats, *Univ. Calif. Publ. Psychol.*, 1929, **4**, 113-114.

9. Blumberg, A. E. and Feigl, H. Logical Positivism, *J. Phil.*, 1931, **28**, 281-296.

10. Bridgman, L. *The logic of modern physics*. New York: The Macmillan Co., 1932.

11. Brown, J. F. A methodological consideration of the problem of psychometrics, *Erkenntnis*, 1934, **4**, 46-61.

12. Brown, J. F. Über die dynamischen Eigenschaften der Realität und Irrealität, *Psychol. Forsch.*, 1932; **14**, 2-26.

13. Brown, J. F. *The social order*. New York: McGraw-Hill, 1936.

14. Carnap, Rudolf. *Physikalische Begriffsbildung*. Karlsruhe: G. Braun, 1926.

15. Chase, Lucile. *Motivation of young children: an experimental study of certain types of external incentives upon the performance of a task*. U. of Iowa Stud. in Child Welfare, 1932, **5**, 119.

16. Crawley, S. L. An experimental investigation of recovery from work, *Arch. of Psychol.*, 1926, No. 85, 1-66.

17. Dashiell, J. F. *Fundamentals of general psychology*. New York: Houghton Mifflin, 1937.

18. Dembo, T. Der Ärger als dynamisches Problem, *Psychol. Forsch.*, 1931, **15**, 1-44.

19. Dembo, T. and Hanfmann, E. The patient's psychological situation upon admission to a mental hospital, *Am. J. Psychol.*, 1935, **47**, 381-408.

20. Dembo, T., Frank, J. D., Lewin, K. and Waring, E. B.   *Studies in social pressure* (in preparation).

21. Fajans, S.   Die Bedeutung der Enfernung für die Stärke eines Aufforderungscharakters beim Säugling und Kleinkind, *Psychol. Forsch.*, 1933, 17, 215-267.

22. Frank, Jerome D.   Some psychological determinants of the level of aspiration, *Am. J. Psychol.*, 1935, 47, 285-293.

23. Frank, J. D.   Individual differences in certain aspects of the level of aspiration, *Am. J. Psychol.*, 1935, 47, 119-128.

24. Frank, J. D.   The influence of the level of performance in one task on the level of aspiration in another, *J. Exp. Psychol.*, 1935, 18, 159-171.

25. Freud, Sigmund.   *New introductory lectures on psycho-analysis.* Trans. W. Y. H. Spratt.   New York: Norton, 1933.

26. Freund, A.   Psychische Sättigung im Menstruum und Intermenstruum, *Psychol. Forsch.*, 1930, 13, 198-217.

27. Gengerelli, J. A.   The principle of maxima plus minima in animal learning, *J. Comp. Psychol.*, 1930, 11, 193-236.

28. Goldstein, Kurt.   *Der Aufbau des Organismus; Einführung in die Biologie unter besonderer Berücksichtigung der Erfahrungen am kranken Menschen.*   Haag: M. Nijhoff, 1934.

29. Hamilton, E. L.   The effect of delayed incentive on the hunger drive in the white rat, *Genet. Psychol. Monog.*, 1929, 5, No. 2.

30. Hausdorff, F.   *Grundzüge der Mengenlehre.*   Leipzig: 1914.

31. Heider, F.   Ding und Medium, *Symposium*, 1927, 1, 109-157.

32. Helmholtz, H. V.   *Zählen und Messen erkenntnistheoretisch betrachtet.*   (In *Schriften zur Erkenntnistheorie.*)   Berlin: Springer, 1921.

33. Heron, W. T. and Skinner, B. F.   Changes in hunger during starvation, *Psychol. Record*, 1937, 1, 51-60.

34. Hilgard, E. R.   The nature of the conditioned response. I. The case for and against stimulus substitution, *Psychol. Rev.*, 1936, 43, 366-385.

35. Hoppe, F.   Erfolg und Misserfolg, *Psychol. Forsch.*, 1931, 14, 1-62.

36. Hull, C. L.   The goal gradient hypothesis and maze learning, *Psychol. Rev.*, 1932, 39, 25-43.

37. Hull, C. L.   The conflicting psychologies of learning—a way out, *Psychol. Rev.*, 1935, 42, 491-516.

38. Hull, C. L.   Differential habituation to internal stimuli in the albino rat, *J. Comp. Psychol.*, 1933, 16, 255-273.

39. Irwin, Orvis C.   The distribution of the amount of motility in young infants between two nursing periods, *J. Comp. Psychol.*, 1932, 14, 429-445.

40. James, William.   *The principles of psychology*, Vol. I.   New York: 1890.

41. Karsten, A. Psychische Sättigung, *Psychol. Forsch.*, 1927, **10**, 142-254.

42. Katz, D. Zur Grundlegung einer Bedürfnispsychologie, *Acta Psychol.*, 1935, **1**, 119-128.

43. Koehler, W. *The mentality of apes.* Trans. E. Hinter. New York: Harcourt, Brace & Co., 1925.

44. Koehler, W. *Gestalt psychology.* New York: Liveright Publishing Co., 1929.

45. Koffka, K. *Principles of gestalt psychology.* New York: Harcourt, Brace & Co., 1935.

46. Koffka, K. *The growth of the mind: an introduction to child psychology.* New York: Harcourt, Brace & Co., 1928.

47. Kounin, Jacob S. A comparative study of initial work outputs and recovery capacities from various work situations. Western Reserve U., Unpublished Master's Thesis, 1936.

48. Krechevsky, I. The genesis of hypothesis in rats, *Univ. Calif. Public. in Psychol.*, 1932, **6**, 1-57.

49. Krechevsky, I. Brain mechanisms and variability I, II, *J. Comp. Psychol.*, 1937, **23**, 121-159.

50. Kuo, Z. Y. The nature of unsuccessful acts and their order of elimination in animal learning, *J. Comp. Psychol.*, 1922, **2**, 1-27.

51. Lashley, K. S. Nervous Mechanisms in Learning, Chap. 10, in *Handbook of general experimental psychology*, ed. Carl Murchison. Worcester: Clark University Press, 1934.

52. Leeper, R. The role of motivation in learning: a study of the phenomenon of differential motivational control of the utilization of habits, *J. Gen. Psychol.*, 1935. **46**, 3-40.

53. Lewin, Kurt. Das Problem der Willensmessung und das Grundgesetz der Association, *Psychol. Forsch.*, 1922, **1**, 191-302.

54. Lewin, Kurt. *A dynamic theory of personality.* Trans. D. K. Adams and K. E. Zener. New York: McGraw-Hill, 1935.

55. Lewin, Kurt. *Principles of topological psychology.* New York: McGraw-Hill, 1936.

56. Lewin, Kurt. Richtungsbegriff in der Psychologie, *Psych. Forsch.*, 1934, **19**, 244-299.

57. Lewin, Kurt. Vectors, cognitive processes, and E. Tolman's criticism, *J. Gen. Psychol.*, 1933, **8**, 318-345.

58. Lewin, Kurt. Some social-psychological differences between the United States and Germany, *Character and Personality*, 1936, **4**, 265-293.

59. Lissner, K. Die Entspannung von Bedürfnissen durch Ersatzhandlungen, *Psychol. Forsch.,* 1933, **18**, 218-250.

60. Line, W., and Wees, W. R. Learning as doing: some suggestions concerning the analysis of direction, *Brit. J. Psychol.*, 1936, **27**, 162-169.

61. Mahler, V. Ersatzhandlungen verschiedenen Realitätsgrades, *Psychol. Forsch.*, 1933, **18**, 26-89.

62. Maier, N. R. F. and Schneirla, T. C. *Principles of animal psychology.* New York: McGraw-Hill Co., 1935.

63. Menger, K. *Dimensionstheorie.* Leipzig: DeGruyter, 1928.

64. Moss, Fred A. Study of animal drives, *J. of Exp. Psychol.*, 1924, **7**, 165-185.

65. Mueller, G. E. Zur Analyse der Gedächtnistätigkeit und des Vorstellungsverlaufes, *Zeitsch. für Psychol.* (Ergänzungsband 8), 1913.

66. Murray, H. A. Facts which support the concept of need or drive, *J. of Psychol.*, 1936, **3**, 27-42.

67. McDougall, W. *The energies of men.* New York: Chas. Scribner's Sons, 1932.

68. Ovsiankina, M. Die Wiederaufnahme unterbrochener Handlungen, *Psychol. Forsch.*, 1928, **11**, 302, 379.

69. Planck, M. *Einführung in die allgemeine Mechanik zum Gebrauch bei Vorträgen sowie zum Selbstunterricht.* Leipzig: Hirzel, 1928.

70. Reichenbach, H. *Philosophie der Raum-Zeitlehre.* Leipzig: De Gruyter, 1928.

71. Richter, C. P. A behavioristic study of the activity of the rat, *Comp. Psychol. Monog.*, 1922, **1**, No. 2.

72. Robinson, E. S. and Heron, W. T. The warming-up effect, *J. Exper. Psychol.*, 1924, **7**, 81-97.

73. Tolman, E. C. and Sams, C. F. Time discrimination in white rats, *J. Comp. Psychol.*, 1925, **5**, 259-263.

74. Skinner, B. F. Drive and reflex strength, I, II, *J. Gen. Psychol.*, 1932, **6**, 22-48.

75. Skinner, B. F. Conditioning and extinction and their relation to drive, *J. Gen. Psychol.*, 1936, **14**, 296-317.

76. Sliosberg, S. Zur Dynamik des Ersatzes in Spiel- und Ernstsituationen, *Psychol. Forsch.*, 1934, **19**, 122-181.

77. Stevens, S. S. The operational basis of psychology, *Am. J. Psychol.*, 1935, **47**, 323-330.

78. Stone, C. P. A sand tube obstruction apparatus, *J. Gen. Psychol.*, 1937, **50**, 203-206.

79. Szymanski, J. S. Versuche über die Wirkung der Faktoren, die als Antrieb zum Erlernen einer Handlung dienen können, *Pflug. Arch. f. d. ges. Physiol.*, 1918, **171**, 374-385.

80. Tolman, E. C. *Purposive behavior in animals and men.* New York: The Century Company, 1932.

81. Tolman, E. C. Psychology versus immediate experience, *Phil. Sci.*, 1935, **3**, 356-380.

82. Tolman, E. C. Demands and conflicts, *Psychol. Rev.*, 1937, **44**, 158-169.

83. Tolman and Honzik. Introduction and removal of reward, and maze performance in rats, *Univ. Calif. Publ. Psychol.*, 1930, **4**, 257-275.

84. Tolman, E. C., Hall, C. S., and Bretnall, E. P. A disproof of the law of effect and a substitution of the laws of emphasis, motivation and disruption, *J. Exper. Psychol.*, 1932, **16**, 601-614.

85. Warden, C. J. *Animal motivation: experimental studies on the albino rat.* New York: Columbia Univ. Press, 1931.

86. Washburn, M. E. *The animal mind: a textbook of comparative psychology.* 2d ed. New York: Macmillan, 1917.

87. Wiehe, F. Die Grenzen des Ichs. (Unpublished manuscript.)

88. Wright, H. F. The influence of barriers upon strength of motivation, *Contributions to Psychological Theory*, 1938, **1**, No. 3.

89. Yerkes, R. M. and Dodson. The relation of strength of stimulus to rapidity of habit formation, *J. Comp. Neurol. and Psychol.*, 1908, **18**, 459-482.

90. Yochelson, S. Effects of rest pauses on work decrement. Thesis 193, Yale University Library.

91. Young, Paul Thomas. *Motivation of behavior: the fundamental determinants of human and animal activity.* New York: J. Wiley & Sons, 1936.

92. Zeigarnik, B. Über das Behalten von erledigten und unerledigten Handlungen, *Psychol. Forsch.*, 1927, **9**, 1-85.

AUTHOR INDEX

[235]

SUBJECT INDEX

A

ability, of individual, 154
acceleration, 134, 149
accessories, unnecessary, 210
achievement, interest in, 160
action, amount of toward goals, 167
action,
  directed, 108, 175
  duration of, 130
  intended, 99
  preparatory, 126
  purposeful, 105
  separated, 32
  toward the goal, 127, 130
  unit of, 208
  variety of, 108
activity, 156
  change of, 134
  goal, 62
  negative valence of, 133
  possible, 77
  speed of, 145
  type of, 125
  velocity of change, 137
adaptation, 81
adit, 169
adult, 97, 102, 103, 156, 202, 203, 204, 205
adulthood, 105
affairs, undecided state, 192
affecting, through a distance, 95
"ahistoric," 2
algebraic, 156
alley, blind, 57, 58, 186
alone, do things, 171
amount of work anticipated, 223
analogy, 87
animal, 133, 138
angle, 55, 84
appetite, 163
approach, 22
  field-theoretical, 96
approximation, first, 96
area, geographical, 156
association, 14, 93
assumption, 18
  implicit, 73
asylum, insane, 63
attachment, emotional, 88
attractiveness, origin of the, 88

automatism, 35
automobile, 157
away from, 51, 55
axiom, 18, 28
axiomatizing, 23

B

barrier, 64, 108. 122, 123, 131, 157
  attack against, 195
  circular, 140
  impassable, 37, 124, 126, 127, 178, 191, 223
  passable, 132, 134
  strength of a, 125
  surrounding, 178
  U-shaped, 67
behavior, 106, 175, 211, 219
  directed, 103
  goal-seeking, 63
  "molar," 117
behaviorism, purposive, 17
being included in, 211
biology, 104
body, solid, 112
boundary, 60
  common, 75
  of a system, 110
brain, 87, 106
breaking, 125
bridge, 61, 103, 181

C

cage, 65
canary, 65
cause,
  historical, 165
  of behavior, 16-17
cell, 24, 30, 58, 70, 117, 118, 215
  neighboring, 118
centimeter, 113
central field, 221
change, 98
  alien, 86
  cause of, 71, 163
  continuous, 38
  imposed, 86
  microscopic, 40
  of cognitive structure, 63, 66
character, of the ground, 153
chewing, 117

CPSIA information can be obtained
at www.ICGtesting.com
Printed in the USA
BVHW080059210122
626528BV00001B/106